TIBETAN
PHRASEBOOK

Sandup Tsering

Tibetan phrasebook
3rd edition – May 2002

Published by
Lonely Planet Publications Pty Ltd, ABN 36 005 607 983
90 Maribyrnong St, Footscray, Victoria 3011, Australia

Lonely Planet Offices
Australia Locked Bag 1, Footscray, Victoria 3011
USA 150 Linden St, Oakland CA 94607
UK 10a Spring Place, London NW5 3BH
France 1 rue du Dahomey, 75011 Paris

Cover illustration
Reflections from Cloud 11 by Yukiyoshi Kamimura

ISBN 1 74059 233 6

text © Lonely Planet Publications Pty Ltd 2002
cover illustration © Lonely Planet Publications Pty Ltd 2002

Printed by The Bookmaker International Ltd
Printed in China

Although the authors and Lonely Planet try to make the information
as accurate as possible, we accept no responsability for any loss,
injury or inconvenience sustained by anyone using this book.

ABOUT THE AUTHOR

Sandup Tsering is a Tibetan Buddhist Scholar, interpreter and language teacher, and was born in Purang in Western Tibet. As a result of the Chinese invasion of Tibet in 1959, his parents fled to India, where they live in a refugee settlement. Sandup moved to Australia in 1984. He has a Bachelor of Arts and a Masters in Buddhism and was the President of the Tibetan Community of Victoria for five years from 1993 until 1998.

FROM THE AUTHOR

My special thanks goes to Ven Thupten Donyo and Kelsang Dhondup for their assistance with typing Tibetan script, and my wife and children for their support. I would also like to thank Alo Bhuti, Sonam Dolkar and Lobsang Dhargye for their help and input.

FROM THE PUBLISHER

Scaling the heights of the *Tibetan phrasebook* was no small task. Sally Steward, Peter D'Onghia and Quentin Frayne arranged all necessary permits and Emma Koch helped with initial preparations. Editor Sophie Putman came on board to organise equipment and supplies, while proofer Adrienne Costanzo lent her keen eye to ensure all went as planned. Experienced trekkers Karina Coates and Karin Vidstrup Monk joined the party and offered support across the most challenging terrain. Jim Jenkin served as a guide along the entire trail, Ben Handicott proved a dependable porter and Annelies Mertens guaranteed no-one was lost for words. Hunor Csutoros provided the trusty map, while Meg Worby contributed to navigation plans with her clever contents. Fabrice Rocher coordinated the final ascent and designers Belinda Campell, Patrick Marris and Yukiyoshi Kamimura ensured it went without a hitch. Yukiyoshi's talented artwork on the cover, and his illustrations of the Tibetan people, flora and fauna, inspired us all. The result: a euphoric summit celebration with chầng all round.

CONTENTS

6   Contents

TIBETAN

INTRODUCTION

Tibetan belongs to the Tibeto-Burman linguistic group of the Sino-Tibetan language family, with Burmese its closest relative. It's spoken by over six million people, mainly in Tibet, but also in neighbouring Nepal, India and Bhutan, and used by Mongolians to study Buddhism.

There are many different Tibetan dialects and, due to differences in pronunciation and vocabulary, it can be difficult for people from different regions to understand one another. The main provinces, U-tsang, Amdo and Kham – all of which have been renamed by China – have their own dialects (and sub-dialects). Other Tibetan dialects can be found in bordering countries. However, greater social interaction among Tibetans from various regions in recent times has led to the development of a standard Tibetan language. In contrast to any of the traditional dialects, it's much closer to classical Tibetan and is also the focus of this book.

Written Tibetan was devised in the 7th century AD by Thumi Sambhota, the minister of the famous Tibetan ruler, King Songtsen Gampo. He was one of 15 scholars sent to India by the king to compile Tibetan scripts so that Buddhist literature could be translated into Tibetan. Under the guidance of his main Indian teachers, Brahmin Lipikara and Devavidyasinha, Sambhota learned a number of classical Indian languages. He developed the Tibetan language based on the Sanskrit characters of the Devanagari script (used for many Indian languages). He also compiled grammar texts which are still the primary source for studying Tibetan grammar today.

Since its introduction, the writing system has barely changed, although the spoken language has evolved considerably. As a result, written and spoken Tibetan are quite different.

Speaking Tibetan is the key to understanding the unique culture, lifestyle and history of the country. This phrasebook will help you communicate with Tibetans and enrich your experience in Tibet.

INTRODUCTION

HOW TO USE THIS PHRASEBOOK
You *Can* Speak Another Language

Anyone can speak another language. Don't worry if you haven't studied languages before, or that you studied a language at school for years and can't remember any of it. You don't need to sit down and memorise endless grammatical details or long lists of vocabulary. You just need to start speaking. Once you start, you'll be amazed how many prompts will help you build on those first words. You'll hear people speaking, pick up sounds from TV, catch a word or two that you think you know from the local radio, see something on a billboard – all these things help to build your understanding.

Plunge In

There's just one thing you need to start speaking another language – courage. Your biggest hurdle is overcoming the fear of saying aloud what may seem to you to be just a bunch of sounds.

The best way to start overcoming your fear is to memorise a few key words. These are the words you know you'll be saying again and again, for example, 'thank you' tu-jay-chay (ཐུགས་རྗེ་ཆེ།).

There's no exact equivalent for 'Hello' in Tibetan – sometimes the greeting ta-shi de-lek (བཀྲ་ཤིས་བདེ་ལེགས།), which literally means 'Good fortune' is used, or Tibetans may just ask a question such as kay-râng ka-bah pay-kay (ཁྱེད་རང་ག་བར་ཕེབས་གས།), 'Where are you going?'. If you're having trouble understanding someone, say ha ko ma-song (ཧ་གོ་མ་སོང་།), 'I don't understand' or yâng-kya ka-lee ka-lee soong nâng da (ཡང་སྐྱར་ག་ལེར་ག་ལེར་གསུང་གནང་དང་།) 'Could you speak more slowly please?'. Other phrases to help you with language difficulties are on page 52.

Abbreviations Used in This Book

adj	adjective		n	noun
f	feminine		pl	plural
inf	informal		pol	polite
lit	literal translation		sg	singular
m	masculine		v	verb

INTRODUCTION

LEGEND

The following notation is used throughout this phrasebook:

( ) parentheses

- indicate words that can be replaced with words of your choice:

> I've been travelling for
> (two) months.
> nga dü-shü da-wa (nyi)   ང་འགྲུལ་བཞུད་ཟླ་བ་(གཉིས་)
> chay-pa yin   བྱས་པ་ཡིན།

- indicate the words are optional:

> Can you show me
> (on the map)?
> (sâp-ta di-nâng)   (ས་བཀྲ་འདི་ནང་)
> tön nâng-da   སྟོན་གནང་དང་།

/ forward slash

- indicates when single words on either side of the slash are interchangeable:

> Turn left/right.
> yön-la/yeh-la   གཡོན་ལ་/གཡས་ལ་སྐྱོགས་གནང་།
> kyog-nâng

- indicates when single words are synonyms:

> necklace   kay-gyen/gü-gyen   སྐེ་རྒྱན་/མགུལ་རྒྱན་

; semicolon

- separates two (or more) alternatives where one (or more) consists of more than one word:

> earrings   ahm-cho gyen;   ཨམ་ཅོག་རྒྱན་/ར་རྒྱན་
>   na-gyen

INTRODUCTION

[ ] square brackets

- contain two (or more) different constructions, separated by a semicolon, or a slash in script. One construction is compulsory in the phrase:

> Please [slow down; go faster].
>   [ka-lee ka-lee; gyok-tsi]   [ག་ལེར་ག་ལེར་/མགྱོགས་ཙི་]
>   do-nâng   འགྲོ་གནང་།
> The guide [has paid; will pay].
>   rin-ba nay-shay gya-khen-gi   རིན་པ་གནས་བཤད་རྒྱག་མཁན་གྱིས་
>   tay-song/tay-gi-ray   སྤྲད་སོང་/སྤྲད་ཀྱི་རེད།

- **bullet points**
- are used in the dictionary only to separate synonyms:

> often   yâng yang • yâng-se   ཡང་ཡང་ • ཡང་སེ་

If it is necessary to clarify the difference between alternatives, this is indicated in parentheses after each word.

PRONUNCIATION

Although there are a few sounds that are not common in English, pronunciation of Tibetan is generally not too difficult. The transliteraton system used in this book has been designed to help you pronounce Tibetan sounds correctly and with ease.

Remember that people will welcome your efforts and won't be concerned if you mispronounce the odd word.

TRANSLITERATION
To assist with pronunciation, all syllables in the transliterations have been hyphenated. As long as you pronounce each of the syllables clearly, you should be understood.

Vowels
Although there are only five vowels indicated in the writing system (see The Tibetan Writing System, page 15), their pronunciation can vary. The vowel ཨི, for example, can be pronounced as i or ee, depending on the sounds around it.

Transliteration	Pronunciation
a	as the 'u' in 'cup'
â	as the 'a' in 'alone'
aw	as the 'aw' in the British 'paw'
e	as the 'e' in 'bet'
i	as the 'i' in 'in'
ee	as the 'ee' in 'see'
o	as the 'o' in 'so'
ö	as the 'er' in 'her'
u	as the 'u' in 'glue'
oo	as the 'oo' in 'soon'
ü	similar to the 'u' in 'flute', but with a raised tongue
ay	as the 'ay' in 'say'

Consonants

Most consonants are pronounced as in English; those that aren't are listed in the box below in Tibetan alphabetical order.

Some consonants in Tibetan can be aspirated or unaspirated. Aspirated consonants are pronounced with a puff of air. An h following the consonant is used to denote aspiration; for example, kh is the aspirated counterpart of k (see below). The difference in pronunciation is important, as it can change the meaning of a word – khâng-pa means 'house', whereas kâng-pa means 'leg'.

Be careful not to confuse th (aspirated t) with the English 'th' in 'thin' – or ph (aspirated p) with the English 'ph' in 'pharmacy'. In the case of zh and sh, however, the h does not indicate aspiration (see below).

Unaspirated	Aspirated	Pronunciation
k		as the 'k' in 'skill'
	kh	as the 'k' in 'kill'
g		always hard, as the 'g' in 'garden'
ng		as the 'ng' in 'sing'
c		as the 'ch' in 'charge'
	ch	as the 'ch' and following 'h' in 'punch hard'
j		as the 'j' in 'jar'
ny		as the 'ny' in 'canyon'
t		as the 't' in 'stop'
	th	as the 't' in 'time'
p		as the 'p' in 'spot'
	ph	as the 'p' in 'pit'
ts		as the 'ts' in 'weights'
	tsh	as the 'ts' and following 'h' in 'fights hard'
dz		as the 'ds' in 'adds'
z		similar to the 'z' in 'zoo'
zh		similar to the 's' in 'pleasure'
r		pronounced deep in the throat, without rolling
s		as the 's' in 'suck'
sh		as the 'sh' in 'shut'

PRONUNCIATION

Nasalised Sounds

An n, m or ng following a vowel indicates a nasalised sound. When pronouncing nasal vowels, the breath escapes partly through the nose and partly through the mouth. The last consonants aren't pronounced, but indicate the nasalisation of the preceding vowel. Imagining an 'ng' at the end of the syllable, as in the word 'sing' can help you make this nasal sound (as long as you remember that the 'g' isn't actually pronounced).

THE TIBETAN WRITING SYSTEM

Tibetan consists of 30 basic characters and four vowels, which can be added to these characters. You'll notice that each of the consonants in the writing system includes an a. This is because consonants in Tibetan are represented as syllabic units and all have an inherent a in their basic form. Symbols are added above or below the consonant to indicate different vowel sounds (see page 16).

ཀ	ཁ	ག	ང	ཅ	ཆ	ཇ	ཉ
ka	kha	ga	nga	ca	cha	ja	nya
ཏ	ཐ	ད	ན	པ	ཕ	བ	མ
ta	tha	da	na	pa	pha	ba	ma
ཙ	ཚ	ཛ	ཝ	ཞ	ཟ	འ	ཡ
tsa	tsha	dza	wa	zha	za	'a	ya
ར	ལ	ཤ	ས	ཧ	ཨ		
ra	la	sha	sa	ha	a		

The symbols added above or below the consonants to indicate different vowel sounds, other than a, are:

Vowel Sound	i	u	e	o
Symbol	�ི	�u	�ེ	�ོ
Position	above	below	above	above

In the following box, we've taken the first consonant ka (ཀ) as an example:

Tibetan	Pronunciation
གི	ki
གུ	ku
གེ	ke
གོ	ko

The Tibetan for each vowel can be pronounced in different ways. Take for example choong, ཆུང ('small') and shu-mah, བཤུམ ('lamp'). Both contain the symbol ༢ but the pronunciation is affected by the letters around it. As a result, the symbol is pronounced as oo and u respectively (see Vowels, page 13, for pronunciation).

Spelling
In Tibetan, certain words may be pronounced the same but have different meanings depending on spelling – just like 'through' and 'threw' in English.

སྔ་མ	nga	before/early
ལྔ	nga	five
ང	nga	drum

PRONUNCIATION

Consonant Stacks

You'll often see characters on top or below other characters, so-called 'consonant stacks'. Some characters take a special form when being stacked; others remain the same. Consonant stacks are generally only formed with certain characters.

Sanskrit Characters

An additional set of 11 characters was created for the purpose of transcribing certain Sanskrit words which can't be represented by the Tibetan writing system, but appear frequently in Tibetan Buddhist literature and occasionally in other contexts. It's unlikely you'll come across any of them while visiting Tibet, but it's useful to know of their existence.

The additional characters are divided into two groups: reverse characters and thick characters. Reverse characters are literally characters of the Tibetan alphabet that have been reversed. Thick characters sound emphatic when pronounced. Again all have an inherent a sound.

Reverse Characters		Thick Characters	
ཊ	ta	གྷ	gha
ཋ	tra	དྷ	dha
ཌ	da	བྷ	bha
ཎ	na	ཛྷ	zha
ཥ	ka	དྲྷ	dhra
ཀྱ	kya		

TONES

Tones (changes in pitch) do exist in Tibetan, but unlike in some Asian languages, they're not crucial to meaning. For this reason, tones haven't been indicated in this book.

STRESS

There's no strong word stress in Tibetan. Generally, if you give equal stress to each syllable, you'll be understood.

PRONUNCIATION

GRAMMAR

Tibetan grammar is quite straightforward, with just a few exceptions. This chapter will give you the basics and you'll soon be stringing your own sentences together.

Although the focus of this book is spoken Tibetan, we've included certain aspects of written Tibetan in this chapter, where relevant to the spoken language.

WORD ORDER

Word order in Tibetan generally follows the pattern subject-object-verb, as opposed to the usual English word order subject-verb-object:

I like Lhasa.	nga lha-sa ga-po yö
	(lit: I Lhasa like)
I need a map.	ngah sâp-ta chig gö
	(lit: I map one need)

ARTICLES
Definite Article

Although the definite article 'the' exists in Tibetan (te), it's rarely used. Where 'the' is used in English, a demonstrative adjective is usually used in Tibetan:

this	di	these	din-tsö
that	pha-gi	those	phân-tsö

The car is white.	mo-ta pha-gi ka-po ray
	(lit: car that white is)
The rooms are dirty.	nye-khâng din-tsö
	tsog-ba ray
	(lit: room these dirty are)

For further examples, see Demonstratives, page 22.

GRAMMATICAL TERMS

A number of basic grammatical terms are used in this chapter. Here's a general summary of them:

adjective	adds information about a noun *red* wine
adverb	adds information about a verb or adjective He runs *quickly*. *very* big
conjunction	joins together sentences or parts of a sentence Wash the car *and* walk the dog.
noun	a person (*John*), thing (*book*), place (*beach*) or concept (*happiness*)
object	refers to the noun or pronoun that is affected by the verb Paul washes the *dog*.
preposition	introduces information about time, place or direction *at* the market *towards* the city
pronoun	usually takes the place of a noun *he* sings instead of Paul sings
subject	refers to the noun or pronoun that is performing an action *The man* washes the dog.
verb	an action or doing word He *runs* fast.

GRAMMAR

Indefinite Article

The indefinite article 'a/an' is expressed in spoken Tibetan by chig, literally meaning 'one':

a yak   yâk chig
                       (lit: yak one)

a book   teb chig
                       (lit: book one)

NOUNS
Plurals

Tibetan nouns have no plural form. Plurals may be indicated through context alone or through the absence of the indefinite article, chig:

There are mountains   bö-la ri yö-ray
   in Tibet.   (lit: Tibet-in mountain are)

Plurals can also be expressed by adding a plural demonstrative adjective (din-tsö, 'these' or phân-tsö, 'those') after the noun:

The bicycles are here.   kâng-ga-ri din-tsö day du
                           (lit: bicycle these here are)

Another alternative is to add a plural word (eg, mâng-po, 'many', nyoong-nyoong, 'a few', nyi, 'two' and ka-shay, 'some') or a numeral (see page 179) after the noun or pronoun:

There are many   bö-la ri mâng-po yö-ray
   mountains in Tibet.   (lit: Tibet-in mountain many are)

DEMONSTRATIVES

Demonstratives are used far more in Tibetan than they are in English. Wherever possible, they're used instead of 'the' to be more specific. There are also more demonstratives in Tibetan than in English, for example, ya-gi, 'that up there' and mân-tsö, 'those down there'.

this	di	these	din-tsö
that	pha-gi	those	phân-tsö
that up there	ya-gi	those up there	yân-tso
that down there	ma-gi	those down there	mân-tsö

Demonstratives are placed after the nouns they refer to:

This country is very beautiful. loong-pa-di nying-je-po
shay-ta du
(lit: country-this
 beautiful very is)

That parcel is mine. cha-lâg pha-gi ngay ray
(lit: parcel that mine is)

That bird up there. chi-hu ya-gi
(lit: bird that-up-there)

ADJECTIVES

Generally, adjectives consist of two syllables in Tibetan. The first syllable is referred to as the root adjective stem and is important when forming comparatives (see opposite) and superlatives (see page 24). Adjectives follow the noun they describe:

red suitcase tog-tay mah-po
(lit: suitcase red)

dirty room nye-khâng tsog-ba
(lit: room dirty)

Comparatives

Comparatives are formed differently in spoken and written Tibetan. In spoken language, comparatives are usually formed by replacing the second syllable of the adjective with the final consonant (along with its inherent a, see the Tibetan alphabet page 15) of the root adjective stem:

good	yâg-po
better	yâg-ga

Sometimes the written form is used in spoken language. The written form replaces the second syllable with pa or wa. There's no rule governing whether to add pa or wa, but even if you add the wrong one you'll still be understood:

good	yâg-po
better	yâg-pa

Here are a few of the more common adjectives with the appropriate endings added. The spoken form is listed first, followed in brackets by the written form. Where the written form is used in spoken language, only one form is given:

bad	dhuk-cha	worse	dhuk-ka (dhuk-pa)
cold	dâng-mo	colder	dâng-nga (dâng-wa)
good	yâg-po	better	yâg-ga (yag-pa)
hot	tsha-po	hotter	tsha-wa
high	tho-po	higher	tho-wa
many	mâng-po	more	mâng-nga (mâng-wa)
small	choong-choong	smaller	choong-nga (choong-wa)

Occasionally, the root adjective stem changes its form when pa or wa is added. Such exceptions are very rare, however:

big	chen-po	bigger	chay-wa

GRAMMAR

To compare two nouns in a sentence, attach -lay (roughly meaning 'than') to the noun that would follow 'than' in English. Note the order of the two nouns is reversed in Tibetan:

Mt Everest is higher than   gâng rim-po-che-lay jo-mo
    Mt Kailash.   lâng-ri tho-wa yö-ray
                                (lit: Mt Kailash-than
                                    Mt Everest higher is)

Superlatives

In both spoken and written language, superlatives are formed by replacing the second syllable of the adjective with -shö. Any root adjective stem changes are the same as for comparatives:

bad	dhuk-cha	worst	dhuk-shö
big	chen-po	biggest	chay-shö
cold	dâng-mo	coldest	dâng-shö
good	yâg-po	best	yâg-shö
high	tho-po	highest	tho-shö
hot	tsha-po	hottest	tsha-shö
many	mâng-po	most	mâng-shö
small	choong-choong	smallest	choong-shö

PRONOUNS
Personal Pronouns

Whether it's acting as the subject (eg, 'I'), or the object (eg, 'me') of a sentence, the pronoun is the same in Tibetan, so nga, for example, means both 'I' and 'me'.

There are many forms of personal pronouns in honorific (for speaking to monks and nuns) and written Tibetan. Those listed below are the most commonly used in the spoken language. You'll notice that all plural pronouns end in -tso

Singular		Plural	
I/me	nga	we/us	ngân-tso
you	kay-râng	you	kay-râng-tso
he/him (inf)	kho	they/them	khong-tso
she/her (inf)	mo	(inf/pol)	
he/she/him/	khong		
her (pol)			
it	te		

When used with intentional verbs (see page 26), the subject changes to mean 'by me', 'by you' etc:

Singular		Plural	
by me	ngay	by us	ngân-tsö
by you	kay-râng-gi	by you	kay-râng-tsö
by him (inf)	khö	by them	kho-tsö
by her (inf)	mö	(m/f, inf)	
by him/	khong-gi	by them	khong-tsö
her (pol)		(m/f, pol)	
by it	tay		

POSSESSIVES

Possessive adjectives (eg, 'my') are the same as possessive pronouns (eg, 'mine'), so ngay is used to mean both 'my' and 'mine'. All plurals end in -tsö:

Singular		Plural	
my/mine	ngay	our/ours	ngân-tsö
your(s)	kay-râng-gi	your(s)	kay-râng-tsö
his (inf)	khö	their(s)	kho-tsö
her/hers (inf)	mö	(m/f, inf)	
his/her (pol)	khong-gi	their(s)	khong-tsö
its	tay	(m/f, pol)	

GRAMMAR

Possessive adjectives, unlike other adjectives, appear before the noun they possess, whereas possessive pronouns always follow the noun to which they refer:

This is my car.	di ngay mo-ta ray (lit: this my car is)
This car is mine.	mo-ta-di ngay-ray (lit: car-this mine-is)

VERBS

Tibetan verbs fall into two classes. One class contains verbs that the subject controls, referred to here as 'intentional verbs'; the other class contains those that represent actions or feelings that the subject does not have direct control over, referred to here as 'unintentional verbs'. 'To eat' and 'to watch' would therefore be intentional verbs, while 'to feel sick' and 'to feel sad' would be unintentional verbs.

Some verbs can have both an intentional and an unintentional form. For example, the verb 'to sleep' has an intentional form, meaning the person went to sleep of their own volition, and an unintentional form, meaning the person fell asleep without wanting or trying to.

It's important to remember that each tense comprises three parts: a main verb, a tense particle and an auxiliary verb, 'to be' (see page 28). For example, 'I'm reading' is ngay log-gi-yö (lit: I read-present-am). In this sentence, the main verb is log 'to read', the tense particle is gi, and yö is the auxiliary verb.

The main verb usually takes the same form in the present, past and future tenses. (See page 30 for a list of Key Verbs.)

The auxiliary verbs and tense particles vary according to subject (me, you, he, she etc) and tense – it's good to try to learn these. The two classes of verbs take different auxiliary verbs and tense particles, so there are two sets to learn.

Intentional Verbs

	Present		Past		Future	
	Tense Particle	Auxiliary Verb	Tense Particle	Auxiliary Verb	Tense Particle	Auxiliary Verb
I/we	-gi	-yö	-pa	-yin	-gi	-yin
you/he/ she/they		-du	-pa song	-ray –		-ray

I listen to music.   ngay rö-ja nyen-gi-yö
(lit: I music listen-present-am)

She listened to music.   mö rö-ja nyen-pâ-ray;
mö rö-ja nyen song
(lit: she music listen-past-was)

They will listen to music.   khong-tsö rö-ja nyen-gi-ray
(lit: they music listen-future-will)

Unintentional Verbs

For unintentional verbs, the tense particle only changes according to person (I, we, he, she etc) in the past tense and the auxiliary verb doesn't change at all according to person. Note that in the past tense, no auxiliary verb is required at all:

	Present		Past	Future	
	Tense Particle	Auxiliary Verb	Tense Particle	Tense Particle	Auxiliary Verb
I/we	-gi	-du	-choong	-gi	-ray
you/he/ she/they			-song		

I'm sick.   nga na-gi-du
(lit: I sick-present-am)

She was sick.   mo na-song
(lit: I sick-past)

They will be sick.   khong-tso na-gi-ray
(lit: I sick-future-will)

GRAMMAR

TO BE

Whereas English uses one verb ('to be') to express both location ('the book is here') and equivalence ('the book is red'), Tibetan uses three different verbs:

1. The verb du is used to express location and also for information gained first-hand.

    The forest is here.   shing-nâg-te day du
                                 (lit: forest-the here is)

    When used with 'I' or 'we', the verb du becomes yö:

    I'm here.   nga day yö
                                 (lit: I here am)

2. To express equivalence the verb ray is used:

    He's Buddhist.   kho nâng-pa ray
                                 (lit: he Buddhist is)
    The rooms are dirty.   nye-khâng din-tsö
                                 tsog-ba ray
                                 (lit: room these dirty are)

    The verb ray becomes yin when it's used with 'I' or 'we':

    I'm a teacher.   nga ge-gan yin
                                 (lit: I teacher am)

3. The verb yö-ray is used to express facts that are general or common knowledge and can be used to express both location and equivalence.

    There are yaks in Tibet.   bö-la yâk yö-ray
                                 (lit: Tibet-in yak are)
    He's a good person.   khong mi yag-po chig yö-ray (pol)
                                 (lit: he person good one is)

All three verbs change when forming a negative sentence (see page 34).

(see page 34).

TO HAVE

There's no equivalent for the verb 'to have' in Tibetan. The idea of possession is expressed by adding -la (usually indicating location, see Postpositions, page 35) to the end of the subject, as well as using the auxiliary verb du/yö at the end of the sentence. Again du is used in all cases except for I/we, when yö is used.

He has a map.   kho-la sâp-ta du
                       (lit: he-la map has)
I have a car.   nga-la mo-ta chig yö
                       (lit: I-la car one have)

MODALS
Want, Need, Must

In Tibetan, the verb gö is used to mean 'want', 'need' and 'must':

I want tea.   nga cha gö
                       (lit: I tea want)
I need two beds.   nga nye-ti nyi gö
                       (lit: I bed two need)

When used in conjunction with another verb, gö takes an auxiliary verb at the end of the sentence:

I must see the   nga shing-nâg-te mig ta-gö-yö
   forest.   (lit: I forest-the see must)

To form a question, gö becomes gö-bay, but the word order remains the same:

Do you want tea?   kay-râng cha gö-bay?
                       (lit: you tea want?)

Alternatively, you can use a question word/phrase, such as 'how much', kâ-tsö: (See page 32 for more question words.)

How much money   kay-râng-la ngü kâ-tsö gö?
   do you want?   (lit: you-la money how-much want?)

To make a negative sentence, add mö to the beginning of gö:

I don't want this.   nga-la di mö-gö
                       (lit: I-la this not-want)

KEY VERBS

Most verbs remain the same for all tenses, but some take a different form depending on the tense, as indicated below. Where present and future columns are blank, those tenses take the same form as the past tense.

Remember the forms listed can be used regardless of the subject (I, you, he, she etc) of the sentence – you just need to add the relevant endings (see page 27).

	Past	Present	Future
to agree	thün		
to arrive	jor		
to borrow/lend	yar		
to break	châg	chok	châg
to bring/take	kay		
to buy	nyö	nyo	nyo
to come	yong		
to cry	ngü	ngu	ngu
to dance	tâb		
to depart (leave)	thön		
to do	chay		
to drink	toong		
to eat	say	sa	sa
to give	tay	tö	tö
to go	chin	doh	doh
to hire	lay	la	la
to hit	doong		
to know (someone/something)	shay		

GRAMMAR

	Past	Present	Future
to like	gah		
to listen	nyen		
to make	sö	so	so
to meet	thoog		
to move	gü		
to need	gö		
to prefer	dâm	dem	dem
to pull	ten		
to receive	jor		
to remember	den		
to say	lâb		
to see	tong		
to send	kur		
to sleep	nyey		
to stay	day	dö	day
to steal	kü	ku	ku
to stop	kâg	gok	gâk
to tell	lâb	so	so
to want	gö		
to wear	gyön		
to write	di		

GRAMMAR

QUESTIONS

There are two main ways to form questions in Tibetan,
depending on whether you want to form a question that requires
a 'yes/no' response, or one that asks for more information.

Information Questions

To form information questions, you'll need to use a question
word. Question words are generally placed before the verb:

What?	kâ-ray?	What did you eat? kay-râng kâ-ray say-bâ-yin? (lit: you what ate?)
Who?	su?	Who's he? khong su ray? (pol) (lit: he who is?)
Where?	ka-bah?	Where's the post office? da-khâng ka-bah yö-ray? (lit: post-office where is?)
When?	ka-dü?	When did you leave? kay-râng ka-dü thön-gay? (lit: you when left?)
Whose?	sü?	Whose is this? di sü ray? (lit: this whose is?)
How?	kân-te-si?	How do I get to ...? ...-la kân-te-si do-gö-ray? (lit: to how go?)
How much/ many?	kâ-tsay/ kât-sö?	How much is the room? khâng-mi te-la gong kâ-tsay ray? (lit: room the cost how-much is?)
Why?	kâ-ray chay-nay?	Why did you go? kay-râng kâ-ray chay-nay chin-bâ-yin? (lit: you why went?)

GRAMMAR

'Yes/No' Questions

To form a question from a sentence that uses one of the three equivalents of the verb 'to be', the endings are as follows:

	du/yö	ray/yin	yö-ray
I/he/she/it/we/they	du-gay	re-bay	yö re-bay
you	yö-bay	yin-bay	

Do you have a pen?   **kay-räng-la nyu-gu-chig yö-bay?**
(lit: you pen-one have?)

For all other verbs, use the following endings:

Intentional Verbs

	Present	Past	Future
I/we	-gi du-gay	-pa re-bay	-gi re-bay
you	-gi yö-bay	verb-bay	-gi yin-bay
he/she/it/they	-gi du-gay	-pa re-bay	-gi re-bay

Unintentional Verbs

	Present	Past	Future
I/we/you/he/she/it/they	-gi du-gay	song-ngey	-gi re-bay

Are you watching the show?   **kay-räng tay-mo ta-gi yö-bay?**
(intentional)   (lit: you show watch-present-are?)

Did you see the show?   **kay-räng tay-mo tong song-ngey?**
(unintentional)   (lit: you show see-past-were?)

GRAMMAR

NEGATIVES

To make a 'to be' sentence negative, use the following forms:

	du/yö	ray/yin	yö-ray
I/we	may	min/ma-yin	yö-ma-ray
you/he/she/it/they	min-du	ma-ray	

This is not a restaurant.   di sa-khâng ma-ray
                               (lit: this restaurant is-not)
There are no hotels here.   day sa-khâng yö-ma-ray
                               (lit: here hotels are-not)

For all other verbs, add the following endings to the main verb:

Intentional Verbs

	Present	Past	Future
I/we	-gi-may	-pa-min	-gi-min
you/he/she/it/they	-gi-min-du	-pa-ma-ray	-gi-ma-ray

Unintentional Verbs

	Present	Past	Future
I/we	-gi-min-du	ma-choong	-gi-ma-ray
you/he/she/it/they		ma-song	

I don't listen to music.   ngay rö-ja nyen-gi-may
  (intentional)   (lit: I music listen-present-not)
I'm not sick.   nga na-gi-min-du
  (unintentional)   (lit: I sick-am-present-not)

GRAMMAR

CONVEYING 'YES' & 'NO'

In Tibetan, the verb form used in the question determines how you say 'yes' and 'no'. Listen out for one of the following forms at the end of a question, and answer with the appropriate 'yes' or 'no':

Question Form	du-gay	yö-bay	re-bay	yin-bay	yö re-bay
Yes	du	yö	ray	yin	yo-ray
No	min-du	may	ma-ray	men	yö mâ-ray

Are yaks big?   yâk chen-po yö re-bay?
                            (lit: yaks big are?)
    Yes./No.   yö-ray/yö mâ-ray

Do you live here?   kay-râng-day shu-gi yö-bay?
                            (lit: you-here live-present-are?)
    Yes./No.   yö/may

There are some exceptions, for example, the past-tense question ending song-ngey (see page 33):

Did you see the show?   kay-râng tay-mo tong song-ngey?
                            (lit: you show see-past-were?)
    Yes./No.   song/ma-song

POSTPOSITIONS

Postpositions are equivalent to prepositions in English; where in English the preposition comes before the noun, in Tibetan it comes after the noun. 'To', 'at', 'for' and 'into' can all be expressed by -la.

I will go to India.   nga gya-ka-la do-gi yin
                            (lit: I India-to go-future-am)

Below is a list of other common postpositions:

above	gâng-la
around	nye-ko-la
behind	gyâb-la/jay-la
beside	tih-la
from	nay
in	nâng-la
in front of	dün-la
of	ki/gi/yi
next to	tih-la
on	gâng-la
opposite	pha-chog-la/kha-trö-la/tog-chog-la
under	wog-la
with	nyâm-du

In front of the house. khâng-bay dün-la
(lit: house in-front-of)

CONJUNCTIONS

Conjunctions are placed in the same position as in English.

and	dâng
because	gâng-yin say-na
but	yin-nay
or	yâng-na
since	tsâng/nay
so (therefore)	te-dah song-tsâng
so that (in order to)	ton-dâ-la/chay-du
then	te-nay/te-dü

I'd like to go to Tsetang, nga tse-tang-la don-dhö-yö,
but I don't have time. yin-nay nga-la dü-tsö may
(lit: I Tsetang-to like but
I time have-no)

You'll find that most Tibetans enjoy having visitors to their country and are keen to talk to you. A good conversation starter is ta-shi de-lek (བཀྲ་ཤིས་བདེ་ལེགས།). Literally meaning 'good fortune', it's often used as an equivalent to 'hello'.

YOU SHOULD KNOW
ཤེས་དགོས་པ།

Hello.	ta-shi de-lek	བཀྲ་ཤིས་བདེ་ལེགས།
Good morning.	nga-to de-lek	སྔ་དྲོ་བདེ་ལེགས།
Goodbye. (staying)	ka-lee pay	ག་ལེར་ཕེབས།
Goodbye. (leaving)	ka-lee shu	ག་ལེར་བཞུགས།
Excuse me; Please. (pol)	tu-jay-sig	ཐུགས་རྗེ་གཟིགས།
Thank you.	tu-jay-chay	ཐུགས་རྗེ་ཆེ།
Many thanks.	tu-jay shay-ta-chay	ཐུགས་རྗེ་ཞི་དྲག་ཆེ།

There's no single word for 'yes' and 'no' – it depends on the verb in the question. Either way, you'll notice that la (ལགས།) is used initially – this is a general marker that politely acknowledges the question. Often the verb that follows will be one of the 'to be' verbs (see Grammar, page 28):

YES		No	
la, yin	ལགས། ཡིན།	la, men	ལགས། མིན།
la, ray	ལགས། རེད།	la, ma-ray	ལགས། མ་རེད།
la, yö	ལགས། ཡོད།	la, may	ལགས། མེད།
la, du	ལགས། འདུག	la, min-du	ལགས། མིན་འདུག

For instance, if asked kay-râng lob-toog yin-bay (ཁྱེད་རང་སློབ་ཕྲུག་ཡིན་པས།), 'Are you a student?', you would reply either la, yin (ལགས། ཡིན།), 'yes' or la, men (ལགས། མིན།), 'no'.

GREETINGS & GOODBYES

Although ta-shi de-lek (བཀྲ་ཤིས་བདེ་ལེགས།) has become popular as a
greeting in Lhasa, it may not always be understood as an equivalent
to 'hello' elsewhere. Traditionally, Tibetans would ask each other
where they were going by way of a greeting; nowadays, people
often just start talking without any greeting at all.

Good morning.	nga-to de-lek	ཞོགས་དྲོ་བདེ་ལེགས།
Good day. (noon)	nyin-mo de-lek	ཉིན་མོ་བདེ་ལེགས།
Good afternoon.	chi-to de-lek	ཕྱི་དྲོ་བདེ་ལེགས།
Good evening.	gong-to de-lek	དགོང་དྲོ་བདེ་ལེགས།

THUMBS UP!

Giving a thumbs up with both hands means 'sorry' in Tibet.

There are two phrases for 'goodbye' in Tibetan: ka-lee shu
(ག་ལེར་བཞུགས།) and ka-lee pay (ག་ལེར་ཕེབས།). The first is said by the
person leaving and literally means 'Stay slowly'; the second is
said to the person leaving and literally means 'Go slowly'. Other
useful phrases include:

It's time to go.
  ta doh-ran-sha   ད་འགྲོ་རན་ཤག

See you tomorrow.
  sa-nyin jay-yong   སང་ཉིན་མཇལ་ཡོང་།

See you later.
  je-ma jay-yong   རྗེས་མ་མཇལ་ཡོང་།

Come again soon.
  yâng-kya pheb-ro-ah   ཡང་སྐྱར་ཕེབས་རོགས་ཨ།

We had a good time.
  ngân-tso kyi-po choong དངོ་སྐྱིད་པོ་བྱུང་།

Good night.
  sim-ja nâng-go   གཟིམ་འཇགས་གནང་དགོས།

MEETING PEOPLE

CIVILITIES

ཨ་རབས

There are two words meaning 'please' in Tibetan: ku-chi (སྐུ་སྐྱིད)
and tu-jay-sig (ཐུགས་རྗེ་གཟིགས). The former is the colloquial and the
latter the polite version. However, neither is used as readily as
'please' in English. Generally, they're reserved for quite desperate
or urgent requests, such as 'Please help me', ku-chi, nga-la rog
nâng-dâ (སྐུ་སྐྱིད་ ང་ར་རོགས་གནང་དང). For day-to-day use, there's a number
of polite expressions for situations where English speakers would
use 'please' or 'thank you'.

(Please) Come in.
  yah pay-nâng   ཡར་ཕེབས་གནང༌།
(Please) Sit down.
  shu-den ja   བཞུགས་གདན་འཇགས།
Excuse me; Sorry.
  gong-da   དགོངས་དག
May I?; Do you mind?
  di-gi re-bay   འགྲིག་གི་རེད་པས།
Thank you (very much).
  tu-jay (shay-ta)-chay   ཐུགས་རྗེ་(ཞེ་དྲག)ཆེ།
Thank you for your hospitality.
  nay-len yak-po nâng-wa   སྐུ་ལེན་ཡག་པོ་གནང་བར་ཐུགས་རྗེ་ཆེ།
  tu-jay-chay
Thank you for your help.
  nga rog nâng-wa tu-jay-chay   ང་ར་རོགས་གནང་བ་ཐུགས་རྗེ་ཆེ།
You're welcome.
  la yin-dâng-yin   ལགས་ཡིན་དང་ཡིན།
Not at all; Don't mention it.
  shu gö-ya yö-ma-ray   ཞུ་དགོས་ཡག་ཡོད་མ་རེད།

NO OFFENCE!

Don't be offended if people don't say 'please' or 'thank
you' to you – these phrases aren't very common in Tibetan.

MEETING PEOPLE

Requests

འབོད་སྐུལ།

I'd like to ask you a favour.
ngay kay-râng-la ray-kü-chig
shu-ya yö

ངས་ཁྱེད་རང་ལ་རེ་སྐུལ་གཅིག
ཞུ་ཡག་ཡོད།

May I ask you a question?
ngay kay-râng-la kân-ti-chig
shu-na di-gi re-bay

ངས་ཁྱེད་རང་ལ་བཀའ་འདྲི་གཅིག
ཞུ་ན་འགྲིག་གི་རེད་པས།

Please can you help me?
ku-chi, nga-la rog nâng-da

སྐུ་མཁྱེན། ང་ལ་རོགས་གནང་དང༌།

(Please) Could you repeat that?
(ku-chi) yâng-kya soong
nâng-da

(སྐུ་མཁྱེན།) ཡང་སྐྱར་གསུང་གནང་དང༌།

(Please) Show me that.
pa-gi nga-la tön nâng da

ཕ་གི་ང་ལ་སྟོན་གནང་དང༌།

Will you pass it to me please?
nga-la shu-ro nâng

ང་ལ་བཤུག་རོགས་གནང༌།

Can I take ... now?
ta ... kye-na di-gi re-bay

ད ... འཁྱེར་ན་འགྲིག་གི་རེད་པས།

May I go now?
ta do-na di-gi re-bay

ད་འགྲོ་ན་འགྲིག་གི་རེད་པས།

Please don't forget!
ku-chi, ma-je-ro nâng

སྐུ་མཁྱེན། མ་བརྗེད་རོགས་གནང༌།

What's the name of this?
dee ming-lâ kâ-ray ray

འདིའི་མིང་ལ་ག་རེ་རེད།

OOH LA LA!

If someone calls you or tries to get your attention, a polite response to show you've heard is **la** (ལགས།). It can also be attached to the end of someone's name to be more polite when calling them. For example, if the person's name is **Tashi**, you would call out **Tashi-la**

FORMS OF ADDRESS འབོད་ཚིག

To attract someone's attention, Tibetans use kinship terms, rather than say 'Excuse me'. Kinship terms vary according to the age and sex of the person you're speaking to. The standard term for someone of about your own age is cho-la (ཇོ་ལགས), literally 'elder brother', for a man, and ah-cha-la (ཨ་ཅག་ལགས), literally 'elder sister', for a woman. For example, to a man on the street who's about your age, but you don't know, you could say cho-la, gom-ba ka-bah du (ཇོ་ལགས། དགོན་པ་ག་བར་འདུག), 'Hey Mister, where's the monastery?'. Other kinship terms include:

To someone ...	male	female
younger	bu (བུ) (lit: son)	bu-mo (བུ་མོ) (lit: daughter)
the same age	cho-la (ཇོ་ལགས) (lit: elder-brother)	ah-cha-la (ཨ་ཅག་ལགས) (lit: elder-sister)
older	pa-la (པ་ལགས) (lit: father)	ah-ma-la (ཨ་མ་ལགས) (lit: mother)
elderly	po-la (པོ་ལགས) (lit: grandfather)	mo-la (མོ་ལགས) (lit: grandmother)

BODY LANGUAGE ལུས་ཀྱི་རྣམ་འགྱུར

In Tibet, people generally admire anyone who shows kindness, generosity and humility in their manner. For instance, if you're serving yourself at a meal, make sure you don't take the last of the food; leave enough for others.

When people meet and also when they farewell each other, they bow their heads slightly. When meeting, they'll also raise their right arm up from the elbow. When farewelling, the person staying may also extend their right hand with the palm facing upwards, as if showing the way for the person departing. Shaking hands has also become fairly common as a greeting.

When closely related people meet after a long absence, or when they're due to part for a long time, they gently touch their foreheads together, while holding each other's hands and saying the relevant phrases. When meeting, they'll say ku-su de-po yin-pay (སྐུ་གཟུགས་བདེ་པོ་ཡིན་པས།), 'How are you?', and when departing they'll say châg-po nâng-ah (ཕྱག་པོ་གནང་ཨ།), 'Take care of yourself', to which the reply is thook-tel nâng mi-gö (ཐུགས་འཁྲལ་གནང་མི་དགོས།), 'You need not worry'.

When giving or receiving items, both hands are usually used. Alternatively, the right hand can be used to give or receive the item with the left hand bent towards the right elbow joint.

Other gestures you may see are head-scratching, which indicates doubt or nervousness, and shaking the index finger, which indicates warning. Sometimes, when listening to the words of a highly respected person, Tibetans may stick their tongue out slightly to show humbleness, respect and loyalty.

When visiting temples, you should take off your shoes, walk slowly and keep noise to a minimum. Hats should not be worn, nor should clothing which exposes the limbs (such as singlets and shorts).

KATA CULTURE

The ka-ta (ཁ་བཏགས་), a white ceremonial scarf, forms an indispensable part of Tibetan culture. It's an auspicious symbol of goodwill, friendship, harmony and love and, similar to flowers in the West, is used in many festivals and ceremonies, such as weddings, New Year and house-warmings. It's also used in greetings and goodbyes, and when people visit temples or lamas they offer ka-ta as a symbol of their faith and respect. Normally, the ka-ta is folded in half lengthwise and draped across both hands and is either placed around the neck of the recipient or given into their hands.

MEETING PEOPLE

FIRST ENCOUNTERS ཐོག་མ་ཐུག་རྒྱུ་གས།

When you first meet someone, use the relevant kinship term to address them (see page 41). Tibetans will be more comfortable giving their name once they've had a bit of a chat with you.

How are you?
  kay-râng ku-su de-po yin-bay   ཁྱེད་རང་སྐུ་གཟུགས་བདེ་པོ་ཨིན་པས།
Fine. And you?
  de-bo-yin. kay-râng-yâng   བདེ་པོ་ཨིན། ཁྱེད་རང་ཡང་སྐུ་གཟུགས་བདེ་པོ་
  ku-su de-po yin-bay   ཨིན་པས།
What's your name?
  kay-râng-gi tsen-lâ kâ-ray-ray   ཁྱེད་རང་གི་མཚན་ལ་ག་རེ་རེད།
My name is ...
  ngay-ming-la ... ray   ངའི་མིང་ལ ... རེད།
I'd like to introduce you to ...
  ngay kay-râng-la ... ngo-tö shu-na   ངས་ཁྱེད་རང་ལ ... ངོ་སྤྲོད་ཞུ་ན།
Pleased to meet you.
  kay-râng jel-pa gâh-po choong   ཁྱེད་རང་མཇལ་པ་དགའ་པོ་བྱུང་།

MAKING CONVERSATION སྐད་ཆ་བྱེད་ཚུལ།

Asking someone where they're going (kay-râng ka-bah pay-kay, ཁྱེད་རང་ག་བར་ཕེབས་གས།) is a good way of opening casual conversation in Tibet.

Do you live here?
  kay-râng-day shu-gi yö-bay   ཁྱེད་རང་འདིར་བཞུགས་ཀྱི་ཡོད་པས།
Where are you going?
  kay-râng ka-bah pay-kay   ཁྱེད་རང་ག་བར་ཕེབས་གས།
What are you doing?
  kay-râng kâ-ray nâng-gi yö   ཁྱེད་རང་ག་རེ་གནང་གི་ཡོད།
This is my partner.
  khong ngay-(tok-po/tok-mo)   ཁོང་ངའི་གྲོགས་པོ་/གྲོགས་མོ་རེད།
  ray (m/f)
What do you think about ...?
  kay-râng ... tog-la sâm-tsü   ཁྱེད་རང ... ཐོག་ལ་བསམ་ཚུལ་
  kâ-ray-yö   ག་རེ་ཡོད།

MEETING PEOPLE

Can I take a photo (of you)?
    (kay-râng) par-chig gyâb-na   (ཁྱེད་རང་)པར་ཆིག་རྒྱབ་ན
    di-giy ray-bay   འགྲིག་གི་རེད་པས།

What's this called?
    di-la kâ-ray sa   འདི་ལ་ག་རེ་ཟ།

Beautiful, isn't it!
    nying-je-po du-kah   སྙིང་རྗེ་པོ་འདུག་ག

It's great here.
    day pay-mi-si kyi-po du   འདིར་དཔེ་མི་སྲི་སྐྱིད་པོ་འདུག

We love it here.
    ngân-tso day kyi-po du   ང་ཚོ་འདིར་སྐྱིད་པོ་འདུག

What a cute baby!
    pu-gu-di nying jay-pa-lah   ཕྲུ་གུ་འདི་སྙིང་རྗེ་པ་ལ།

Are you waiting too?
    kay-râng-yâng gook-tay yö-bay   ཁྱེད་རང་ཡང་སྒུག་ནས་ཡོད་པས།

That's funny/strange.
    te kyen-tsa-po ray   དེ་ཁྱད་མཚར་པོ་རེད།

Are you here on holiday?
    kay-râng day goong-seng yin-bay   ཁྱེད་རང་འདིར་གུང་གསེང་ཡིན་པས།

I'm here ...   nga day ... yin   ང་འདིར་ ... ཡིན།
    for a holiday   goong-seng-chay   གུང་གསེང་ཆེད
    on business   tsong-lay-chay   ཚོང་ལས་ཆེད
    to study   lob-jong je-chay   སློབ་སྦྱོང་བྱེད་ཆེད

How long are you here for?
    kay-râng-day yün ring-lö   ཁྱེད་རང་འདིར་ཡུན་རིང་ལོས
    day-ki-yin   བསྡད་ཀྱི་ཡིན།

I'm here for ... weeks/days.
    nga day dün-ta/   ང་འདིར་བདུན་ཕྲག/
    nyin-ma ... day-ki-yin   ཉིནམ ... བསྡད་ཀྱི་ཡིན།

Do you like it here?
    kay-râng-day kyi-po du-gay   ཁྱེད་རང་འདིར་སྐྱིད་པོ་འདུག་གས།

Yes, a lot.
    kyi-po shay-ta du   སྐྱིད་པོ་ཤེ་དྲག་འདུག

We're here with our family.
    ngân-tso-day nâng-mi
    nyâm-tu leb-yö ཨ་ཚོ་འདིར་ནང་མི ཉམ་དུ་ས�་ེབས་ཡོད།

I'm here with my boyfriend/girlfriend.
    nga-day tok-po/tok-mo
    nyâm-tu leb-yö ང་འདིར་གྲོགས་པོ/གྲོགས་མོ ཉམ་དུ་ས�་ེབས་ཡོད།

Isn't the weather good today?
    te-ring nâm-shi yâg-po du-gah དེ་རིང་གནམ་གཤིས་ཡག་པོ་འདུག་ག

Please sit here.
    day shu-ro-nâng འདིར་བཞུགས་རོགས་གནང་།

Sure.	yin-da-yin	ཡིན་དང་ཡིན།
Just a minute.	teh-si gu-ah	ཏོག་ཙམ་སྒུག་ག
I see.	ah-leh	ཨ་ལེ།
It's OK.	di-gi ray	འགྲིག་གི་རེད།
It's (not) important.	kay-chen-po (ma)-ray	གལ་ཆེན་པོ་(མ)རེད།
It's (not) possible.	si-ki (ma)-ray	སྲིད་ཀྱི་(མ)རེད།
Look!	mik ta-dâ	མིག་བལྟ་དང་།
Listen (to this)!	(di) nyön-da	(འདི)ཉོན་དང་།
I'm ready.	nga ta-dig-yin	ང་གྲ་འགྲིག་ཡིན།
Are you ready?	kay-râng ta-dig yin-bay	ཁྱེད་རང་གྲ་འགྲིག་ཡིན་པས།
Go away!	pah gyu	ཕར་རྒྱུགས།
Be quiet!	kah-ga shu	ཁ་ཁ་བཀག་གས།
Never mind.	kay chay-kiy ma-ray	གར་བྱེད་ཀྱི་མ་རེད།

MEETING PEOPLE

NATIONALITIES

ཡུལ་ལུགས

If your country isn't listed here, try pointing on a map.

Where are you from?

kay-râng loong-pa ka-nay yin   ཁྱེད་རང་ལུང་པ་ཀ་ནས་ཡིན།

I'm from ...	nga ...-nay yin	ང་ ...ནས་ཡིན།
We're from ...	ngân-tso ...-nay yin	ང་ཚོ་ ...ནས་ཡིན།
Africa	ah-fi-ri-ka	ཨ་ཕི་རི་ཀ
Asia	ay-shi-ya	ཨེ་ཤི་ཡ
Australia	o-ta-li-ya	ཨོ་ས་ཀ་ལི་ཡ
Canada	ka-na-da	ཁེ་ན་ད
China	gyâ-nak	རྒྱ་ནག
England	in-ji loong-pa	དབྱིན་ཇི་ལུང་པ
Europe	yu-rop	ཡུ་རོབ
Finland	fin-land	ཕིན་ལནྡ
France	fa-ren-si	ཕ་རན་སི
Germany	jar-man	འཇར་མན
Holland	ho-land	ཧོ་ལནྡ
India	gya-ga	རྒྱ་གར
Ireland	ah-ri-len	ཨེ་རི་ལནྡ
Israel	e-za-rel	ཨི་ཛ་རེལ
Italy	e-ta-lee	ཨི་ཊ་ལི
Japan	ree-bin	རི་ཕིན
the Middle East	shar-kyil gya-kab	ཤར་དཀྱིལ་རྒྱལ་ཁབ
New Zealand	nu-zee-land	ནིའུ་ཛི་ལནྡ
Norway	naw-way	ནོར་ཝེ
Scotland	so-kot-land	སོ་ཀོཊ་ལནྡ
South America	lho ah-mi-ri-ka	ལྷོ་ཨ་མི་རི་ཀ
Spain	se-pan	སེ་པན
Sweden	sü-den	སུད་ཏན
Switzerland	sü-zee	སུད་སི
the USA	yu-es-ay/ah-mi-ri-ka	ཡུ་ཨེས་ཨེ/ཨ་མི་རི་ཀ
Wales	welz	ཝེལས

We come from a/the ...	ngân-tso ...-nay yin	ngâ ...-nay yin
I live in/at the/a ...	nga ...-la dö-ki-yö	
city	dong-kay	
countryside	dong-seb	
mountains	ri gâng	
seaside	tso-dâm	
suburbs of ...	... dong-kay sa-kü	
village	dong-seb	

CULTURAL DIFFERENCES

How do you do this in your country?
kay-râng-gi loong-pay loog-sö-la
di kân-teh-si chay-gö-ray
Is this a local or national custom?
di sa-nay-ki loog-sö yin-na,
gyâ-kâb-ki loog-sö yin-na

| local | sa-nay-ki |
| national | gyâ-kâb-ki |

I don't want to offend you.
ngay kay-râng-la pok-tu
chay-sâm may
I'm sorry, it's not the custom
in my country.
gong-ta te-da ngân-tsö
loong-pay loog-sö-la yö-ma-ray

THE PATH TO HAPPINESS

All Tibetan houses have an altar room and monks or nuns are frequently invited to perform rituals or recite religious books for the prosperity and happiness of the family. Outside each house, you'll find a Buddhist flag.

I'm not accustomed to this.
    nga di-la gom-di may   ང་འདི་ལ་གོམས་འདྲིས་མེད།

I don't mind watching, but I'd
prefer not to participate.
    nga tay-mo ta-ya-tsâm ma-tok   ང་ལྟད་མོ་ལྟ་ཡག་ཚམ་མ་གཏོགས་བྱེད་བྱེ་གཏོགས
    thay-tog chay-dö may   བྱེད་འདོད་མེད།

I'll give it a go.
    ngay ta-tsö chay-go   ངས་ལྟ་ཚོད་བྱེད་གོ

I'm sorry, it's	gong-ta di ngay	དགོངས་དག་འདི་ངའི
against my ...	...-dâng tün-gee min-du	...དང་མཐུན་གྱི་མིན་འདུག
beliefs	ta-wa	ལྟ་བ
culture	rig-shoong	རིག་གཤུང
religion	chö-loog	ཆོས་ལུགས

AGE   རང་ལོ

How old are you?
    kay-râng lo kâ-tsay yin   ཁྱེད་རང་ལོ་ག་ཚོད་ཡིན།

How old is your ...?	... lo kâ-tsay ray	... ལོ་ག་ཚོད་རེད།
son	kay-râng-gi bu	ཁྱེད་རང་གི་བུ
daughter	kay-râng-gi bu-mo	ཁྱེད་རང་གི་བུ་མོ

I'm ... years old.	nga lo ... yin	ང་ལོ ... ཡིན།
18	chö-gye	བཅོ་བརྒྱད
25	nyi-shu tsay-nga	ཉི་ཤུ་ཙ་ལྔ

(See Numbers & Amounts, page 179, for your age.)

OCCUPATIONS   འཚོ་བའབས
The list opposite includes both local and Western occupations.

What do you do (for a living)?
    kay-râng (tso-tâb-che) lay-kâ   ཁྱེད་རང་(འཚོ་བའབས་ཆེད་)
    kâ-ray chay-ki-yö   ལས་ཀ་ག་རེ་བྱེད་ཀྱི་ཡོད།

I'm a/an ...	nga ... yin	᠍᠍᠍ ... ཡིན།
actor	tâb tön-pa	འཁྲབ་སྟོན་པ་
artist	ri-mo khen	རི་མོ་མཁན་
businessperson	tsong-pa	ཚོང་པ་
carpenter	shing-so-wa	ཤིང་བཟོ་བ་
chef	ma-chen	མ་བྱན་
doctor	ahm-chi	ཨེམ་ཆི་
driver	mo-ta tong-khen	མོ་ཊ་གཏོང་མཁན་
engineer	so-tün chen-mo-wa	བཟོ་སྟུན་ཆེན་མོ་བ་
factory worker	so-ta lay-ka chay-khen	བཟོ་གྲྭའི་ལས་ཀ་བྱེད་མཁན་
farmer	shing-pâ	ཞིང་པ་
journalist	tsâg-ba gya-khen	ཚགས་པར་རྒྱགས་མཁན་
labourer	ngay-tsö gyu-khen	ངལ་རྩོལ་རྒྱུ་མཁན་
lawyer	tim tsö-pa	ཁྲིམས་རྩོད་པ་
manual worker	ngay-tsö gyu-khen	ངལ་རྩོལ་རྒྱུ་མཁན་
mechanic	trü-lay pa	འཕྲུལ་ལས་པ་
musician	ro-ja tong-khen	རོལ་ཆ་གཏོང་མཁན་
nomad	dok-pa	འབྲོག་པ་
nurse	men-khâng nay-yok	སྨན་ཁང་གི་ནད་གཡོག
office worker/ clerk	lay-koong lay-ka chay-khen; doong-yig	ལས་ཁུངས་ལས་ཀ་བྱེད་ མཁན་/དྲུང་ཡིག
scientist	tsen-rig pa	མཚན་རིག་པ་
secretary	doong-yig	དྲུང་ཡིག
student	lob-toog	སློབ་ཕྲུག
tailor	tsen-po-wa	ཚེམ་པོ་བ་
teacher	gay-gan	དགེ་རྒན་
university lecturer	tsu-la lob-tay lek-chah shö-khen	གཙུག་ལག་སློབ་གྲྭའི་ ལེགས་བཤད་འཆད་མཁན་
waiter	se-dim shâb-shu-wa	ཟས་འབྲིམ་ཞབས་ཞུ་བ་
writer	tsom-di-pa	རྩོམ་འབྲི་པ་

I'm retired.
   nga gen-yö yin   ང་རྒན་ཡོལ་ཡིན།

I'm unemployed.
   ngah lay-ka may   ངར་ལས་ཀ་མེད།

What are you studying?
   kay-râng lob-jong kâ-ray   ཁྱེད་རང་སློབ་སྦྱོང་ག་རེ་
   nâng-gi yö   གནང་གི་ཡོད།

I'm studying ...	nga ... lob-jong	ང་ ... སློབ་སྦྱོང་
	chay-ki yö	བྱེད་ཀྱི་ཡོད།
art	ri-mo	རི་མོ
arts/humanities	gyu-tse rig-nay	རྒྱུ་སྐྱལ་རིག་གནས
Buddhism	nâng-chö	ནང་ཆོས
business	tsong-lay	ཚོང་ལས
engineering	so-tün rig-nay	བཟོ་སྐྲུན་རིག་གནས
English	in-ji kay-yig	དབྱིན་ཇིའི་སྐད་ཡིག
languages	kay-yig	སྐད་ཡིག
law	tim	ཁྲིམས
medicine	men	སྨན
science	tsen-rig	མཚན་རིག
teaching	gay-gan ö-jong	དགེ་རྒན་འོས་སྦྱོང
Tibetan	bö-kay	བོད་སྐད

FEELINGS
ཚོར་སྣང་

I'm ...	nga ...-gi du	ང་ ...གི་འདུག
Are you ...?	kay-râng ...-gi du-gay	ཁྱེད་རང་ ...གི་འདུག་གས།
afraid	tah	སྐྲག
angry	loong lâng	རྫོང་ལང་
cold	khya	འཁྱག
depressed	sem-shu bay-ti châg	སེམས་ཤུགས་ཆུང་དེ་ཆགས
hot	tsa-wa tsi	ཚ་བ་ཚིག
hungry	drö-kog tog	གྲོད་ཁོག་ལྟོགས
sad	sem kyo	སེམས་སྐྱོ
sleepy	nyi ku	གཉིད་ཁུག
sorry (regret)	gyö-pa kye	འགྱོད་པ་སྐྱེ
thirsty	ka kom	ཁ་སྐོམ
tired	kâ-lay ka	དཀའ་ལས་ཁ
worried	sem-tel lâng	སེམས་འཚབ་ལང་

I'm grateful.	kay-râng nga-la kâ-tin chen-po yin	ཁྱེད་རང་ང་ལ་བཀའ་དྲིན་ཆེན་པོ་ཡིན
I'm happy.	nga kyi-po du	ང་སྐྱིད་པོ་འདུག
I'm in a hurry.	nga te-wa yö	ང་འཕྲལ་བ་ཡོད
I'm keen to ...	nga ...-la dö-pa yö	ང་ ...ལ་འདོད་པ་ཡོད
I'm sorry. (condolence)	nga lo-phâm yö	ང་བློ་ཕམ་ཡོད
I'm well.	nga de-po yin	ང་བདེ་པོ་ཡིན

MEETING PEOPLE

BREAKING THE LANGUAGE BARRIER

གོ་བརྡ་མི་འཕྲོད་པའི་དཀའ་ངལ་སེལ་བ།

You'll find that English isn't widely spoken in Tibet, particularly in the more remote areas. Even in Lhasa the number of English speakers is relatively small.

Do you speak English?
  kay-râng in-ji-kay shing-gi
  yö-bay

ཁྱེད་རང་དབྱིན་ཇི་སྐད་
ཤེས་ཀྱི་ཡོད་པས།

Yes, I do.
  la, yö

ལགས། ཡོད།

No, I don't.
  la, may

ལགས། མེད།

Does anyone speak English?
  in-ji-kay shay-khen yö ray-bay

དབྱིན་ཇི་སྐད་ཤེས་མཁན་ཡོད་རེད་པས།

I speak a little.
  teh-si shin-gi yö

ཏོག་ཙམ་ཤེས་ཀྱི་ཡོད།

Do you understand?
  ha ko song-ngay

ཧ་གོ་སོང་ངས།

I understand.
  ha ko-song

ཧ་གོ་སོང་།

I don't understand.
  ha ko ma-song

ཧ་གོ་མ་སོང་།

Could you speak more slowly please?
  yâng-kya ka-lee ka-lee soong
  nâng da

ཡང་སྐྱར་ག་ལེར་ག་ལེར་གསུང་གནང་དང་།

Could you repeat that?
  te yâng-kya soong nâng-da

དེ་ཡང་སྐྱར་གསུང་གནང་དང་།

Please write it down.
  ku-chi, shu-gü-tog ti nâng-da

སྐུ་མཁྱེན། ཤོག་བུའི་ཐོག་འབྲི་གནང་དང་།

How do you say ...?
  ... kân-te-si lâb gö ray

... གང་འདྲས་ལབ་དགོས་རེད།

What does ... mean?
   ...-gi tön-tåg kâ-ray ray ...གི་དོན་དག་ག་རེ་རེད།

What does this mean?
   di tön-tåg kâ-ray ray འདི་དོན་དག་ག་རེ་རེད།

What's this called?
   di-la kâ-ray sa འདི་ལ་ག་རེ་ཟ།

Just a moment, I'll try to find
it in this book.
   teh-si goo-ah, teb-di nâng ཏོག་ཙམ་འགུགས་ཨ། དེབ་འདི་ནང་
   yö-may ta-gi-yin ཡོད་མེད་བལྟ་གི་ཡིན།

Can you read this script for me please?
   nga-la yi-ge-di lo-rog nâng-da ང་ལ་ཡི་གེ་འདི་ཀློག་རོགས་གནང་དང་།

Can you show me (in this book)?
   (teb di-nâng) mig tön-da (དེབ་འདིའི་ནང་)མིག་སྟོན་དང་།

STAYING IN TOUCH སྐུ་མཉུད་འབྲེལ་བ

Tomorrow is my last day here.
   sa-nyin nga day dö-ya nyin སང་ཉིན་ང་འདིར་སྡོད་ཡག་ཉིན་མཐའ་
   ta-ma-te yin མ་དེ་ཡིན།

Let's swap addresses.
   ka-chång je-ray chay-na ཁ་བྱང་བརྗེ་རེས་བྱེད་ན།

Do you have a pen and paper?
   kay-rång-la nyu-gu dång ཁྱེད་རང་ལ་སྙུ་གུ་དང་ཤོག་གུ་ཡོད་པས།
   shu-gu yö-bay

What's your address?
   kay-rång-gi ka-chång ཁྱེད་རང་གི་ཁ་བྱང་ག་རེ་རེད།
   kâ-ray ray

What's your email address?
   kay-rång-gi ee-mel ཁྱེད་རང་གི་ཨི་མེལ་ཁ་བྱང་ག་རེ་རེད།
   ka-chång kâ-ray ray

Here's my address.
   ngay ka-chång di-ray ངའི་ཁ་བྱང་འདི་རེད།

If you ever visit (Scotland) you
must come and visit us.

    kay-râng gay-si (so-kot-land)-la
    pheb-na nga-tsö-sah ngay-pa-du
    pheb-nâng

ཁྱེད་རང་གལ་སྲིད་（སོ་ཀོཊ་ལེན་）ལ་ཕེབས་ནང་
ཚོའི་སར་དེས་པ་དུ་ཕེབས་གནང་།

If you come to (Birmingham) you've
got a place to stay.

    kay-râng gay-si (ba-min-gâm)-la
    pheb-na shoog-sa nga-tsö-sah yö

ཁྱེད་རང་གལ་སྲིད་（བྱར་མིང་བགྷམ་）ལ་
ཕེབས་ན-ར་བཞུགས་ས-ར་ཚོའི་སར་ཡོད།

Do you have an email address?

    kay-râng-la ee-mel ka-châng
    yö-bay

ཁྱེད་རང་ལ་ཨཱི་མེལ་ཁ་བྱང་ཡོད་པས།

Do you have access to a fax machine?

    kay-râng-la faks-tog day-wa
    chay thoob-ki re-bay

ཁྱེད་རང་ལ་ཕེག་སི་ཐོག་འབྲེལ་བ་བྱེད་
ཐུབ་ཀྱི་རེད་པས།

I'll send you copies of the photos.

    ngay kay-râng-la par tâng
    yong-gi yin

ངས་ཁྱེད་རང་ལ་པར་གཏང་ཡོང་གི་ཡིན།

Don't forget to write!

    nga-la yig-day nâng-ya ma-jay-ah

ང་ལ་ཡི་གེ་འབྲེལ་གནང་ཡ་མ་བརྗེད་ཨ།

It's been great meeting you.

    kay-râng jay-wa ka-bo
    shay-ta choong

ཁྱེད་རང་མཇལ་བར་དགའ་པོ་ཞེ་དྲག་བྱུང་།

Keep in touch!

    mu-tü-nay day-wa nâng-ah

མུ་མཐུད་ནས་འབྲེལ་བ་གནང་ཨ།།

འགྲིམ་འགྲུལ་བྱེད་པ།

GETTING AROUND

There's a number of ways you can travel around in Tibet. For longer distances, buses, minibuses, taxis or hire vehicles are available; for shorter distances – or for the energetic – cycling or walking are also options.

FINDING YOUR WAY
འགྲོ་ལམ་འཚོལ་བ།

Where's the ...?	... ka-bah yö-ray	... ག་བར་ཡོད་རེད།
bus station	chi-chö lâng-kho bâb-tsoog	སྤྱི་སྤྱོད་རྡུངས་འཁོར་ བབས་ཚུགས།
road to ...	...-la doh-say lâm-ga	...ལ་འགྲོ་སའི་ལམ་ག

What time does the ... leave/arrive?	... chu-tsö kâ-tsay-la doh-ki-ray/leb-ki-ray	... ཆུ་ཚོད་ག་ཚོད་ལ་ འགྲོ་གྱི་རེད།/སྲེབས་ཀྱི་རེད།
aeroplane	nâm-du	གནམ་གྲུ།
boat	dru-zing	གྲུ་གཟིངས།
bus	chi-chö lâng-kho	སྤྱི་སྤྱོད་རྡུངས་འཁོར།

What ... is this?	... di-ming-la ka-ray-sa	... འདིའི་མིང་ལ་ག་རེ་ཟ།
street	lâm-ga	ལམ་ག
village	loong-pa/dong-seb	ལུང་པ/གྲོང་གསེབ།

How do I get to ...?
...-la kân-teh-si doh-gö ray
...ལ་གང་འདྲས་འགྲོ་དགོས་རེད།

Is it far/near?
[ta ring-po; ta nye-po] re-bay
[ཐག་རིང་པོ/ཐག་ཉེ་པོ] རེད་པས།

Can I walk there?
gom-pa gyâb-nay leb thoob-ki re-bay
གོམ་པ་བརྒྱབ་ནས་སྲེབས་ཐུབ་ཀྱི་ རེད་པས།

Can you show me (on the map)?
(sâp-ta di-nâng) tön nâng-da
(ས་བཀྲའ་འདི་ནང་) སྟོན་གནང་དང་།

Are there other means of getting there?
pha-kay do-ya tâb-lâm shen-da yö re-bay
ཕ་གིར་འགྲོ་ཡག་ཐབས་ལམ་གཞན་དག ཡོད་རེད་པས།

GETTING AROUND

Directions
ལམ་སྟོན་གནས།

Turn (left/right)	...-la (yön/yeh)	...ལ་(གཡོན་/གཡས་)
at the ...	kyog-nâng	སྐྱོགས་གནང་།
next corner	su-dong jay-ma	ཟུར་གདོང་རྗེས་མ།
traffic lights	lâm-gay log-da	ལམ་གའི་གློག་བརྡ།
Go straight ahead.	ka-toog-do	ཁ་ཐུག་འགྲོ།
Turn left/right.	yön-la/yeh-la	གཡོན་ལ་/གཡས་ལ།
	kyog-nâng	སྐྱོགས་གནང་།
Thank you for	lâm-ga tön-nâng-wa	ལམ་ཀ་སྟོན་གནང་བར་
showing us the way.	tu-jay-chay	ཐུགས་རྗེ་ཆེ།

north	châng	བྱང་
south	lho	ལྷོ་
east	shâr	ཤར་
west	noob	ནུབ་

inside	nâng-lâ	ནང་ལ་
outside	chi-lo-lâ	ཕྱི་ལོག་ལ་
behind	gyâb-lâ	རྒྱབ་ལ་
in front of	dün-lâ	མདུན་ལ་
opposite	dog-cho/	ཕྱོག་ཕྱོགས་/
	pha-chog/ka-trö	ཕར་ཕྱོགས་/ཁ་གྲོད་
far	ta ring-po	ཐག་རིང་པོ་
near	tee-lâ/ta nye-po	བཞིས་ལ་/ཐག་ཉེ་པོ་
here	day	འདིར་
there	pha-kay	ཕ་གིར་

DISTANCE LEARNING

Along the roads in Tibet, distance is typically cited in do-ban (དོ་སྦུང་), the road repair stations which can be seen every 10 km.

How many *doban* is it to the
Saga district?
sa-ga zong bâ-tu do-ban   ས་སྐྱ་རྫོང་བར་དུ་དོ་སྦུང་
kâ-tsay yö-ray   ག་ཚད་ཡོད་རེད།

TAXI

ཏེག་སི

Taxis are readily available for travel outside Lhasa, but tend not to be used within the city. In certain towns, you'll also find rick-shaws (rik-sha, རིག་ཤ) available, offering a relaxed way to get around.

Where can I find a taxi?
  tek-si la-sa ka-bah yö-ray

ཏེག་སི་ཀླ་ས་ག་པར་ཡོད་རེད།

Please hire us a taxi.
  tek-si-chig dâ-la tong nâng-dâng

ཏེག་སི་གཅིག་ང་ཚོ་ལ་གཏོང་གནང་དང་།

Is this taxi free?
  tek-si-di tong-pa re-bay

ཏེག་སི་འདི་སྟོང་པ་རེད་པས།

Can you take me to ...?
  ...-la kye-rog nâng

...ལ་སྐྱེལ་རོགས་གནང་།

I want a taxi to the airport.
  nâm-tâng-ba tek-si-chig gö-ki-du

གནམ་ཐང་བར་ཏེག་སི་གཅིག་དགོས་ཀྱི་འདུག།

How much is it to go to ...?
  ...-la doh-wa-la la-ja kâ-tsay yin

...ལ་འགྲོ་བ་ལ་གླ་ཆ་ག་ཚད་ཡིན།

How much is the fare?
  khor-la-la kâ-tsay yin

འཁོར་གླ་ལ་ག་ཚད་ཡིན།

Do we pay extra for luggage?
  cha-lâg-la la-ja tö-ba tay-gö re-bay

ཅ་ལག་ལ་གླ་ཆ་འཕར་ལ་སྟེར་དགོས་རེད་པས།

Instructions

ལམ་སྟོན་བྱེད་པ

Continue!	mu thü-nâng
Please wait here.	day gu-rog nâng
Stop here!	day kâg-rog nâng

སྨུ་མཐུད་གནང་།
འདིར་འགུག་རོགས་གནང་།
འདིར་བཀག་རོགས་གནང་།

Stop at the corner.
  su-dong-tay kâg-rog nâng

གཟུར་གདོང་དེར་བཀག་རོགས་གནང་།

It's the next street to the left/right.
  lâm-ga jay-ma-tay yön-la/
  yeh-la kyog-nâng

ལམ་ག་རྗེས་མ་དེར་གཡོན་ལ་/
གཡས་ལ་སྐྱོག་གནང་།

Please [slow down; go faster].
  [ka-lee ka-lee; gyok-tsi] doh-nâng

[ག་ལེར་ག་ལེར་/མགྱོགས་ཙི་] འགྲོ་གནང་།

GETTING AROUND

BUYING TICKETS   ཏེ་ཀ་སི་ཉོ་ཝ།

Where can I buy a ticket?

    ti-ka-si nyo-sa ka-bah yö-ray   ཏེ་ཀ་སི་ཉོ་ས་ག་པར་ཡོད་རེད།

I want to buy a ticket to ...

    nga ...-la doh-ya-gi ti-ka-si   ང་ ...ལ་འགྲོ་ཡག་གི་ཏེ་ཀ་སི་

    nyo-gö-yö   ཉོ་དགོས་ཡོད།

How much is a	...-la doh-ya ti-ka-si	...ལ་འགྲོ་ཡག
ticket to ...?	gong kâ-tsay ray	གི་ཏེ་ཀ་སི་གོང་ག་ཚོད་རེད།
Ganden	gân-den	དགའ་ལྡན
Gyantse	gyân-tse	རྒྱལ་རྩེ
Shigatse	shi-gâ-tse	གཞིས་ཀ་རྩེ

Do I need to book?

    (ti-ka-si) ngön-la nyo-gö re-bay   (ཏེ་ཀ་སི་)སྔོན་ལ་ཉོ་དགོས་རེད་པས།

Can I reserve a place?

    dö-sa ngön-nay ngâg thoob-ki   སྡོད་ས་སྔོན་ནས་མངགས་ཐུབ་ཀྱི་རེད་པས།

    re-bay

It's full.

    kâng tsa-sha   གང་ཚར་ཤག

Please refund my ticket.

    ti-ka-si ngü tsoo lo-rog nâng   ཏེ་ཀ་སི་དངུལ་ཚུར་སློག་རོགས་གནང་།

Can I get a stand-by ticket?

    dö-sa tan ma-kay-way ti-ka-si   སྡོད་ས་གཏན་མ་ཁེལ་བའི་ཏེ་ཀ་སི་

    thob-ki re-bay   འཐོབ་ཀྱི་རེད་པས།

I'd like (a) ...	ngah ... gö	ང་ ... དགོས།
one-way ticket	ya-lâm chig-pö	ཡར་ལམ་གཅིག་པོའི་
	ti-ka-si	ཏེ་ཀ་སི
return ticket	ya-lâm ma-lâm	ཡར་ལམ་མར་ལམ
	nyi-kay ti-ka-si	གཉིས་ཀའི་ཏེ་ཀ་སི
two tickets	ti-ka-si nyi	ཏེ་ཀ་སི་གཉིས

GETTING AROUND

AIR

 གནམ་ཐོག

When's the next flight to ...?
...-la doh ya-gi nâm-du
jay-ma-de kâ-dü ray

...ལ་འགྲོ་ཡས་གནམ་གྲུ་རྗེས་མ་དེ་གདུས་རེད།

How long does the flight take?
nâm-dru-nâng yün ring-lö
doh-gö ray

གནམ་གྲུ་ནང་ཡུན་རིང་ལོས་འགྲོ་དགོས་རེད།

Is it a direct route?
sha-kyâg doh-ya re-bay

ཤར་རྒྱག་འགྲོ་ཡས་རེད་པས།

What time do I have to check in
at the airport?
ti-ka-si to-dâm-che nâm-tâng-la
chu-tsö ka-tsay jor-gö-ray

ཏི་ཀ་སི་དོ་དམ་ཆེད་གནམ་ཐང་ཆུ་ཚོད་
ག་ཚད་འབྱོར་དགོས་རེད།

Where's the baggage claim?
tog-tay tsi-len chay-sa ka-bah
yö-ray

དོག་ཐེལ་རྩིས་ལེན་བྱེད་ས་ག་བར་
ཡོད་རེད།

My luggage hasn't arrived.
ngay tog-tay jor min-du

ངའི་དོག་ཐེལ་འབྱོར་མིན་འདུག

At Customs

འགག་སྒོ་ལས་འཁུངས

I have nothing to declare.
nyen-seng shu gö-yeh cha-lâg
kay may

སྙན་སེང་ཞུ་དགོས་ཡས་ཅ་ལག་གང་ཡང་མེད།

I have something to declare.
ngah nyen-seng shu gö-yeh
cha-lâg-chig yö

ངར་སྙན་སེང་ཞུ་དགོས་ཡས་ཅ་ལག་ཅིག་ཡོད།

Do I have to declare this?
di nyen-seng shu gö re-bay

འདི་སྙན་སེང་ཞུ་དགོས་རེད་པས།

This is all my luggage.
ngay cha-lâg di-ga-râng yin

ངའི་ཅ་ལག་འདི་དགའ་རང་ཡིན།

That's not mine.
pa-gi ngay ma-ray

ཕ་གི་ངའི་མ་རེད།

I didn't know I had to declare it.
te nyen-seng shu-gö-pa ngay
ha-go-ma-song

དེ་སྙན་སེང་ཞུ་དགོས་པ་ངས་ཧ་གོ་མ་སོང་།

GETTING AROUND

BUS

བུ་སྐྱོད་རྫས་འཁོར་

Most public bus services are based in Lhasa and run to Shigatse,
Tsetang and the border. Privately run minibus services, however,
run to many other areas. You'll find that minibuses are cheaper
than public buses, as foreigners are charged local prices.

Where is the bus (stop) for ...?
  ...-lâ dro-khen gi chi-chö lâng-kho
  (kâg-sa) ka-bah yö-ray
...ལ་འགྲོ་མཁན་གྱི་སྤྱི་སྐྱོད་རྫས་འཁོར་
(བཀག་ས)ག་བར་ཡོད་རེད།

Where is this (bus) going?
  (chi-chö lâng-kho-di) ka-bah
  doh-gi ray
(སྤྱི་སྐྱོད་རྫས་འཁོར)འདི་ག་པར་
འགྲོ་གི་རེད།

Will it go to ...?
  ...-lâ doh-gi re-bay
...ལ་འགྲོ་གི་རེད་པས།

How often do buses come?
  chi-chö lâng-kho teng mâng-lö
  yong-gi yö-ray
སྤྱི་སྐྱོད་རྫས་འཁོར་ཐེང་མང་
ལོས་ཡོང་གི་ཡོད་རེད།

How long does the trip take?
  gyün ring-lö doh-ya yö-ray
རྒྱུན་རིང་ལོས་འགྲོ་ཡག་ཡོད་རེད།

What time's the ... bus?	chi-chö lâng-kho ... chu-tsö kâ-tsay-la doh-gi ray	སྤྱི་སྐྱོད་རྫས་འཁོར་ ... ཆུ་ཚོད་ག་ཚད་ལ་འགྲོ་གི་རེད།
first	tâng-po-te	དང་པོ་དེ་
last	tha-ma-te	མཐའ་མ་དེ་
next	je-ma-te	རྗེས་མ་དེ་

What time will it leave ...?	... chu-tsö kâ-tsay thon-gi ray	... ཆུ་ཚོད་ག་ཚད་ལ་འཐོན་གྱི་རེད།
this evening	dho-gong	དོ་གོང་
today	te-ring	དེ་རིང་
tomorrow	sa-nyin	སང་ཉིན་

The (bus) is ...   (chi-chö lâng-kho) ... sha   (ক্সু'র্শ্বৃক্সম'বর্ষের্) ... ꣃ
   cancelled   chi-ten chay   ক্সুর'বৃৰ্বৃন'ৰ্শ্বৃৰ্
   delayed   jay-lü teb   ৰ্বৃৰ'শ্লম'থেবৰা
   on time   dü-tog-ray   ৰ্বৃৰ'র্শ্বৃৰ'ৰৃৰ

Is that seat taken?
   koob-kyâg pâ-gay mi dö-khen   ক্সুব'শ্বৃশ্বৃর'ৰী'র্শ্বৃৰ'ৰ্শ্বৃর
   yö re-bay   র্শ্বৃৰ'ৰৃৰ'থৰা
Could you let me know when we get to ...?
   ngân-tso ...-la leb-dü nga-la len   ৰ'র্শ্বৃ ...'থম্বৃৰ'ৰুৰ'ৰ'থম'থৰৰ
   kye-rog nâng   শ্বৃৰ'র্শ্বৃৰ'ৰৰ'
How far to go?
   tâg ring-lö doh-ya yö-ray   থৰ'ৰৃৰ'থৰ'থর্শ্বৃৰ'থৰৰ'র্শ্বৃৰ'ৰৃৰ
I want to get off!
   nga mah bâb-ki-yin   ৰ'ৰৰৰ'থৰৰ'ক্সু'থৰা

CAR   র্শ্বৃৰ

Vehicle rental is a popular option in Tibet, especially with travellers
who have limited time. There are plenty of rental agencies to choose
from in Lhasa and also a few in Shigatse. Since tourists aren't
allowed to drive rental vehicles in Tibet, agencies will organise a
driver – and also a guide, if required. It's wise to arrange to pay in
two instalments – half before the trip and half on your return.

Where can I hire a car (and driver)?
   mo-ta (dâng mo-ta tong-khen)   র্শ্বৃৰ (ৰৰ'র্শ্বৃৰ'শ্বৃৰ'র্শ্বৃৰ'ৰৰৰ)
   la-sa ka-bah yö-ray   শ্বৃৰম'ৰৰৰ'র্শ্বৃৰ'ৰৃৰ

I'd like to   nga ...-chig yar   ৰ ...'শ্বৃৰৰ'বৃৰ্শ্বৃৰ'র্শ্বৃৰ
hire a ...   dhö-yö
   jeep   jip   ক্সুৰ
   landcruiser   len cu-ru-sa   থেৰ'ক্সু'ৰু'ম
   minibus   chi-chö lâng-kho   ক্সু'র্শ্বৃৰ'ৰৰম'বর্ষের্
       choong-choong   ক্সুৰ'ক্সুৰ

For ... day(s).   nyin-ma ...   ৰৰ্শ্বৃৰ ...
For ... week(s).   dün-tâ ...   ৰৰৰৰ'ৰ্শ্বৃ ...

GETTING AROUND

How much does it cost per kilometre?

ki-lo-mi-tar re-ray-la gong kâ-tsay nay-ki ray

གི་ལོ་མི་ཊར་རེ་རེ་ལ་གོང་གཚང་གནད་ཀྱི་རེད།

Does that include insurance?

tay khong-su in-shu-ren thob-tâng tsi yö re-bay

དེ་འི་ཁོངས་སུ་ཨིན་ཤུ་རན་འཐོབ་ཐང་ བརྩི་ཡོད་རེད་པས།

I'll pay half now, and half at the end of the trip.

khor-la che-kâ dân-ta tay-ki yin, che-kâ jay-ma doh-tsa-nay tay-ki yin

འཁོར་ལ་ཕྱེད་ཀ་ད་ལྟ་སྤྲོད་ཀྱི་ཡིན། ཕྱེད་ཀ་རྗེས་ མ་འགྲོ་ཚར་ནས་སྤྲད་ཀྱི་ཡིན།

I'd like to see the car.

nga mo-ta mig tân-dhö yö

ང་མོ་ཊ་མིག་བལྟ་འདོད་ཡོད།

I'd like to meet the driver.

nga mo-ta tong-khen thoog-dhö yö

ང་མོ་ཊ་གཏོང་མཁན་ཐུག་འདོད་ཡོད།

How many people does the vehicle take?

mo-tay-nâng mi kâ-tsay shong-gi ray

མོ་ཊ་འི་ནང་མི་ག་ཚད་གཤོང་གི་རེད།

How much is it daily/weekly?

[nyin ray-ray; dun-tâg ray-ray] gong kâ-tsay ray

[ཉིན་རེ་རེར།/བདུན་ཕྲག་རེ་རེར།] གོང་ག་ཚད་རེད།

Does that include mileage?

may-le kâ-tsay doh-men-gi gong-tsay nyâm-tu tsi yö re-bay

མེ་ལེ་ག་ཚད་འགྲོ་མིན་གྱི་གོང་ཚད་མཉམ་དུ་ བརྩིས་ཡོད་རེད་པས།

How long can we park here?

day mo-ta yun ring-lö shah cho-gi ray

འདིར་མོ་ཊ་ཡུན་རིང་ལོས་བཞག་ཆོག་གི་རེད།

Does this road lead to ...?

lâm-ga-di ... doh-ya re-bay

ལམ་ཀ་འདི་ ... འགྲོ་ཡག་རེད་པས།

Please stop (the car).
  (mo-ta) kâ-rog nâng   (མོ་ཊ་)བཀག་རོགས་གནང་།
I want to take a picture.
  nga par chig gyâ-gi-yin   ང་པར་ཅིག་རྒྱག་གི་ཡིན།

fastest route   lâm-chog gyog-shö   ལམ་ཕྱོགས་མགྱོགས་ཤོས
short route   lâm-chog tâg nye-wa   ལམ་ཕྱོགས་ཐག་ཉེ་བ

BICYCLE   ཀང་རྒྱ་རིལ

Several hotels in Lhasa hire out bicycles and they're a great way to
get around the capital. If you're a guest of the hotel, you won't
have to worry about a deposit.

Is it within cycling distance?
  kâng-ga-ri-tog leb thoob-ya-ki   ཀང་རྒྱ་རིལ་ཐོག་སླེབས་ཐུབ་ཡས་ཀྱི་ས
  sa-tâg re-bay   ཐག་རེད་པས།
Is there a bike path?
  kâng-ga-ri tong-yeh lâm-ga   ཀང་རྒྱ་རིལ་གཏོང་ཡས་ལམ་ཁ་འདུག་གས།
  du-kay
Is there a guide to bicycle paths?
  kâng-ga-ri lâm-ga tön-chay   ཀང་རྒྱ་རིལ་ལམ་ཁ་སྟོན་བྱེད་གནས་ཡིག་འཆོབ
  nay-yig thob-ki re-bay   ཀྱི་རེད་པས།
Where can I hire a bicycle?
  kâng-ga-ri la-sa ka-bah yö-ray   ཀང་རྒྱ་རིལ་གླ་ས་ག་བར་ཡོད་རེད།
Do you hire bicycles?
  kâng-ga-ri la-ya yö-bay   ཀང་རྒྱ་རིལ་གླ་ཡག་ཡོད་པས།
You have to leave your passport
here (as security).
  kay-râng-gi pa-se-pot   ཁྱེད་རང་གི་སྤུ་སེ་པོ་ཊ
  (ta-ma-chay) day shâ-go-ray   (གཏའ་མ་ཆེད་)འདིར་བཞག་དགོས་རེད།
Where can I find (second-hand)
bikes for sale?
  kâng-ga-ri (nying-pa) nyo-sa   ཀང་རྒྱ་རིལ་(རྙིང་པ་)ཉོ་ས
  ka-bah yö-ray   ག་བར་ཡོད་རེད།

GETTING AROUND

How much is it for a/an ...?	... la-ja kâ-tsay ray	... ལ་ཇ་ག་ཚད་རེད།
hour	chu-tsö-chig	ཆུ་ཚོད་གཅིག
morning	sho-kay-chig	ཞོགས་ཀའི་གཅིག
afternoon	chi-toh-chig	ཕྱི་དྲོ་གཅིག
day	nyin-ma-chig	ཉིན་མ་གཅིག
week	dün-tâ-chig	བདུན་ཕྲག་གཅིག
month	da-wa-chig	ཟླ་བ་གཅིག

Can you fix this bicycle?
  kâng-ga-ri-di sob-chö gya
  thoob-ki re-bay

ཀང་སྒ་རི་འདི་བཟོ་བཅོས་རྒྱག་ཐུབ་ཀྱི་རེད་པས།

It has a puncture.
  khor-lo dhö sha

འཁོར་ལོ་བརྫོལ་ཤག

bicycle path	kâng-ga-ri lâm-ga	ཀང་སྒ་རི་ལམ་ག
brakes	kha kâ-ya bay-rek	ཁ་བཀག་ཡ་ལ་བྱེད་རེག
chain	khor-lö châg-tâg	འཁོར་ལོའི་ལྕགས་ཐག
gears	so-khor gi-yar	སོ་འཁོར་གྱི་ཡར
handlebars	lâg-ju yook-ba	ལག་འཇུ་དགུགས་པ
helmet	châg-sha	ལྕགས་ཞ
inner tube	khor-lo nâng-gi-shoob	འཁོར་ལོའི་ནང་གི་ཤུབ
lights	log	གློག
mountain bike	ri-zek kâng-ga-ri	རི་འཛེག་ཀང་སྒ་རི
padlock	go-châg	སྒོ་ལྕགས
pump	poom-da/pom	ཕུ་མདའ/ཕོམ
puncture	yi-koong	ཡི་ཁུང
racing bike	gyook-den kâng-ga-ri	རྒྱུག་འགྲན་ཀང་སྒ་རི
saddle	(kâng-gâ-ri) koob-kyâg	(ཀང་སྒ་རི)སྐུབ་ཀྱག
tools	lâg-cha	ལག་ཆ

ཕྱོང་གནས་ ACCOMMODATION

There's a variety of accommodation in Lhasa, Shigatse and Tsetang, ranging from small inns to luxury hotels. In more remote areas, your options will be limited – you'll either have to take a tent or try to convince a villager to let you stay. Alternatively, you could try a truck stop. Truck stops offer basic, often dorm-style, rooms and can be found in all districts (zong, རྫོང་, or shen, གཞན་) in Tibet.

FINDING ACCOMMODATION ཕྱོང་གནས་འཚོལ་བ་

See Trekking, page 113 for words and phrases on camping.

I'm looking for a ...	...-chig mig ta-gi-yö	...གཅིག་མིག་བལྟ་གྱི་ཡོད།
campsite	gur gyâb-nay	གུར་བརྒྱབ་ནས་ཕྱོང་
	dö-say sa-cha	སྡོད་ས་ཆ་
guesthouse	drön-khâng	མགྲོན་ཁང་
hotel	drü-khâng/fan-dian	འགྲུལ་ཁང་/ཧྥན་ཏི་ཡན་
Where can I	drü-khâng ...-chig	འགྲུལ་ཁང་ ...གཅིག་
find a ... hotel?	ka-bah ra-gi ray	རག་གི་རེད།
clean	tsâng-ma	གཙང་མ་
good	yâg-po	ཡག་པོ་
nearby	tâg nye-po	ཐག་ཉེ་པོ་
Where's the	drü-khâng ... ka-bah	འགྲུལ་ཁང་ ...
... hotel?	yö-ray	ག་བར་ཡོད་རེད།
best	yâg-shö	ཡག་ཤོས་
cheapest	ke-shö	ཁེ་ཤོས་

What's the address?
ka-châng kâ-ray ray   ཁ་བྱང་ག་རེ་རེད།

Could you write down the address?
ka-châng day ti-rog nâng   ཁ་བྱང་འདིར་འབྲི་རོགས་གནང་།

BOOKING AHEAD

�སྔོན་ནས་བྱ་འགྲིགས་པ

I'd like to book a (single/double)
room, please.

> khâng-mi [mi-chig kay-kyâng
> dö-sa; mi-nyi dö-sa]-chig la gö-yö

For (three) nights.

> tsen (soom) ring

མཚན་(གསུམ་)རིང་

How much for ...?   ...-la gong kâ-tsay ray   ...ལ་གོང་ག་ཚད་རེད་

one night	tsen chig	མཚན་གཅིག
a week	dun-tâ chig	བདུན་ཕྲག་གཅིག
two people	mi-nyi	མི་གཉིས

I'll/We'll be arriving at ...

> nga/ngân-tso ...-la yong-gi-yin   ང་/ང་ཚོ་ ...ལ་ཡོང་གི་ཡིན

My name's ...

> ngay ming ... yin   ངའི་མིང་ ... ཡིན

THEY MAY SAY ...

gong-da, khâng-mi tong-pa min-du
Sorry, we're full.

CHECKING IN

འབྱོར་བར་གཏོང་བ

Do you have any rooms/beds
available?

> khâng-mi/nye-ti tong-pa
> yö-bay

Do you have a room with two beds?

> nye-ti-nyi chay-pay khâng-mi
> yö-bay

Do you have a room with a
double bed?
  mi-nyi shong-say nye-ti   མི་གཉིས་ཤོང་སའི་ཉལ་ཁྲི
  chay-pay khâng-mi yö-bay   བྱེད་པའི་ཁང་མི་ཡོད་པས།
I'm not sure how long I'm staying.
  nga yün-ring-lö day-gö   ང་ཡུན་རིང་ལོས་བསྡད་དགོས
  ten-ten may   གཏན་གཏན་མེད།
Are there any private rooms here?
  day nye-khâng kâb-tsâng yö   འདིར་ཉལ་ཁང་ཁབ་གཙང་ཡོད
  re-bay   རེད་པས།

I'd like ...   ngah ...-chig gö   ང་ ...ཅིག་དགོས།
  to share a dorm   chi-khâng-nâng   སྤྱི་ཁང་ནང་སྡོད་ས
                          dö-sa
  a single room   mi chig-kay-kyâng   མི་གཅིག་ཁེར་རྐྱང་སྡོད
                          dö-say khâng-mi   སའི་ཁང་མི

I need ... bed(s).   nga-la nye-ti ... gö   ང་ལ་ཉལ་ཁྲི ... དགོས།
  one   chig   གཅིག
  two   nyi   གཉིས
  three   soom   གསུམ

I/We want a   nga/ngân-tso   ང་/ངཚོ་ ... ཡོད་པའི་ཁང་མིག
room with (a) ...   ... yö-pay   ཅིག་དགོས།
                        khâng-mi-chig gö
  air-conditioning   dâng-log   གྲང་གློག
  bathroom   trü-khâng   ཁྲུས་ཁང
  hot water   chu tsa-po   ཆུ་ཚ་པོ
  private toilet   sâng-chö râng-da   གསང་སྤྱོད་རང་བདག
  shower   soog-po tru-ya   གཟུགས་པོ་བཁྲུ
                         tor-chu   ཡག་ཐོར་ཆུ
  telephone   kha-pah   ཁ་པར
  TV   dian-shi;   ཌེན་ཤི;
                         soog-tong nyen-tin   གཟུགས་མཐོང་ཉན་འཛིན
  window   gay-koong   སྒེ་ཁུང

ACCOMMODATION

Can I see the room?
    nye-khâng mig ta-na di-gi re-bay   ཉལ་ཁང་མིག་བལྟ་ན་འགྲིག་གི་རེད་པས།
I don't like this room.
    khâng-mi-di lo-la bah ma-song   ཁང་མི་འདི་བློ་ལ་བབ་ཀྱི་མིན་འདུག
Do you have another (room)?
    (nye-khâng) shen-da yö-bay   (ཉལ་ཁང་)གཞན་དག་ཡོད་པས།
It's fine. I'll take it.
    yâg-po du. khâng-pa-di   ཡག་པོ་འདུག ཁང་པ་འདི་
    la-gi yin   ང་གི་ཡིན།

REQUESTS & QUERIES   འབོད་སྐུལ་དང་འདྲི་རྩད་བྱེད་པ།

Can I get ... here?   day ... râ-gee   འདིར་ ... རག་གི་རེད་པས།
                   re-bay
   food/meals   kha-la   ཁ་ལག
   boiled water   chu khö-ma   ཆུ་འཁོལ་མ

Where's the bathroom?
    trü-khâng ka-bah   ཁྲུས་ཁང་ག་བར།
Where's the toilet?
    sâng-chö ka-bah yö-ray   གསང་སྤྱོད་ག་བར་ཡོད་རེད།
Is there hot water (all day)?
    chu tsa-po (nyin-gâng) yö re-bay   ཆུ་ཚ་པོ་(ཉིན་གང་)ཡོད་རེད་པས།
Is there electricity (all day)?
    (nyin-gâng) log yö re-bay   (ཉིན་གང་)གློག་ཡོད་རེད་པས།
Where's breakfast served?
    shog-cha ka-bah tâng-gi-ray   ཞོགས་ཇ་ག་བར་གཏང་གི་རེད།
Is there somewhere to wash clothes?
    du-log trü-sa yö re-bay   དུག་ལོག་འཁྲུས་ས་ཡོད་རེད་པས།
Can we use the kitchen?
    tâb-tsâng bay-chö chay-na   ཐབ་ཚང་བེད་སྤྱོད་བྱེད་ན་འགྲིག་གི་རེད་པས།
    di-gi re-bay
Can we use the telephone?
    kha-pah bay-chö chay-na   ཁ་པར་བེད་སྤྱོད་བྱེད་ན་འགྲིག་གི་རེད་པས།
    di-gi re-bay

I need a/another ...
    ngah ...-chi/-shen-da-chi gö   ངར་ ...ཅིག/གཞན་དག་ཅིག་དགོས།

Do you have a safe where I
can leave my valuables?
    rin-tâng-chen cha-lâg   རིན་ཐང་ཅན་ཅ་ལག་བཅོལ་ས་ཡོད་པས།
    chö-sa yö-bay

Could you store this/these for me?
    di/din-tsö nyâh nâng-gay   འདི/འདི་ཚོ་ཉར་གནང་གས།

Could I have a receipt for them?
    choong-zin-chig nâng-dâ   བྱུང་འཛིན་ཅིག་གནང་དང་།

Do you change money here?
    day chi-gye-ngü jay-gee yö-bay   འདིར་ཕྱི་རྒྱལ་དངུལ་བརྗེ་གྱི་ཡོད་པས།

Do you arrange tours?
    yu-kor tow-châm doh-ya ko-dik   ཡུལ་སྐོར་སྤྲོ་འཆམ་འགྲོ་ཡལ་གོ་སྒྲིག
    shu-gi yö-bay   ཞུ་གྱི་ཡོད་པས།

Is there a message board?
    kha-len shâg-sa shog-pâng yö-bay   ཁ་ལན་བཞག་ས་ཤོག་པང་ཡོད་པས།

Can I leave a message?
    len-chi shâg-na di-gi re-bay   ལན་གཅིག་བཞག་ན་འགྲིག་གི་རེད་པས།

Is there a message for me?
    ngah len du-gay   ངར་ལན་འདུག་གས།

Please wake me up   **sa-nyin ... nyi**   སང་ཉིན་ ... གཉིད་
at ... tomorrow.   **say-rog nâng**   སད་རོགས་གནང་།
    five o'clock   **chu-tsö nga-pah**   ཆུ་ཚོད་ལྔ་པར་
    six o'clock   **chu-tsö doog-pah**   ཆུ་ཚོད་དྲུག་པར་

Please change the sheets.
    cha-tah-di je-rog-nâng   ཅག་དར་འདི་བརྗེ་རོགས་གནང་།

The room needs to be cleaned.
    khâng-mi-di tsâng-ma so-gö-du   ཁང་མིག་འདི་གཙང་མ་བཟོ་དགོས་འདུག

Can you wash this?
    di trü thoob-gi re-bay   འདི་འཁྲུ་ཐུབ་ཀྱི་རེད་པས།

Please iron these.
    din-tso u-ti kyön nâng-dâ   འདི་ཚོར་ཡུར་ཏི་བརྒྱབ་གནང་དང་།

ACCOMMODATION

ACCOMMODATION

Could we have (a/an) ...?	ngân-tsoh ... gö	ངན་ཚོ་ ... དགོས།
(extra) blanket	nye-chay (tö-bâ)	ཉལ་ཆས་(ཐོལ་བ)
(extra) quilt	pho-gay (tö-bâ)	ཕོ་ཐེལ་(ཐོལ་བ)
mosquito net	nye-gur	ཉལ་གུར་
pillow	nyen-go	སྔས་མགོ་
pillowcase	nyen-shoob	སྔས་ཤུབ་
our key	ngân-tsö di-mig	ངན་ཚོའི་ལྡེའི་མིག
sheet	cha-tah/nye-keb	ཐལ་དར་/ཉལ་ཁེབས་

I've locked myself out of my room.
ngay go-châg gyâb-nay di-mig nâng-la lâg-sha   ངས་སྒོ་ལྕགས་བརྒྱབ་ནས་ལྡེའི་མིག་ནང་ལ་ ལུག་ཤག

We left the key at reception.
di-mig ngân-tsö nay-len-sah shâg yö   ལྡེའི་མིག་ང་ཚོས་སྐྱེ་ལེན་ས་བཞག་ཡོད།

COMPLAINTS   སྐྱོན་བརྗོད་

I can't open/close the window.
gay-koong chay/gyâb thoob-ki min-du   སྐེ་ཁུང་ཕྱེ་/བརྒྱབ་ཐུབ་ཀྱི་མིན་འདུག

The toilet won't flush.
sâng-chö-di kâg sha   གསང་སྤྱོད་འདག་གགས་ཤག

Can I change to another (room)?
(khâng-mi) shen-ta chig-la po-na di-gi re-bay   (ཁང་མི་)གཞན་དག་གཅིག་ལ་ སྤོ་ན་འགྲིག་གི་རེད་པས།

The ... doesn't work.	... di kyön shor-sha	... འདི་སྐྱོན་ཤོར་ཤག
heater	tsa-log	ཚ་ལོག
lamp	shu-mah	བཞུ་མར་
light bulb	log shay-do	གློག་ཤེལ་རྡོག
telephone	kha-pah	ཁ་པར་
TV	dian-shi;	ཏེན་ཤི/
	soog-tong nyen-tin	གཟུགས་མཐོང་ཉན་འཕྲིན་

This room is dirty.
nye-khâng-di tsog-pa ray-sha ཁང་མིག་འདི་བཙོག་པ་རེད་ཤག

This room is too ...	khâng-mi-di ... ta-shâg	ཁང་མིག་འདི་ ... དྲག་ཤག
big	chay	ཆེ་
cold	dâng	གྲང་
dark	nâg	ནག
light/bright	öh chay	འོད་ཆེ་
noisy	kay-jö tsa	སྐད་ཅོར་ཚ
small	choong	ཆུང་

This ... is not clean.	... di tsâng-ma min-du	... འདི་གཙང་མ་མིན་འདུག
blanket	nye-chay	ཉལ་ཆས
pillow	nyen-go	སྔས་མགོ
pillowcase	nyen-shoob	སྔས་ཤུབ
sheet	cha-tah/nye-keb	ཅ་དར་/ཉལ་ཁེབས

Please fix ...	... so-ro nâng	... བཟོ་རོགས་གནང
this	di	འདི་
the bed	nye-ti-di	ཉལ་ཁྲི་འདི་

ACCOMMODATION

CHANGING ROOMS

Traditionally, Tibetans don't have private bedrooms, so if you stay in a Tibetan house, don't be surprised if your host wanders into your room!

Most houses have one large bedroom, which is also used as a lounge. Each morning the bedding is folded away, so that the bed can be used during the day for people to sit on.

CHECKING OUT ··· འཆོར་བ·ད་གཏོང་བ

What time do we have to check out?
ngân-tso chu-tsö ka-tsay ·ང་ཚོ་ཆུ་ཚོད་ག་ཚོད
tön-gö-ray འཆོར་དགོས་རེད

I'd like to check nga ... tön-gi yin ·ང ... འཆོར་གྱི་ཡིན
out ...
  now tân-da ·ད་ལྟ
  at noon nyin-goong ·ཉིན་གུང
  tomorrow sa-nyin ·སང་ཉིན

We had a great stay, thank you.
ngân-tso kyi-po shay-ta choong, ·ང་ཚོ་སྐྱིད་པོ་ཞེ་དྲག་བྱུང
tu-jay-chay nâng ·ཐུགས་རྗེ་ཆེ་གནང

You've been wonderful.
kay-râng-nay pay-mi-si yâk-po ·ཁྱེད་རང་ནས་དཔེ་མི་སྲིད་ཡག་པོ
nâng-choong ·གནང་བྱུང

Thank you for all your help.
kay-râng-nay rog nâng-wa ·ཁྱེད་རང་ནས་རོགས་གནང་བར
tsâng-mah tu-jay-chay ·ཚང་མར་ཐུགས་རྗེ་ཆེ

The room was perfect.
nye-khâng pay-mi-si yâg-po du ·ཉལ་ཁང་དཔེ་མི་སྲིད་ཡག་པོ་འདུག

We hope we can return some day.
ngân-tso jay-ma yâng-kya yong ·ང་ཚོ་རྗེས་མ་ཡང་བསྐྱར
thoob-pay re-wa-yö ·ཡོང་ཐུབ་པའི་རེ་བ་ཡོད

I'd like to pay the bill.
ngü-tsi gya-gi yin ·དངུལ་རྩིས་རྒྱག་གི་ཡིན

Can I pay with a travellers cheque?
drü-shü ngü-zin-tog ngü pü-na ·འགྲུལ་བཞུད་དངུལ་འཛིན་ཏོག་དངུལ་སྤྲད་ན
di-gi re-bay ·འགྲིག་གི་རེད་པས

Can I pay by credit card?
ngü bu-lön shog-jâng-tog ·དངུལ་བུ་ལོན་ཤོག་བྱང་ཏོག
tay-na di-gi re-bay ·སྤྲད་ན་འགྲིག་གི་རེད་པས

ACCOMMODATION

There's a mistake in the bill.
    ngü-tsi-nâng non-tü shor-sha   དངུལ་རྩིས་ནང་ནོར་འཁྲུལ་ཤོར་ཤག

Can I leave my luggage here?
    ngay cha-lâg day shâg-na di-gi   ངའི་ཅ་ལག་འདིར་བཞག་ན་འགྲིག་གི
    re-bay   རེད་པས།

We'll be back in (three) days.
    ngân-tso nyin-ma-(soom)   ང་ཚོ་ཉིན་མ་(གསུམ)
    je-la yong-gi-yin   རྗེས་ལ་ཡོང་གི་ཡིན།

Can you call a taxi for me?
    ngah tek-si-chig kay tong-da   ང་ལ་ཊེག་སི་གཅིག་སྐད་གཏོང་དང་།

RENTING   གླ་བ

I'm here about your ad for a
room to rent.
    khâng-la tong-ya kyâb-da nâng-du,   ཁང་ག་གཏོང་ཡ་ཁྱབ་བརྐྱགས
    chay-tsâng nga day yong-wa-yin   གནང་དུག་ལུས་ཚང་ང་འདིར་ཡོང་བཡིན།

Do you have any flats to rent?
    khâng-la tong-ya khâng-pa   ཁང་ག་གཏོང་ཡ་ཁང་པ་ཡོད་པས།
    yö-bay

I'm looking for a flat to rent for
(two) months.
    ngah da-wa (nyi)-ring khâng-pa-chig   ང་ཟླ་བ་(གཉིས)་རིང་ཁང་པ་གཅིག
    la-ya tâb-shay chay-ki yö   གླ་ཡག་ཐབས་ཤེས་བྱེད་ཀྱི་ཡོད།

I'm looking for   ... tee-la khâng-pa-chig   ... འཁྲིས་ལ་ཁང་པ་ཅིག
something close   râg-gi yö-may ta-gi-yö   རག་གི་ཡོད་མེད་བལྟ་གི་ཡོད།
to the ...
    city centre   dong-kay-kyil   གྲོང་འཁྱེར་དཀྱིལ
    market   trom   ཁྲོམ
    monastery   gom-pa   དགོན་པ

ACCOMMODATION

How much is it per ...?	... ray-ray-la gong kâ-tsay ray	... རེ་རེ་ལ་གོང་ག་ཚད་རེད།
week	dün-tâ	བདུན་ཕྲག
month	da-wa	ཟླ་བ

Is there anything cheaper?
   gong ke-wa yö-bay
   གོང་ཁེ་བ་ཡོད་པས།
Could I see it?
   nga mig ta-na di-gi re-bay
   ང་མིག་བལྟ་ན་འགྲིག་གི་རེད་པས།
Do you need a deposit?
   ngü nga-dön tay gö-ki re-bay
   དངུལ་སྔ་འདོན་སྤྲད་དགོས་ཀྱི་རེད་པས།
I'd like to rent it for (one) month.
   da-wa (chig)-ring la-gi yin
   ཟླ་བ་(གཅིག)་རིང་གླ་རྒྱུ་ཡིན།

Lhasa is not only the capital, but the heart and soul of Tibet. The vast white and ochre Potala Palace dominates the city and is considered one of the wonders of Eastern architecture. The Jokhang, the most sacred and active of Lhasa's temples, is another key sight. Surrounding the Jokhang is the Barkhor circuit, the most famous of Lhasa's pilgrimage circuits and also a popular spot for souvenir shopping.

Modern Lhasa is divided into two sections: a western Chinese section and an eastern Tibetan section.

LOOKING FOR ...   ... འཚོལ་བ

I'm looking for a/the ...	... ka-bah yö-may ta-gi yö	... ག་བར་ཡོད་མེད་བལྟ་གི་ཡོད།
art gallery	låg-tse dem-tön-khâng	ལག་རྩལ་འགྲེམས་སྟོན་ཁང་
bank	ngü-khâng	དངུལ་ཁང་
church/temple	lha-khâng	ལྷ་ཁང་
cinema	log-nyen ta-sa	གློག་བརྙན་བལྟ་ས
city centre	drong-kay-kyil	གྲོང་ཁྱེར་དཀྱིལ
... consulate	... dön-chö lay-khoong	... དོན་གཅོད་ལས་ཁུངས
... embassy	... shung-tsâb lay-khoong	... གཞུང་ཚབ་ལས་ཁུངས
... hotel	... drü-khâng	... འགྲུལ་ཁང་
market	trom	ཁྲོམ
museum	dem-tön-khâng	འགྲེམས་སྟོན་ཁང་
police station	kor-soong lay-koong	སྐོར་སྲུང་ལས་ཁུངས
post office	da-khâng	སྒྲག་ཁང་
public telephone	mi-mâng kha-pah	མི་དམངས་ཁ་པར
public toilet	mi-mâng sâng-chö	མི་དམངས་གསང་སྤྱོད
restaurant	sa-khâng	ཟ་ཁང་
telephone centre	kha-pah lay-khoong	ཁ་པར་ལས་ཁུངས
tourist information office	yu-kor to-châm lay-khoong	ཡུལ་སྐོར་སྤྲོ་འཆམ་གྱི་ལས་ཁུངས
town square	dong-kay mi-mâng zom-sa te-wa	གྲོང་ཁྱེར་མི་དམངས་འཛོམས་ས་སྟེ་བ

(See Getting Around, page 56, for directions.)

AT THE BANK

དངུལ་ཁང་ནས་ལ།

In rural areas it can be difficult to change large notes, so try to carry cash in small denominations.

What time does the bank open?
ngü-khâng chu-tsö kâ-tsay go chay-gi ray

དངུལ་ཁང་ཆུ་ཚོད་ག་ཚོད་ལ་སྒོ་ཕྱེ་གི་རེད།

I want to exchange some money.
nga chi-gay ngü jay-gö-yö

ང་ཕྱི་རྒྱལ་དངུལ་བརྗེ་དགོས་ཡོད།

Where can I cash a travellers cheque?
drü-shü ngü-zin jay-sa ka-bah yö-ray

འགྲུལ་བཞུད་དངུལ་འཛིན་བརྗེ་ས་ག་བར་ཡོད་རེད།

Please change this travellers cheque.
drü-shü ngü-zin-dee jay nâng-da

འགྲུལ་བཞུད་དངུལ་འཛིན་འདི་བརྗེ་གནང་དང་།

Can I use my credit card to withdraw money?
bu-lön shog-châng-tog ngü tön cho-gee re-bay

བུ་ལོན་ཤོག་བྱང་ཐོག་དངུལ་བཏོན་ཆོག་གི་རེད་པས།

Can I exchange money here?
day chi-gye-ngü jay-gi re-bay

འདིར་ཕྱི་རྒྱལ་དངུལ་བརྗེ་གི་རེད་པས།

What's the exchange rate?
ngü-je-gong-tsay kâ-ray ray

དངུལ་བརྗེའི་གོང་ཚད་ག་རེ་རེད།

What's your commission?
kay-râng-gi keb-sâng ten-cha kâ-tsay ray

ཁྱེད་རང་གི་ཁེ་གཙང་འབབ་ཆ་ག་ཚོད་རེད།

Please write it down.
day di-rog nâng

འདིར་འབྲི་རོགས་གནང་།

Where do I sign?
sa-yig ka-bah gya-go ray

ས་ཡིག་ག་བར་རྒྱག་དགོས་རེད།

Can I have smaller notes?
ngü-shog rin-tâng choong-wa nâng thoob-ki re-bay

དངུལ་ཤོག་རིན་ཐང་ཆུང་ཆུང་བ་གནང་ཐུབ་ཀྱི་རེད་པས།

Can I have money transferred
here from my bank?

    ngay-ngü chö-say ngü-khâng-nay ་བདི་དངུལ་འཚོལ་སའི་དངུལ་ཁང་ནས་དངུལ་
    ngü-day tâng thoob-ki re-bay འདིར་གཏོང་ཐུབ་ཀྱི་རེད་པས།

Can I transfer money overseas?

    chi-gay-la ngü tâng thoob-ki ཕྱི་རྒྱལ་ལ་དངུལ་གཏོང་ཐུབ་ཀྱི་རེད་པས།
    re-bay

How long will it take to arrive
(here/there)?

    (day/pha-kay) jor-pa-la (འདིར་ / ཕགིར་)འབྱོར་པ་ལ་རྒྱུན་རིང་
    gyün ring-lö gâ-ki-ray ལོས་འགག་གི་རེད།

Has my money arrived yet?

    tân-da ngay ngü jor ད་ལྟ་བདི་དངུལ་འབྱོར་སོང་ངས།
    song-ngay

I'm expecting some money from ...

    nga la ...-nay ngü ga-shay ང་ལ ...ནས་དངུལ་ག་ཤས་ལེབ་ཡོང་
    leb yong-wa-yö བའོད།

black market	nâg-tsong	ནག་ཚོང་
cashier	ngü-nye	དངུལ་གཉེར་
counterfeit	zü-ma	རྫུས་མ་
signature	sa-yig	ས་ཡིག

AROUND TOWN

AT THE POST OFFICE ཕྱག་འཁང་རྣམ་ཚང་

The international postal service offered in Tibet is generally reliable
and efficient. However, if you have mail to send, it's best to do
so in Lhasa, Shigatse or Tsetang. For faxes, head to the main
communication centre or any top-end hotel. Note that while
service varies little, prices vary a lot.

I want to buy ...	nga ...-chig gö-yö	ང ...ཅིག་དགོས་ཡོད།
postcards	dâg-shog	ཕྱག་ཤོག
stamps	ti-ka-si/dâg-tag	ཏི་ཀ་སི / ཕྱག་རྟགས་

would like to send a ...	nga ...-chig tâng-go yö	ང་ ...གཅིག་གཏང་དགོས་ཡོད།
fax	faks	ཕེག་སེ།
letter	yi-ge	ཡིག་གེ།
parcel	cha-lâg	ཅ་ལག
postcard	dâg-shog	སྐྱག་ཤོག
telegram	tar	དར།

Please send it by air/surface mail.
    nâm-tog/sa-tog tâng nâng-ro   གནམ་ཐོག/ས་ཐོག་གཏང་གནང་རོགས།

How much does it cost to send this to ...?
    di ... tâng-na gong kâ-tsay nay-ki-ray   འདི་ ...གཏང་ན་གོང་ག་ཚད་གནད་ཀྱི་རེད།

Where's the poste restante section?
    da-trö may-pay dâg-yi jo-khâng ka-bah yö-ray   བདག་སྟོང་མེད་པའི་སྐྱག་ཡིག་འཇོག་ཁང་ག་བར་ཡོད་རེད།

Is there any mail for me?
    nga-la dâg du-gay   ང་ལ་སྐྱག་འདུག་གས།

aerogram	nâm-tog tong-yâg yi-kog	གནམ་ཐོག་གཏོང་ཡག་ཡི་ཀྲོགས།
air mail	nâm-tog dâg-kay	གནམ་ཐོག་སྐྱག་སྐྱེལ།
envelope	yi-gok	ཡིག་ཀྲོགས།
express mail	nyur-kye-dâg	མྱུར་སྐྱེལ་སྐྱག
mailbox	dâg-gâm	སྐྱག་སྒམ།
registered mail	teb-kay dâg	དེབ་སྐྱེལ་སྐྱག
surface mail	sa-tog dâg-kay	ས་ཐོག་སྐྱག་སྐྱེལ།

GIVING LIP!

Don't be alarmed if someone pouts at you – they're probably just showing you which way to go. Tibetans often use their lips to indicate direction.

TELECOMMUNICATIONS   ཁ་པར་ཤོག་འཕྲུལ་སྐྱལ།

For international telephone calls, try the major post offices or
telecommunication centres. Calls are charged per minute and often
there's a one-minute minimum charge – check before you call.

Where's the nearest public phone?
    mi-mâng kha-pah tong-sa   མི་དམངས་ཁ་པར་གཏོང་ས་བག་
    tah nye-shö ka-bah yö-ray   ཉེ་ཤོས་ག་བར་ཡོད་རེད།

Could I use the telephone?
    kha-pah bay-chö chay-na   ཁ་པར་བེད་སྤྱོད་བྱེད་ན་འགྲིག་གི་རེད་པས།
    di-gi re-bay

I want to call ...
    nga ...-la kha-pah tâng-go yö   ང་ ...ལ་ཁ་པར་གཏང་དགོས་ཡོད།

How much does a (one)-minute
call cost?
    ka-ma-(chig) kay-cha shay-na   སྐར་མ་(གཅིག)་སྐྱེད་ཆ་བཤད་ན་གོང་ག་
    gong kâ-tsay ray   ཚད་རེད།

How much does each extra
minute cost?
    ka-ma tö-pa ray-ray-la   སྐར་མ་ལྷོད་པ་རེ་རེ་ལ་གོང་ག་ཚད་གནང་གི་
    gong kâ-tsay ray   རེད།

The number is ...
    kha-pah ahng-dâng ... ray   ཁ་པར་ཨང་གྲངས་ ... རེད།

What's the area code for ...?
    ... sa-nay-ki kha-pah ahng-ta   ... ས་གནས་ཀྱི་ཁ་པར་ཨང་རྟགས་ག་རེ་རེད།
    kâ-ray ray

I want to make a long-distance call
to (Australia).
    nga (o-ta-li-ya)-la kha-pah   ང་(ཨོ་ཏ་ལི་ཡ་)ལ་ཁ་པར་གཏང་དགོས་ཡོད།
    tâng-go yö

I want to make a reverse-charges/
collect call.
    kha-pah tong-la phâ-chog-nay   ཁ་པར་གཏོང་ལ་ཕ་ཕྱོགས་ནས་རྩི་རྒྱ་ཆོག་
    tsi-gya chog-pay kha-pah-chi   པའི་ཁ་པར་གཅིག་གཏང་དགོས་ཡོད།
    tâng go-yö

AROUND TOWN

It's engaged.
    kha-pah de-wa ray-sha   ཁ་པར་བྲེལ་བ་རེད་ཤག

I've been cut off.
    nga kay-cha shay-ki shay-ki   ང་སྐད་ཆ་བཤད་ཀྱི་བཤད་ཀྱི་ཁ་པར་མཚམས་ཆད་
    kha-pah tsâm chay-song   སོང་།

engaged	de-wa	བྲེལ་བ
fax	faks	ཕེག་སེ
modem	mo-dem	མོ་ཌེམ
mobile/cell	mo-ba-yel/po-kay	མོ་བྱེལ་ཁ་པར་/
phone	kha-pah	པོ་འཕྲིང་ཁ་པར
operator	kha-pah lay-chay-pa	ཁ་པར་ལས་བྱེད་པ
phone book	kha-pah ahng-dâng-teb	ཁ་པར་ཨང་གྲངས་དེབ
phone box	kha-pah tong-say	ཁ་པར་གཏོང་སའི་ཁང་ཆུང
	khâng-choong	
phone card	kha-pah tong-ya la-kay	ཁ་པར་གཏོང་ཡག་ལག་འཁྱེར
public telephone	mi-mâng kha-pah	མི་དམངས་ཁ་པར
reverse charges	la pha-chog nay tsi	གླ་ཕ་ཕྱོགས་ནས་རྩིས་ཀྲུག་
	gyâ-chog-pa	ཚོགས་པ

Making a Call   ཁ་པར་གཏོང་བ

Hello, do you speak English?
    ta-shi de-lek, kay-râng in-ji-kay   བཀྲ་ཤིས་བདེ་ལེགས།
    shin-gi yö-bay   ཁྱེད་རང་དབྱིན་ཇི་སྐད་ཤེས་ཀྱི་ཡོད་པས།

Hello, is ... there?
    ha-lo, ...-la shoog du-gay   ཧ་ལོ། ...ལགས་བཞུགས་འདུག་གས།

Hello. (answering a call)
    ha-lo   ཧ་ལོ

Can I speak to ...?
    nga ...-la kah-mö shu-gö yö   ང་ ...ལགས་ལ་ཁ་མོ་ཞུ་དགོས་ཡོད།

Who's calling?
    su yin-bâh   སུ་ཡིན་པ།

It's ...
    nga ... yin   ང་ ... ཡིན

Yes, he's/she's here.
la-wong, khong day shoog-du ལགས་ཡོད། ཁོང་འདིར་བཞུགས་འདུག

One moment, please.
teh-si gu-nâng ཏིག་ཙམ་བསྐུག་གནང་།

I'm sorry, he's/she's not here.
khong day shoog min-du ཁོང་འདིར་བཞུགས་མིན་འདུག

What time will he/she be back?
kho/mo chu-tsö kâ-tsay-la
yong-gi ray ཁོ་/མོ་ཆུ་ཚོད་ག་ཚོད་ལ་ཡོང་གི་རེད།

Can I leave a message?
kha-len-chi shâ-na di-gi re-bay ཁ་ལན་གཅིག་བཞག་ན་འགྲིག་གི་རེད་པས།

Please tell ... I called.
...-la ngay kha-pah tâng-so
shu-rog ...ལ་ངས་ཁ་པར་བཏང་སོང་ཞུ་རོགས།

My number is ...
ngay kha-pah ahng-dâng ... ray ངའི་ཁ་པར་ཨང་གྲངས་ ... རེད།

I don't have a contact number.
ngah kha-pah ahng-dâng may ངར་ཁ་པར་ཨང་གྲངས་མེད།

I'll call back later.
ngay jay-la kha-pah tâng-go ངས་རྗེས་ལ་ཁ་པར་གཏང་གོ

The Internet ཨིན་ཊར་ནེཊ་

Is there a local Internet cafe?
sa-nay-day in-ta-net bay-chö
tong-sa yö-pay cha-khâng
yö re-bay ས་གནས་དེར་ཨིན་ཊར་ནེཊ་བེད་སྤྱོད་གཏོང་ས་ཡོད་པའི་ཇ་ཁང་ཡོད་རེད་པས།

I'd like to get Internet access.
nga in-ta-net bay-chö chay-go yö ང་ཨིན་ཊར་ནེཊ་བེད་སྤྱོད་བྱེད་དགོས་ཡོད།

I'd like to check my email.
ngah ee-mel yö-may ta-go yö ངར་ཨི་མེལ་ཡོད་མེད་བལྟ་དགོས་ཡོད།

I'd like to send an email.
nga ee-mel-chig tâng-go yö ང་ཨི་མེལ་ཞིག་གཏང་དགོས་ཡོད།

SIGHTSEEING

ཁྱབ་སྐོར་འགྲོ་བ

Where can I get a local map?
  sa-nay-ki sâp-ta kâ-nay ra-gi-ray

ས་གནས་ཀྱི་ས་བཀྲག་ནས་རག་གི་རེད།

Do you have a guidebook in English?
  in-ji kay-tog drü-shü
  nay-yig yö-bay

དབྱིན་ཇི་སྐད་ཡིག་འཁྱུལ་བསྟུད་གནས་ཡིག་
ཡོད་པས།

What are the main attractions?
  ta-kor dro-sa tso-wo
  kâ-ray yö-ray

བལྟ་སྐོར་འགྲོ་ས་གཙོ་བོ་ག་རེ་ཡོད་རེད།

We only have [one day; two days].
  ngân-tso nyin-ma
  chig-lay/nyi-lay de-ya may

ང་ཚོ་ཉིན་མ་གཅིག་/གཉིས
ལས་བསྡད་ཡག་མེད།

I'd like to see ...
  ... mig ta-dö yö

... མིག་བལྟ་འདོད་ཡོད།

Is it OK if I take a photo?
  par gyâb-na di-gi re-bay

པར་རྒྱབ་ན་འགྲིག་གི་རེད་པས།

Can I take your photograph?
  kay-râng par gyâ-na di-gi re-bay

ཁྱེད་རང་པར་རྒྱབ་ན་འགྲིག་གི་རེད་པས།

Could you take a photograph of me?
  nga-la par-chig gyâ nâng-da

ང་ལ་པར་ཅིག་རྒྱབ་གནང་དང་།

Would you like a copy?
  kay-râng par gö-bay

ཁྱེད་རང་པར་དགོས་པས།

I'll send you one.
  ngay-chig tâng yong-gö

ངས་གཅིག་གཏང་ཡོང་དགོས།

What's your address?
  kay-râng-gi ka-châng kâ-ray ray

ཁྱེད་རང་གི་ཁ་བྱང་ག་རེ་རེད།

Getting In

ནང་དུ་འཛུལ་བ

What time does it open/close?
  chu-tsö kâ-tsay-la go
  chay-gi/gyâb-gi ray

ཆུ་ཚོད་ག་ཚད་ལ་སྒོ་ཕྱེ་/སྒོ་བརྒྱབ་གི་རེད།

Is there an admission charge?
  zü-la tay-go re-bay

འཛུལ་ལ་གླ་སྤྲད་དགོས་རེད་པས།

You don't have to pay.
    la tay-go ma-ray   ལ་སྤྲོད་དགོས་མ་རེད།
Can I make a donation?
    shen-deb bü-na di-gi re-bay   ཞལ་འདེབས་ཕུལ་ན་འགྲིག་གི་རེད་པས།

The Sights   བལྟ་སྐོར་

What's that ...?	... pha-gi kâ-ray ray	... ཕ་གི་ག་རེ་རེད།
building	khâng-pa	ཁང་པ་
monument	den-ten	རྟེན་རྟེན་
place	sa-cha	ས་ཆ་
How old is it?	nying-lö ray	ཉིང་ལོ་ལོས་རེད།
ancient	na ngâ-mo	གནའ་སྔ་མོ་
archaeological	na-ngö chay-pay	གནའ་རྫོས་དཔྱད་པའི་
	rig-nay	རིག་གནས་
cinema	log-nyen ta-sa	གློག་བརྙན་བལྟ་ས་
concert	ro-yâng tro-tön	རོ་དབྱངས་སྟོན་སྟོན་
crowded	tsâng-ga shi-shi	འཛང་ག་ཞེ་ཞེ་
flag	dar-cho	དར་ཅོག་
gardens	may-tog doom-ra	མེ་ཏོག་སྡུམ་ར་
market	trom	ཁྲོམ་
monastery	gom-pa	དགོན་པ་
mosque	ka-chay lha-khâng	ཁ་ཆེའི་ལྷ་ཁང་
museum	dem-tön khâng	འགྲེམས་སྟོན་ཁང་
old city	dron-kay nying-ba	གྲོང་ཁྱེར་རྙིང་པ་
palace	pho-dâng	ཕོ་བྲང་
park	ling-ga	གླིང་ག་
statues	dâ-ku	འདྲ་སྐུ་
temple	lha-khâng	ལྷ་ཁང་
university	tsoog-la lob-ta chen-mo	གཙུག་ལག་སློབ་གྲྭ་ཆེན་མོ་

Tours བསྐོར་སྐོར་

Are there regular tours we can join?
cha-chen drü-pa ta-kor ti-gi
yö-na teh nyâm-tu ngân-tso
yong-na di-gi re-bay

ཚར་ཅན་འགྲུལ་པ་བལྟ་སྐོར་འཁྱིད་ཀྱི་ཡོད་ན་
དེ་དང་མཉམ་དུ་ཚོ་ཡོང་ན་འགྲིག་གི་རེད་པས།

How much is [the tour; a guide]?
[ta-kor do-ya; nay-shay
gya-khen] la-cha kâ-tsay ray

[བལྟ་སྐོར་འགྲོ་ཡག/གནས་བཤད་
རྒྱག་མཁན་]ཀྲ་ཆ་ག་ཚད་རེད།

How long is the tour?
ta-kor gyün ring-lö do-ya
yö-ray

བལྟ་སྐོར་རྒྱུན་རིང་ལོས་འགྲོ་ཡག་ཡོད་རེད།

Will we have free time?
ngân-tsoh dü-tsö tong-ba
yö re-bay

ང་ཚོར་དུས་ཚོད་སྟོང་པ་ཡོད་རེད་པས།

What time should we be back?
ngân-tso chu-tsö kâ-tsay
chi-log teb-ki ray

ང་ཚོ་ཆུ་ཚོད་ག་ཚད་ལ་ཕྱིར་ལོག་སྐེབས་ཀྱི་རེད།

The guide [has paid; will pay].
rin-ba nay-shay gya-khen-gi
tay-song/tay-gi-ray

རིན་པ་གནས་བཤད་རྒྱག་མཁན་གྱིས་
སྤྲད་སོང་/སྤྲད་ཀྱི་རེད།

I'm with them.
nga khong-tsö nyâm-du yö

ང་ཁོང་ཚོའི་མཉམ་དུ་ཡོད།

I've lost my group.
nga rog-pa tsâng-ma lâg-sha

ང་རོགས་པ་ཚང་མ་བརྫགས་ཤག

Have you seen a group of
(Australians)?
kay-râng-nay (o-ta-li-ya) drü-ba
kyu-chig tong song-ngay

ཁྱེད་རང་ནས་(ཨོ་སི་ཊ་ལི་ཡ)
འགྲུལ་པ་ཁྱུ་གཅིག་མཐོང་སོང་ངས།

AROUND TOWN

VISITING TEMPLES   ལྷ་ཁང་མཇལ་གནང་བ

Tibetans are deeply religious and you'll see monks, nuns and other local people walking around temples, saying prayers, lighting butter lamps and incense, and turning prayer wheels to show their spiritual devotion. Throughout the year, there are many religious festivals (see Festivals & Holidays, page 174).

If you want to address a monk or a nun and you don't know their name, you can use the honorific titles **ku-sho-la** (སྐུ་ཞབས་ལགས) for monks and **ani-la** (ཨ་ནི་ལགས) for nuns. Other titles for people associated with Buddhism are:

abbot	khen-po	མཁན་པོ
lama (teacher)	la-ma	བླ་མ
layperson	kyâ-wo	སྐྱ་བོ
monastic disciplinarian	gay-kö	དགེ་སྐོས
shrine keeper	kö-nyey	བསྐོ་གཉེར
student	gay-toog/lob-toog	དགེ་ཕྲུག / སློབ་ཕྲུག
What is that ... called?	... pha-gi ming-la kâ-ray ray	... ཕ་གིའི་མིང་ལ་ག་རེ་རེད
monastery	gom-pa	དགོན་པ
nunnery	ah-ni gom-pa	ཨ་ནི་དགོན་པ
shrine/temple	lha-khâng	ལྷ་ཁང

MONUMENTALLY SACRED

Chö-ten (མཆོད་རྟེན) are religious monuments that can be found throughout Tibet. When Buddhism was first introduced, there were no images of Buddha and chö-ten became symbolic of Buddhism. Often you'll see piles of stones around the base of the chö-ten inscribed with the sacred words 'Om Mani Padme Hum' the mantra of Avalokiteshvara, the Bodhisattva of Compassion.

Am I allowed to go inside
(the temple)?
    (gom-bay)-nâng doh cho-ki
    re-bay   (དགོན་པའི་)ནང་འགྲོ་ཆོག་གི་རེད་པས།

Am I allowed to go upstairs?
    toh-ga doh cho-ki re-bay   ཐོག་ཁར་འགྲོ་ཆོག་གི་རེད་པས།

How many monks/nuns are there?
    tâ-pa/ah-ni kâ-tsay yö-ray   གྲྭ་པ / ཨ་ནི་ག་ཚོད་ཡོན་རེད།

I'd like to meet the abbot.
    nga khen-po-dâng jen-dö yö   ང་མཁན་པོ་དང་མཇལ་འདོད་ཡོད།

May I offer ...?	...-chi bü-na di-gi re-bay	...ཕུལ་ན་འགྲིག་གི་རེད་པས།
a butter lamp	chö-may	མཆོད་མེ་
incense	pö	སྤོས།

SIGNS

སྒོ་རྒྱག་	CLOSED
གྲང་མོ་	COLD
ཉེན་ཁ་	DANGER
འཛུལ་ཡས་	ENTRANCE
དོན་ས་	EXIT
ཚ་པོ་	HOT
འཛུལ་མི་ཆོག	NO ENTRY
པར་རྒྱག་མི་ཆོག	NO PHOTOGRAPHS
ཐ་མག་འཐེན་མི་ཆོག	NO SMOKING
སྒོ་ཕྱེ་	OPEN
བཀག་སྡོམ་བྱེད་པ་	PROHIBITED
ཁ་བཀག	STOP
གསང་སྤྱོད་	TOILETS

Can I sit here for a while?

    day te-tsi day-na di-gi re-bay   འདིར་ཏོག་ཙམ་བསྡད་ན་འགྲིག་གི་རེད་པས།

Please say a prayer for me.

    ngah mön-lâm kyön nâng-ro   ང་ར་སྨོན་ལམ་བསྐྱོན་གནང་རོགས།

I'd like to learn about meditation.

    nga gom châng-dö yö   ང་སྒོམ་སྦྱང་འདོད་ཡོད།

altar	chö-shom	མཆོད་གཤོམས་
assembly hall	tsog-khâng	ཚོགས་ཁང་
bell	tih-bu	དྲིལ་བུ་
Buddha	sâng-gye	སངས་རྒྱས་
circumambulation	ko-ra	སྐོར་བ་
cymbal	boog-chel	སྦུག་ཆལ་
drum	nga	ང་
gods/goddesses	lhâ/lhâ-mo	ལྷ་/ལྷ་མོ་
karma	lay	ལས་
meditate	gom	སྒོམ་
non-virtue	mi-ge-wa	མི་དགེ་བ་
offering	chö-pa	མཆོད་པ་
prayer wheel	mâ-ni kho-lo	མ་ཎི་འཁོར་ལོ་
prostrate	châg-tsay	ཕྱག་འཚལ་
reliquary	chor-ten	མཆོད་རྟེན་
rosary	tren-ngâ	ཕྲེང་བ་
spiritual dance	châm	འཆམ་
trumpet (small)	gyâ-ling	རྒྱ་གླིང་
trumpet (big)	doong-chen	དུང་ཆེན་
vajra (a tantric ritual sceptre)	dor-je	རྡོ་རྗེ་
vase	boom-pa	བུམ་པ་
virtue	gay-wa	དགེ་བ་

For phrases on Pilgrimage & Religion, see Specific Needs, page 166.

KEEPING THE FAITH

Buddhism first appeared in Tibet in the 7th century AD. It gained popularity during the reign of King Trisong Detsen (755-97) and King Tritsug Detsen Ralpachen (817-36). However, following the reign of the next king, Langdharma, the Tibetan state collapsed and Buddhism was attacked. The faith didn't revive until the 11th century, when Tibetans began travelling to India to study. New ideas were brought back and eventually three further schools of Buddhism developed: Kagyupa, Sakyapa and Gelugpa. The Nyingmapa order, referred to as the 'Old School' already existed.

PAPERWORK

ཡིག་ཆ།

name	ming	མིང་
address	ka-châng	ཁ་བྱང་
date of birth	kye-tse	སྐྱེས་ཚེས་
place of birth	kye-yül	སྐྱེས་ཡུལ་
birth certificate	kye-tse lâg-kay	སྐྱེས་ཚེས་ལག་ཁྱེར་
age	lo	ལོ་
sex	pho-mo tâg	ཕོ་མོ་དག་
female	mo	མོ་
male	pho	ཕོ་
nationality	loong-ba	ལུང་པ་
profession/work	tso-tâb châng-sha	འཚོ་བབས་སྐྱོངས་ལ་འཚོ་བའི་
	tön-pay lay-rig/lay-ka	ལས་རིགས་ / ལས་ཀ་
marital status	châng-sa gyâb yö-may	ཆང་ས་བརྒྱབ་ཡོད་མེད་གནས་
	nay-bâb	བབས་
single	mi-hreng	མི་ཧྲེང་
married	châng-sa gyâb yö-ba	ཆང་ས་བརྒྱབ་ཡོད་པ་
divorced	sa-tsâng ka day-wa	བཟའ་ཚང་ཁ་བྲལ་བ་
widow	kyo-da de-pö mo-hreng	ཁྱོ་ག་འདས་པའི་མོ་ཧྲེང་
widower	kye-man de-pö pho-hreng	སྐྱེ་དམན་འདས་པའི་ཕོ་ཧྲེང་

AROUND TOWN

religion	chö-loog	ཆོས་ལུགས་
identification	ngo-trö lâg-kay	ངོ་སྤྲོད་ལག་ཁྱེར་
passport	pa-se-pot/chi-kyö lâg-teb	སྤ་སེ་པོཊ་ / ཕྱི་སྐྱོད་ལག་དེབ
passport number	pa-se-pot âhng-dâng	སྤ་སེ་པོཊ་ཨང་གྲངས
visa	vi-za/tong-chen	ཝི་ཟ / མཐོང་མཆན
car owners title	mo-ta dâg-pö ming	མོ་ཊ་བདག་པོའི་མིང་
car registration	mo-tay teb-kye	མོ་ཊའི་དེབ་སྐྱེལ
drivers licence	mo-ta tong-ya lâg-kay	མོ་ཊ་གཏོང་ཡག་ལག་ལག་ཁྱེར
tourist card	yu-kor tro-châm lâg-kay	ཡུལ་སྐོར་སྤྲོ་འཆམ་ལག་ཁྱེར
reason for travel	drü-kyö chay-ya gyu-tsen	འགྲུལ་སྐྱོད་བྱེད་ཡག་རྒྱུ་མཚན
purpose of visit	drü-shü chay-ya gyu-tsen	འགྲུལ་བཞུད་བྱེད་ཡག་རྒྱུ་མཚན
business	tsong-lay	ཚོང་ལས
holiday	goong-seng	གུང་གསེང
visiting relatives	nyen-tay	གཉེན་འཕྲད
visiting the homeland	râng-gi pha-yu ta-ga	རང་གི་ཕ་ཡུལ་བལྟ་བག
border	sa-tsâm	ས་མཚམས
customs	gâ-go	བག་གོ
immigration	gyâ-khâb shen-du shi châg-pa	རྒྱལ་ཁབ་གཞན་དུ་ གཞིས་ཆགས་པ

FAMILY

ཁྱིམ་ཚང་

Tibetans may well refer to themselves as husband, **kyo-ka** (ཁྱོ་ག),
literally meaning 'man', and wife, **kye-man** (སྐྱེ་དམན་), literally
meaning 'woman', even if they're not married. For Tibetans, it's
more appropriate for an unmarried foreign couple to introduce
themselves as husband and wife, if they're in a serious relationship
– otherwise **tok-po** (གྲོགས་པོ་), 'boyfriend', and **tok-mo** (གྲོགས་མོ་),
'girlfriend', are fine.

QUESTIONS

འདྲི་རྩད་

Are you married?

   kay-râng châng-sa   ཁྱེད་རང་ཆང་ས
   kyön tsa-bay   བརྒྱོན་ཚ་བས།

Is your husband/wife here?

   kay-rârng-gi kyo-ka/   ཁྱེད་རང་གི་ཁྱོ་ག/སྐྱེ་དམན་འདིར་ཡོད་པས།
   kye-man day yö-bay

Do you have a boyfriend/girlfriend?

   kay-rârng-la tok-po/tok-mo   ཁྱེད་རང་ལ་གྲོགས་པོ་/གྲོགས་མོ་ཡོད་པས།
   yö-bay

How many children do you have?

   kay-rârng-la pu-gu kâ-tsay yö ཁྱེད་རང་ལ་ཕྲུ་གུ་ག་ཚོད་ཡོད།

How many brothers/sisters do
you have?

   kay-rârng-la pün-kya bu/bu-mo ཁྱེད་རང་ལ་སྤུན་སྐྱ་བུ/བུ་མོ་ག་ཚོད་
   kâ-tsay yö   ཡོད།

How old are they?

   khong-tso lo kâ-tsay kâ-tsay ray ཁོང་ཚོ་ལོ་ག་ཚོད་ག་ཚོད་རེད།

Do you live with your family?

   kay-rârng nârng-mi nyâm-tu   ཁྱེད་རང་ནང་མི་མཉམ་དུ་སྡོད་ཀྱི་ཡོད་པས།
   dö-ki yö-bay

Do you get along with your family?

   nârng-mi-dârng châm-bo yö-bay ནང་མི་དང་འཆམ་པོ་ཡོད་པས།

FAMILY

REPLIES

ལན་འདེབས།

I'm ...   nga ...   ང་ ...

  single ·   mi-hreng yin   མི་ཧྲེང་ཡིན།

  married   châng-sa gyâb-tsah   ཆང་ས་བརྒྱབ་ཚར།

  separated/   [kye-man/kyo-ka]-dâng   [སྐྱེས་དམན་/ཁྱོ་ག]

    divorced   ka-ka châh song (m/f)   དང་ཁ་ཁ་ཆགས་སོང་།

I'm a widower/widow.

  ngay kye-man/kyo-ka dong-song   ངའི་སྐྱེས་དམན་/ཁྱོ་ག་གྲོང་སོང་།

I have a girlfriend/boyfriend.

  ngah tok-mo/tok-po yö   ངར་གྲོགས་མོ་/གྲོགས་པོ་ཡོད།

We live together, but we're not married.

  nga-nyi nyâm-tu dö-ki yö-te   ང་གཉིས་མཉམ་དུ་སྡོད་ཀྱི་ཡོད་དེ་

  châng-sa gyâb-may   ཆང་ས་བརྒྱབ་མེད།

I don't have any children.

  nga pu-gu chig-kyâng may   ང་ཕྲུ་གུ་གཅིག་ཀྱང་མེད།

I have a daughter/son.

  nga-la pu-gu bu-mo-chig/bu-chig yö   ང་ལ་ཕྲུ་གུ་བུ་མོ་གཅིག་/བུ་གཅིག་ཡོད།

I live with my family.

  nga nâng-mi nyâm-tu dö-ki yö   ང་ནང་མི་མཉམ་དུ་སྡོད་ཀྱི་ཡོད།

FAMILY

ཁྱིམ་ཚང་

aunt	ah-nay/su-mo	ཨ་ནེ/སུ་མོ
baby	pu-gu	ཕྲུ་གུ
boy	bu	བུ
brother	pün-kya bu	སྤུན་སྐྱག་བུ
children	pu-gu	ཕྲུ་གུ
dad	pa-la	པ་ལགས
daughter	bu-mo	བུ་མོ
daughter-in-law	bü kye-man	བུའི་སྐྱེས་དམན
family	nâng-mi	ནང་མི
family name	nâng-mi ming	ནང་མིའི་མིང
father	pa-pha	པ་ཕ
father-in-law	sa-tsâng-gi pa-pha	བཟའ་ཚང་གི་པ་ཕ
girl	bu-mo	བུ་མོ
given name	bhö-ming	འབོད་མིང
grandfather	po-po	པོ་པོ
grandmother	mo-mo	མོ་མོ
husband	kyo-ka	ཁྱོ་ག
mother	ah-ma	ཨ་མ
mother-in-law	sa-tsâng-gi ah-ma	བཟའ་ཚང་གི་ཨ་མ
mum	ah-ma	ཨ་མ
nickname	ming-tog	མིང་འདོགས
sister	pün-kya bu-mo	སྤུན་སྐྱག་བུ་མོ
son	bu	བུ
son-in-law	bu-mö kyo-ka	བུ་མོའི་ཁྱོ་ག
uncle	ah-shâng/ah-ku	ཨ་ཞང/ཨ་ཁུ
wife	kye-man	སྐྱེས་དམན

HELP THE AGED

Younger people are expected to respect older people, and children are expected to support their aged parents.

TALKING WITH PARENTS ཕ་མ་དང་སྐད་ཆ་ཤོད་པ།

When's the baby due?
pu-gu ka-dü kye-ren yö-ray ཕྲུ་གུ་ག་དུས་སྐྱེ་རེན་ཡོད་རེད།

What are you going to call the baby?
pu-gu-la ming kâ-ray ta-gi yin ཕྲུ་གུ་ལ་མིང་ག་རེ་བཏགས་ཀྱི་ཡིན།

Is this your first child?
**di kay-râng-gi pu-gu dâng-po
re-bay** འདི་ཁྱེད་རང་གི་ཕྲུ་གུ་དང་པོ་རེད་པས།

How old are your children?
**kay-râng-gi pu-gu-tso lo
kâ-tsay kâ-tsay ray** ཁྱེད་རང་གི་ཕྲུ་གུ་ཚོ་ལོ་ག་ཚོད་ག་ཚོད་རེད།

I can't believe it! You look
too young.
**ngön-nay re-bay. kay-râng
dân-ta-ahng shön-sha töh-po
shay-ta du** དངོས་གནས་རེད་པས།
ཁྱེད་རང་ད་ལྟ་འང་གཞོན་ཤ་འདོད་པོ་
ཤེད་ཀ་འདུག

Does he/she attend school?
**kho/mo lob-ta doh-ki yö
re-bay** ཁོ་/མོ་སློབ་གྲྭ་འགྲོ་གི་ཡོད་རེད་པས།

Is it a private or state school?
**te gay-pay/shoong-gi lob-ta
re-bay** དེ་སྒེར་པའི་/གཞུང་གི་སློབ་གྲྭ་རེད་པས།

Who looks after the children?
pu-gu sü ta-gi yö-ray ཕྲུ་གུ་སུས་བལྟ་གི་ཡོད་རེད།

Do you have grandchildren?
**kay-râng-la pu-gü pu-gu
yö-bay** ཁྱེད་རང་ལ་ཕྲུ་གུའི་ཕྲུ་གུ་ཡོད་པས།

What's the baby's name?
pu-gü ming kâ-ray ray ཕྲུ་གུའི་མིང་ག་རེ་རེད།

Is it a boy or a girl?
pu-gu bu ray, bu-mo ray ཕྲུ་གུ་བུ་རེད། བུ་མོ་རེད།

Is he/she well-behaved?
kho/mo chö-lâm yâg-po yö-bay ཁོ་/མོ་སྤྱོད་ལམ་ཡག་པོ་ཡོད་པས།

Does he/she let you sleep at night?

   khö/mö kay-râng tsen-la ཁོས་/མོས་ཁྱེད་རང་མཚན་ལ་གཉིད་
nyih khoog chu-gi du-gay ཁུག་བཅུག་གི་འདུག་གས།

He's/She's very big for his/her age!

   kho/mo râng-gi lo-tsay-la ཁོ་/མོ་རང་གི་ལོ་ཚད་ལ་དཔགས་པས་གཟུགས་
pâg-bay soog-po chen-po པོ་ཆེན་པོ་ཞིག་འདུག
shay-ta du

What a beautiful child!

   pu-gu nying jay-wa-la ཕྱུ་གུ་སྙིང་རྗེ་བ་ལ།

He/She looks like you.

   kho/mo kay-râng dâng da-wo du ཁོ་/མོ་ཁྱེད་རང་དང་དར་པོ་འདུག

He/She has your eyes.

   khö/mö mig kay-râng ཁོའི་/མོའི་མིག་ཁྱེད་རང་མིག་དང་དར་པོ་འདུག
mig-dâng da-wo du

Who does he/she look like, mum
or dad?

   kho/mo pa-pha-dâng ཁོ་/མོ་པ་ཕ་དང་ཨ་མ་གཉིས་སུ་འདར་པོ་འདུག
ah-ma-nyi su da-wo du

TALKING WITH CHILDREN ཕྱུ་གུ་དང་སྐད་ཆ་ཤོད་པ།

What's your name?

   kay-râng ming-la kâ-ray sa ཁྱེད་རང་མིང་ལ་ག་རེ་ཟ།

How old are you?

   kay-râng lo kâ-tsay yin ཁྱེད་རང་ལོ་ག་ཚད་ཡིན།

When's your birthday?

   kay-râng-gi kye-tsay ka-dü ray ཁྱེད་རང་གི་སྐྱེ་ཚེས་ག་དུས་རེད།

Do you have brothers and sisters?

   kay-râng-la pün-kya bu dâng ཁྱེད་རང་ལ་སྤུན་རྐྱ་བུ་དང་སྤུན་
pün-kya bu-mo yö-bay རྐྱ་བུ་མོ་ཡོད་པས།

Do you go to school or kindergarten?

   kay-râng lob-ta do-gi ཁྱེད་རང་སློབ་གྲྭ་འགྲོ་གི་ཡོད་ན། ཕྱུ་གསོ་ཁང་
yö-na, bu-so-khâng do-gi འགྲོ་གི་ཡོད་ན།
yö-na

Is your teacher nice?

    gay-gan-gi yag-po chay-kee
    du-gay   དགེ་རྒན་གྱིས་ཡག་པོ་བྱེད་ཀྱི་འདུག་གས།

Do you like school?

    lob-ta do-ya gah-po yö-bay   སློབ་གྲྭ་འགྲོ་ཡག་དགའ་པོ་ཡོད་པས།

Do you play sport?

    tse-mo tsi-gi yö-bay   རྩེད་མོ་རྩེ་གྱི་ཡོད་པས།

What sport do you play?

    tse-mo kâ-ray tsi-gi yö   རྩེད་མོ་ག་རེ་རྩེ་གྱི་ཡོད།

What do you do after school?

    lob-da do-jay kâ-ray
    chay-ki yö   སློབ་གྲྭ་གྲོལ་རྗེས་ག་རེ་བྱེད་ཀྱི་ཡོད།

Do you learn English?

    in-ji-kay jong-gi yö-bay   དབྱིན་ཇི་སྐད་སྦྱོང་གི་ཡོད་པས།

We speak a different language in
my country, so I don't understand
you very well.

    ngân-tsö loong-pâh kay
    shen-da gya-gi yö-ray,
    song-tsâng, ngay kay-râng-gi
    kay-cha yâg-po ha go-ki
    min-du   ང་ཚོའི་ལུང་པར་སྐད་གཞན་དག་རྒྱག་གི་ཡོད་རེད། སོང་ཙང་ངས་ཁྱེད་རང་གི་སྐད་ཆ་ཡག་པོ་ཧ་གོ་གི་མིན་འདུག

I come from very far away.

    nga loong-ba tâg ring-po
    shig-nay yong-wa yin   ང་ལུང་པ་ཐག་རིང་པོ་ཞིག་ནས་ཡོང་བ་ཡིན།

Do you want to play a game?

    ngah nyâm-du tse-mo tsi-gay   ང་མཉམ་དུ་རྩེད་མོ་ཞིག་རྩེ་གས།

What will we play?

    kâ-ray tse-gâh   ག་རེ་རྩེ་ག

FAMILY

དགའ་མོས། INTERESTS

Tibetans generally don't have hobbies – any spare time they have is spent resting at home, praying, or socialising with friends.

COMMON INTERESTS ཕྱིར་བཏང་དགའ་མོས་བྱེད་ས།

What do you do in your spare time?

kay-râng thoog day-pö-kâb
kâ-ray nâng-gi yö

ཁྱེད་རང་ཐུགས་དལ་པོའི་སྐབས་ག་རེ་གནང་གི་ཡོད།

Do you like ...?	kay-râng ...-la ka-bo yö-bay	ཁྱེད་རང་ ...ལ་དགའ་པོ་ཡོད་པས།
I like ...	nga ...-la ka-bo yö	ང་ ...ལ་དགའ་པོ་ཡོད།
I don't like ...	nga ...-la ka-bo may	ང་ ...ལ་དགའ་པོ་མེད།
cooking	kha-la so-ya	ཁ་ལག་བཟོ་ཡག
shopping	nyo-cha gya-ya	ཉོ་ཆ་རྒྱག་ཡག
reading	teb lo-ya	དེབ་ཀློག་ཡག
travelling	yu-ko tro-châm doh-ya	ཡུལ་སྐོར་སྤྲོ་འཆམ་འགྲོ་ཡག
talking	kay-cha-shö-ya	སྐད་ཆ་ཤོད་ཡག
watching football	kâng-bol ta-ya	རྐང་པོལ་བལྟ་ཡག
watching TV	dian-shi ta-ya; soog-tong loong-tin ta-ya	ཏེན་ཞི་བལྟ་ཡག/གཟུགས་མཐོང་རླུང་འཕྲིན་བལྟ་ཡག
I like ...	nga ... gya-ya ka-bo yö	ང་ ... རྒྱག་ཡག་དགའ་པོ་ཡོད།
dancing	shâb-doh	ཞབས་བྲོ
discos	dis-ko	ཌིས་ཀོ
diving	chu-ting kay	ཆུ་གཏིང་རྐྱལ
hiking	kâng-dü	རྐང་འགུལ
meditation	gom	སྒོམ
photography	par	པར
swimming	kay	རྐྱལ
yoga	yo-ga-gom	ཡོ་ག་སྒོམ

INTERESTS

I like ...	nga ... tsi-ya ka-bo yö	ང་... རྩེ་ཡག་དགའ་པོ་ཡོད།
aerobics/ athletics	lü-tsay	ལུས་རྩལ།
baseball	bas-bol	བེས་བོལ།
basketball	bis-ket-bol/sihn-bol	བུས་ཀེ་ཏ་བོལ།/སིན་བོལ།
boxing	bok-sing	བོག་སིང་།
cricket	kri-ket	ཀིརི་ཀེཏ།
football (soccer)	kâng-bol	རྐང་བོལ།
gymnastics	lü-tsay	ལུས་རྩལ།
hockey	hoc-key	ཧོག་ཀི།
judo	ju-doh	འཇུ་དོ།
martial arts	râng-soong dâg-tsay	རང་སྲུང་དག་རྩལ།
playing games	tsay-mo	རྩེད་མོ།
playing sport	tsay-mo/lü-tsay	རྩེད་མོ།/ལུས་རྩལ།
rugby	râg-bi po-lo	རག་བྱི་པོ་ལོ།
tennis	ten-nis	ཊེ་ནི་སི།
Tai Chi	tai-chi	ཐའི་ཅི་ལུས་རྩལ།
volleyball	vo-lee-bol/dra-bol	ཝོ་ལི་བོལ།/དྲ་བོལ།
weightlifting	ji-deg lü-tsay	ལྗིད་འདེགས་ལུས་རྩལ།

I like ...	nga ... tong-ya ka-bo yö	ང་... གཏོང་ཡག་དགའ་པོ་ཡོད།
cycling	kâng ga-ri	རྐང་སྒ་རི།
music	rö-ja	རོལ་ཆ།
rowing	dru	གྲུ།
skiing	gang-shü	གངས་ཤུད།

ART

སྒྱུ་རྩལ་རིག་གནས།

When's the gallery open?
  dem-tön-khâng ka-dü
  go chay-ki-ray

འགྲེམས་སྟོན་ཁང་ག་དུས་སྒོ་ཕྱེ་གྱི་རེད།

What kind of art are you interested in?
  kay-râng lâg-tsay rig-nay
  kân-day-la ying-yö

ཁྱེད་རང་ལག་རྩལ་རྩལ་རིག་གནས་གང་
འདྲ་ལ་ན་འབྲིངས་ཡོད།

I'm interested in ...   nga ...-la ying yö   ང་...ལ་ན་འབྲིངས་ཡོད།
  painting   tsön-ti ri-mo   ཚོན་ཏིས་རི་མོ
  performance art   tâb-tön   བཏབ་སྟོན
  sand mandalas   dü-tsön kyi-khoh   དུལ་ཚོན་དཀྱིལ་འཁོར
  sculpture   bu-kö   འབུར་སྐོས

altarpiece	chö-shom	མཆོད་གཤོམས
curator	dem-tö cha-lâg	འགྲེམས་སྟོན་ཅ་ལག་ལྟ་རྒྱམས
	nyâm-so chay-khen	གསོས་བྱེད་མཁན
gardens	doom-ra	སྒུམ་ར
photographer	pâh gya-khen	པར་རྒྱག་མཁན
sculptor	kö gya-khen	སྐོས་རྒྱག་མཁན
slide	sa-le-di log-nyen-pâh	སའེ་ཌེ་སྒོག་གཉན་པར
souvenir shop	den-ten cha-lâg	དན་རྟེན་ཅ་ལག་ཚོང་ཁང
	tsong khâng	
statue	dâ-ku	འདྲ་སྐུ

TALKING ABOUT TRAVELLING

ཡུལ་སྐོར་སྒྲོ་འཆམས་སྐོར་སྐད་ཆ་ཤོད་པ

Have you travelled much?
  kay-râng loong-pa mâng-boh
  dü-shü chay-nyong bay

ཁྱེད་རང་ལུང་པ་མང་པོ་འགྲུལ་བཞུད་
བྱེད་སྦྱོང་པས།

How long have you been travelling?
  kay-râng dü-shü yün ring-lö
  chay-pa yin

ཁྱེད་རང་འགྲུལ་བཞུད་ཡུན་རིང་ལོས་
བྱེད་པ་ཡིན།

INTERESTS

I've been travelling for (two) months.
    nga dü-shü da-wa (nyi)   ང་བརྒྱལ་བཞུད་ཟླ་བ་(གཉིས་)ཕྱས་པ་ཡིན།
    chay-pa yin
Where have you been?
    kay-râng ka-bah ka-bah chin-ba   ཁྱེད་རང་ག་བར་ག་བར་ཕྱིན་པ།
I've been to ...
    nga ...-la chin yin   ང་ ...ལ་ཕྱིན་ཡིན།
What did you think of ...?
    kay-râng-gi thong-tsü-la   ཁྱེད་རང་གི་མཐོང་ཚུལ་ལ་
    ... kân-day du   ... གང་འདྲས་འདུག

I thought it was ...	**ngay sâm-pâh**	དའི་བསམ་པར་
	te ...-chi ray-sha	དེ་ ...ཅིག་རེད་ཤག
boring	**nyob-to**	ཉོ་ཏོ་
great	**pay yâg-po**	དཔེ་ཡག་པོ་
horrible	**pay doog-châg**	དཔེ་སྡུག་ཆག
OK	**dig-tsâm**	འགྲིག་ཙམ་
too expensive	**doh-song chen-po**	འགྲོ་སོང་ཆེན་པོ་

There are too many tourists there.
    pha-gay yu-kor toh-châm-pa   ཕ་གིར་ཡུལ་སྐོར་སྤྲོ་འཆམས་པ་
    pay mâng-po du   དཔེ་མང་པོ་འདུག
Not many people speak (English).
    (in-ji-kay) shin-khen   (དབྱིན་ཇི་སྐད་)ཤེས་མཁན་ཞེ་དྲག
    shay-ta min-du   མིན་འདུག
I was ripped off in ...
    ngah ...-la shen-ta-gi   ང་ ...ལ་གཞན་དག་གི་མགོ་རྡུང་བྱུང་།
    go doong-choong
People are really friendly there.
    mi-tso pay ka-bo nye-po   མི་ཚོ་དཔེ་དགའ་པོ་ཉེ་པོ་བྱེད་ཀྱི་འདུག
    chay-ki du
What's there to do in ...?
    ...-la ka-ray ka-ray   ...ལ་ག་རེ་ག་རེ་བྱེད་ཡ་ཡོད་རེད།
    chay-ya yö-ray

There's a really good restaurant/
hotel there.

    sa-khâng/don-khâng ngön-nay   ཟ་ཁང་/མགྲོན་ཁང་དངོས་གནས་ལས་

    yâg-po-chi du   པོ་ཅིག་འདུག

INTERESTS

I'll write down the details for you.

    ka-bah yö-may ngay shu-gü   ག་བར་ཡོད་མེད་ངས་ཤོག་བུའི་སྟེང་

    gâng-la say-po-chay di-ko   ལ་གསལ་པོ་བྱེད་བྲིས་བོ

The best time to go is in (December).

    do-ya-ki dü-tsö yâg-shö   འགྲོ་ཡག་གི་དུས་ཚོད་ཡག་ཤོས་

    (chin-da chu-nyi)-la ray   (ཕྱི་ཟླ་བཅུ་གཉིས་)ལ་རེད་ལག

Is it expensive?

    doh-song chen-po re-bay   འགྲོ་སོང་ཆེན་པོ་རེད་པས།

Did you go alone?

    kay-râng chig-bo chin-bay   ཁྱེད་རང་གཅིག་པུ་ཕྱིན་པས།

Is it safe for women travellers on
their own?

    kye-man chig-bo doh-na   སྐྱེས་དམན་གཅིག་པོ་འགྲོ་ན་ཉེན་

    nyen-ga yö ma-re-bay   ཁ་ཡོད་མ་རེད་པས།

Is it safe to hitchhike?

    te-po ten-nay mo-tah dü-shü   མཐེའུ་བསྟན་ནས་མོ་ཊ་འགྱུལ་བཏང་

    chay-na nyen-ga yö ma-re-bay   བྱེད་ན་ཉེན་ཁ་ཡོད་མ་རེད་པས།

GOING OUT
Where to Go

                                   ཕྱི་ལོགས་སུ་སྐྱོད་སྐྱོད་གཏོང་དུ་འགྲོ་བ

                                   ག་པར་འགྲོག

What's there to do in the evenings?

    göng-da nâng-wa kyi-kyi   དགོང་དག་སྣང་བ་སྐྱིད་སྐྱིད་ག་རེ་གཏོང་

    kâ-ray tong-ya yö-ray   ཡག་ཡོད་རེད།

Is there a local entertainment
guide in English?

    sa-nay-la tay-mo gâng ta-gyu   ས་གནས་ལ་ལྟད་མོ་ག་གང་བལྟ་རྒྱུ་

    yö-may kyâb-ta-teb in-ji-tog   ཡོད་མེད་ཁྱབ་སྒྲགས་དེབ་དབྱིན་ཇི་ཐོག

    yö re-bay   ཡོད་རེད་པས།

Are there any discos?

    dis-ko tâb-sa yö re-bay   ཌིས་ཀོ་འཐབ་ས་ཡོད་རེད་པས།

INTERESTS

How much is it to get in?
    zü-la kâ-tsay tay-go-ray   འཛུལ་ལྭ་ག་ཚད་སྤྲད་དགོས་རེད།

Are there places where you
can hear local music?
    yü-mee rö-ja nyen-sa yö re-bay   ཡུལ་མིའི་རོལ་ཆ་ཉན་ས་ཡོད་རེད་པས།

Where can I find out what's on?
    nâng-wa kyi-kyi tong-ya   སྣང་བ་སྐྱིད་སྐྱིད་གཏོང་ཡག་རེ་ག་རེ་
    kâ-ray kâ-ray yö-may ka-nay   ཡོད་མེད་ག་ནས་གོ་ཐུབ་ཀྱི་རེད།
    ha-go thoob-ki ray

What's on tonight?
    ta-ring gong-ta kâ-ray yö-ray   ད་རིང་དགོངས་དག་ག་རེ་ཡོད་རེད།

I feel like going (for a) ...	nga ... dro-nying dö-ki du	ང་ ... འགྲོ་སྙིང་འདོད་ཀྱི་འདུག
stroll	châm-châm	འཆམ་འཆམ
dancing	shay tâb-gah	གར་ལ་བཏབ་བག
coffee/drink	ka-bi toong-gâh;	ཀོ་ཕི་འཐུང་བ/
	chig toong-gâh	གཅིག་འཐུང་བ

I feel like going to a/the ...	nga ... dro-nying dö-ki du	ང་ ... འགྲོ་སྙིང་འདོད་ཀྱི་འདུག
bar/pub	châng-khâng	ཆང་ཁང
cafe	cha-khâng	ཇ་ཁང
cinema	log-nyen ta-sa	གློག་བརྙན་བལྟ་ས
concert	rö-yâng tro-tön ta-sa	རོལ་དབྱངས་སྟོ་སྟོན་བལྟ་ས
monastery	gom-pa	དགོན་པ
nightclub	tsen-tsog tro-kyi tong-sa	མཚན་ཚོགས་སྤྲོ་སྐྱིད་གཏོང་ས
opera	dö-ga ta-sa	ཟློས་གར་བལྟ་ས
restaurant	sa-khâng	ཟ་ཁང
temple	lha-khâng	ལྷ་ཁང
theatre	tâb-tön-khâng	འཁྲབ་སྟོན་ཁང

Invitations

 མགྲོན་འབོད།

What are you doing this
evening/weekend?

kay-râng [ta-ri gong-ta; ray-sa
pen-pa dâng nyin-ma]-la
kâ-ray nâng-gi yö

ཁྱེད་རང་[ད་རིས་དགོང་དག/རེས་གཟའ་
སྤེན་པ་དང་ཉི་མ་]ལ་ག་རེ་གནང་གི་ཡོད།

Would you like to go out
somewhere?

kay-râng chi-log chig-la
don-dhö yö-bay

ཁྱེད་རང་ཕྱི་ལོག་ཅིག་ལ་
འགྲོ་འདོད་ཡོད་པས།

Karaoke

ག་ལ་ཨོ།

Nightlife and entertainment are not big in Tibet. In the country,
electric lighting is very rare, so people rise with the sun and go
to bed at sunset. In the towns and cities, however, karaoke
has become a popular pastime, particularly in Lhasa, and can
provide a good night's entertainment. Drink prices tend to be
comparatively high and you also have to pay to sing a song.
You're unlikely to hear any Tibetan music at a karaoke bar –
most of the songs are Chinese.

Do you want to go to a karaoke bar?
ga-la-wa châng-khâng-la doh-gay   ག་ལ་ཝ་ཆང་ཁང་ལ་འགྲོ་གས།
Do you have to pay to enter?
zü-la tay-go re-bay   འཛུལ་ལ་སྤྲད་དགོས་རེད་པས།
No, it's free.
ma-ray, la tay-go ma-ray   མ་རེད། ལ་སྤྲད་དགོས་མ་རེད།
Which song do you want to sing?
shay ga-gi tâng-dö yö   གཞས་ག་གི་གཏང་འདོད་ཡོད།
Do you like this song?
shay di-la ga-bo yö-bay   གཞས་འདི་ལ་དགའ་པོ་ཡོད་པས།
Do you want to sing this with me?
ngay nyâm-tu shay-di tâng-gay   ངའི་མཉམ་དུ་གཞས་འདི་གཏང་གས།
Who's this singer?
shay tong-khen-di su ray   གཞས་གཏོང་མཁན་འདི་སུ་རེད།

INTERESTS

Do you know a good restaurant
(that's cheap)?

sa-khâng yâg-po
(gong kay-po)-chig ka-bah
yö-may ha-go-ki yö-bay

ཟ་ཁང་ཡག་པོ་(གོང་ཁེ་པོ་)ཅིག་ག་བར་
ཡོད་མེད་ང་གོ་གྱི་ཡོད་པས།

Would you like to go for a
drink/meal?

chig toong-gâh/sa-gâh doh-gay

གཅིག་འཐུང་ག/ཟ་ག་འགྲོ་གས།

My shout. (I'll buy)

jin-dâk nga yin

སྦྱིན་བདག་ང་ཡིན།

Do you want to come to the ...
concert with me?

ngay nyâm-tu ... rö-yâng
tro-tön ta-gâh doh-gay

ངའི་མཉམ་དུ་ ... རོལ
དབྱངས་སྟོན་སྟོན་པ་ལྟ་ག་འགྲོ་གས།

We're having a party.

ngân-tso thuk-tro tâng-gi yö

ང་ཚོ་ཐུགས་སྤྲོ་གཏོང་གི་ཡོད།

Come along.

pheb nâng

ཕེབས་གནང་།

Responding to Invitations   བདའ་ལན་སློག་པ

Sure!

la-se, yin-dâng yin

ལགས་སེ། ཡིན་དང་ཡིན།

Yes, I'd love to.

la-se, nga dö-pa yö

ལགས་སེ། ང་འདོད་པ་ཡོད།

Yes. Where shall we go?

la-se. ngân-tso ka-bah doh-ga

ལགས་སེ། ང་ཚོ་ག་བར་འགྲོ་ག

No, I'm afraid I can't.

la, yong thoob-sa ma-ray,
gong-gay may-pa-chi

ལགས། ཡོང་ཐུབ་ས་མ་རེད།
དགོངས་དག་མེད་པ་ཅི

What about tomorrow?

sa-nyin chay-na gâng-day du

སང་ཉིན་བྱེད་ན་གང་འདྲས་འདུག

Arranging to Meet

 དུས་བཀག་རྒྱུག་པ།

What time shall we meet?

ngân-tso chu-tsö kâ-tsay
thoog-pa chay-kah

ང་ཚོ་ཆུ་ཚོད་ག་ཚོད་ཐུག་པ་བྱེད་ག

Where will we meet?

ka-bah thoog-pa chay-gay

ག་བར་ཐུག་པ་བྱེད་གས།

Let's meet at (eight) o'clock
at the ...

ngân-tso chu-tsö (gye-pa)-la
...-la thoog-pa chay-na

ང་ཚོ་ཆུ་ཚོད་(བརྒྱད་པ་)ལ
...ལ་ཐུག་པ་བྱེད་ན།

OK. I'll see you then.

la-ray. o-na je-yong

ལགས་རེད། ོ་ན་མཇལ་ཡོང་།

Agreed/OK!

mö-thün yö; di-gi ray

མོས་མཐུན་ཡོད་/འགྲིག་གི་རེད།

I'll come over at (six) o'clock.

nga chu-tsö (doog-pa)-la
yong-gi yin

ང་ཆུ་ཚོད་(དྲུག་པ་)ལ་ཡོང་གི་ཡིན།

I'll pick you up at (nine) o'clock.

ngay kay-râng chu-tsö (gu-pa)
len-gâh yong-gi yin

ངས་ཁྱེད་རང་ཆུ་ཚོད་(དགུ་པ་)
ལེན་གར་ཡོང་གི་ཡིན།

I'll try to make it (on time).

nga (dü-tsö tâg-tâg-la) leb
thoob-pa chay-ki yin

ང་(དུས་ཚོད་ཐག་ཐག་ལ་)
སླེབས་ཐུབ་པ་བྱེད་ཀྱི་ཡིན།

If I'm not there by (nine), don't
wait for me.

gay-si nga chu-tsö (gu-pa) gong-
gong-la ma-joh-na ngah
ma-gu-ro nâng

གལ་སྲིད་ང་ཆུ་ཚོད་(དགུ་པ་)གོང་
ལ་མ་འབྱོར་ན་ངར་མ་བསྒུག་རོགས་གནང་།

INTERESTS

I'll be along later. Where will you be?

   nga je-la yong-gee yin. kay-râng   ང་རྗེས་ལ་ཡོང་གི་ཡིན། ཁྱེད་རང་

   ka-bah thoog thoob-ki ray   ག་བར་ཐུག་ཐུབ་ཀྱི་རེད།

See you later/tomorrow.

   je-ma/sa-nyin jay-yong   རྗེས་མ། སང་ཉིན་མཇལ་ཡོང་།

Sorry I'm late.

   gong-da nga je-lü teb-song   དགོངས་དག ང་རྗེས་ལུས་ཐེབས་སོང་།

Never mind.

   kay chay-kiy ma-ray   གའི་བྱེད་ཀྱི་མ་རེད།

TREKKING

It's well worth travelling to the more remote areas of Tibet and exploring the country's natural diversity. The further away from the main towns you travel, however, the more you'll have to rely on Tibetan, as few people will understand English.

GETTING INFORMATION གནས་ཚུལ་ཞིབ་འབས་བྱེད་པ

Given the challenges of trekking in Tibet, many travellers wisely opt to hire a pack animal (usually a yak or a donkey) to carry their kit. It's best to swot up on your Tibetan before you enter into negotiations (see Bargaining, page 124), as there's generally haggling involved. It's worth it though – you'll have an easier trek and your yak driver will also serve as a guide, so you won't have to worry about getting lost.

Where can I find out about
hiking trails in the region?

sa-kü-day kâng-tâng-tog	ས་ཁུལ་འདིར་རྐང་འཐང་ཐོག
gyâng-ring châm-châm doh-ya	རྒྱང་རིང་ཆམ་ཆམ་འགྲོ་ཡག
lâm-gay-koh kay-cha di-sa	ལམ་གའི་སྐོར་སྐད་ཆ་འདྲི་ས
ka-bah yö-ray	ག་བར་ཡོད་རེད།

I want to rent a ...	nga ...-chig la-gö-yö	ང་ ...གཅིག་གླ་འགོས་ཡོད།
donkey	boong-gu	བོང་གུ
horse	ta	རྟ
yak	yâk	གཡག

How much does it cost for each ...?	... ray-ray-la la-ja kâ-tsay ray	... རེ་རེ་ལ་གླ་ཆ་ ག་ཚོད་རེད།
day	nyi-ma	ཉིན་མ
week	dün-tâ	བདུན་ཕྲག

I need a ...   nga ...-chig gö   ང་ ... གཅིག་དགོས།
  guide   lâm-gyü chay-khen   ལམ་རྒྱུས་བྱེད་མཁན་
  pack animal   kay-ma   ཁལ་མ་
  porter   do-bo kay-ngen   དོ་པོ་འཁྱེར་མཁན་

Is it safe to climb this mountain?
  ri-di gâng-la zâg-na nyen-ga   རི་འདིའི་སྒང་ལ་འཛེག་ན་ཉེན་ག་ཡོད་མ་རེད་པས།
  yö ma-re-bay

Is there a hut up there?
  ya-gay khâng-pa yö re-bay   ཡ་གེར་ཁང་པ་ཡོད་རེད་པས།

Do I need a guide?
  lâm-gyü chay-khen gö-ki   ལམ་རྒྱུས་བྱེད་མཁན་དགོས་ཀྱི་རེད་པས།
  re-bay

Are there guided treks?
  kâng-dü gyâb-nay doh-sa   གྱང་འགུལ་བརྒྱབ་ནས་འགྲོ་ས་
  de-po yö re-bay   འདེ་པོ་ཡོད་རེད་པས།

I'd like to talk to someone
who knows this area.
  sa-kü-te gyü-yö-khen mi-shig-la   ས་ཁུལ་འདི་རྒྱུས་ཡོད་མཁན་མི་ཞིག་ལ་
  kân-ti shu-dhö-yö   བཀའ་འདྲི་ཞུ་འདོད་ཡོད།

How long is the trail?
  kâng-lâm-te tâg ring-lö yö-ray   གྱང་ལམ་དེ་ཐག་རིང་ལོས་ཡོད་རེད།

Is the track (well-)marked?
  lâm-ga-te kha-chog ka-ba   ལམ་ག་དེ་ཁ་ཕྱོགས་ག་བར་འཆན་རྟགས་
  do-man tâg (say-bo) gyâb   (གསལ་པོ་)བརྒྱབ་ཡོད་རེད་པས།
  yö re-bay

How high is the climb?
  yâh toh-lö za-ya yö-ray   ཡར་མཐོ་ལོས་འཛེག་ཡག་ཡོད་རེད།

Which is the shortest route?
  lâm-chog tâg nye-shö ka-gi-ray   ལམ་ཕྱོགས་ཐག་ཉེ་ཤོས་ག་གི་རེད།

Which is the easiest route?
  lâm-chog lay la-shö ka-gi-ray   ལམ་ཕྱོགས་ལས་སླ་ཤོས་ག་གི་རེད།

Is the path open?
  lâm-ga go chay-yö re-bay   ལམ་ག་སྒོ་ཕྱེ་ཡོད་རེད་པས།

When does it get dark?
   na-koong ka-dü cha-gi yö-ray
   ནག་ཁུང་ག་དུས་ཆགས་ཀྱི་ཡོད་རེད།

Is it very scenic?
   yü-jong nying-je-po du-gay
   ཡུལ་ལྗོངས་སྙིང་རྗེ་པོ་འདུག་གས།

Where can I hire mountain gear?
   **ri za-gyü kho-chay ya-sa
   ka-bah yö-ray**
   རི་ར་རྒྱུའི་མཁོ་ཆས་གཡར་ས་
   ག་བར་ཡོད་རེད།

Where can we buy supplies?
   sa-chay nyo-sa ka-bah yö-ray
   བཟའ་ཆས་ཉོ་ས་ག་བར་ཡོད་རེད།

Do you have any food suitable
for trekking?
   **ri-loong-la kyâm-kyâm dro-tü
   kye-ya ka-la yö-bay**
   རི་ལུང་ལ་འཁྱམ་འཁྱམ་འགྲོ་དུས་འཁྱེར་
   ཡག་ཁ་ལག་ཡོད་པས།

Do you have any dried fruit?
   shing-toh kâm-bo yö-bay
   ཤིང་ཏོག་སྐམ་པོ་ཡོད་པས།

TREKKING

ON THE PATH འགྲོ་ལམ་ཐོག

Once you get off the main roads in Tibet, there's very little in the way of accommodation and food. However, you may be able to buy grain and other items of food from villagers and they may even allow you to stay in their homes on some trekking routes.

What is the name of that ...?	... pha-gi ming-la kâ-ray ray	... ཕ་གིའི་མིང་ལ་ག་རེ་རེད།
bridge	sâm-pâ	ཟམ་པ།
lake	tsho	མཚོ།
river	tsâng-po	གཙང་པོ།
village	loong-pa/dong-seb	ལུང་པ/གྲོང་གསེབ།

Is this the trail/ road to ...?	di ... do-ya-gi lâm-ga re-bay	འདི ... འགྲོ་ཡག་གི་ལམ་ཁ་ རེད་པས།
Drigung	di-goong	འབྲི་གུང་
Mt Kailash	gâng rim-po-che	གངས་རིན་པོ་ཆེ་
Samye	sâm-ye	བསམ་ཡས་
Tsetang	tse-tang	རྩེད་ཐང་

Which way to ...?
... doh-ya-gi lâm-ga ka-gi-ray ... འགྲོ་ཡག་གི་ལམ་ཁ་ག་གི་རེད།
Where have you come from?
kay-râng ka-nay yong-ba ཁྱེད་རང་ག་ནས་ཡོང་བ།
How long did it take you?
gyün ring-lö goh-song རྒྱུན་རིང་ལོས་འགོར་སོང་།
Where can we spend the night?
ngân-tso gong-da ka-bah day-go-ray ང་ཚོ་དགོང་དག་ག་བར་བསྡད་དགོས་རེད།
Can I leave some things here for a while?
ngay cha-lâg ga-shay nay-kâb day shâg-na di-gi re-bay ངའི་ཅ་ལག་འགའ་ཤས་གནས་སྐབས་ འདིར་བཞག་ན་འདྲིག་གི་རེད་པས།
Can we go through here?
dee bah-la do-na di-gi re-bay འདིའི་བར་ལ་འགྲོ་ན་འགྲིག་གི་རེད་པས།
Is the water OK to drink?
chu-di toong lo-gi re-bay ཆུ་འདི་འཐུང་ལོ་གི་རེད་པས།

What is the next village on the trail?
    lâm-ga te-nay chin-na dâng-po   ལམ་ག་དེ་ནས་ཕྱིན་ན་དང་པོ་ལུང་པ་ག་
    loong-pa ka-ray leb-ki-ray   རེ་ས�لེབས་ཀྱི་རེད།

Will we reach (Samye) before dark?
    sa ma-roop gong-la (sâm-ye)   ས་མ་རུབ་གོང་ལ་(བསམ་ཡས་)ས�لེབས་ཀྱི་
    leb-gi re-bay   རེད་པས།

I have to rest.
    nga ngay-so gyâb gö-ki-du   ང་ངལ་གསོ་བརྒྱབ་དགོས་ཀྱི་འདུག

I need to go to the toilet.
(urinate/defecate)
    nga chim-ba/tsok-pa tâng-ga   ང་གཅིན་པ་/བཙོག་པ་གཏང་དག།
    doh gö-ki-du   འགྲོ་དགོས་ཀྱི་འདུག

Are there any other areas to stay
apart from here?
    di mem-bay loong-pa shen-da   འདི་མིན་པའི་ལུང་པ་གཞན་དག
    dö-sa du-gay   ལ་སྡོད་ས་འདུག་གས།

Can we get accommodation at ...?
    ...-lâ nay-tsâng râ-gi re-bay   ...ལ་གནས་ཚང་རག་གི་རེད་པས།

How many ...	(sâm-ye) bah-tu ...	(བསམ་ཡས་)བར་དུ་ ...
to (Samye)?	kâ-tsay go-gi-ray	ག་ཚོད་འགྲོར་གྱི་རེད།
hours	chu-tsö	ཆུ་ཚོད་
days	nyin-ma	ཉིན་མ་
kilometres	ki-lo-mi-tar	ཀི་ལོ་མི་ཏར་

Is the trail ...?	lâm-ga ... du-gay	ལམ་ག་ ... འདུག་གས།
bad	dhuk-cha	སྡུག་ཆགས་
good	yâg-po	ཡག་པོ་
narrow	tog-po	དོག་པོ་
safe	ten-po	བརྟན་པོ་
steep (uphill/ downhill)	(gyen/tu) sah-po	(གྱེན་/ཐུར་)
		ཟར་པོ་
wide	gya chem-po	རྒྱ་ཆེན་པོ་

Do we have to pay to sleep in your house?
kay-râng-gi khang-pah nay-la
tay-go re-bay
ཁྱེད་རང་གི་ཁང་པར་གནས་སྣ་
སྡོད་དགོས་རེད་པས།

Can we stay here tonight?
ngân-tso dho-gong day day-nâ
di-gi re-bay
ང་ཚོ་དགོང་འདིར་བསྡད་ན་འགྲིག་
གི་རེད་པས།

Please make a meal for us tonight.
dho-gong ngân-tsoh
kha-la-chi so nâng-dâ
དོ་དགོང་ང་ཚོ་ལ་ཁ་ལག་གཅིག་
བཟོ་གནང་དང་།

I'll pay you.
ngay kay-râng-la la-ja tay-go
ངས་ཁྱེད་རང་ལ་གླ་ཆ་སྤྲད་གོ།

Can we get food in that village/place?
loong-pa/sa-cha pha-gay
kha-la râ-gi re-bay
ལུང་པ/ས་ཆ་ཕ་གིར་
ཁ་ལག་རག་གི་རེད་པས།

Is there a restaurant?
sa-khâng du-gay
ཟ་ཁང་འདུག་གས།

Is there firewood and water here?
day chu-dâng may-shing du-gay
འདིར་ཆུ་དང་མེ་ཤིང་འདུག་གས།

Where is the leader?
go-tih ka-bah
འགོ་འཛིན་ག་བ།

Do you have any	... tsong-ya	... བཙོང་ཡག
... to sell?	yö-bay	ཡོད་པས།
meat	sha	ཤ
potatoes	sho-gok	ཞོག་ཁོག
rice	dray	འབྲས
roasted barley flour	tsâm-pa	ཙམ་པ
wholemeal flour	dro-shib	གྲོ་ཞིབ

Please lend me	nga ...-chig	ང་ ...གཅིག་གནང་རོགས་གནང་དང་།
a ...	ya-nâng-da	
ladle	kyok	སྐྱོག
pot	nö-chay	སྣོད་ཆས

CAMPING

གུར་རྒྱག་ནས་སྡོད་པ

Where's the nearest campsite?
  gur gyâb-sa tâg nye-shö
  ka-bah yö-ray

གུར་རྒྱག་ས་ཐག་ཉེ་ཤོས་ག་བར་ཡོད་རེད།

Do you have any sites available?
  gur gyâb-sa sa-cha
  tong-pa yö-bay

གུར་རྒྱག་ས་ས་ཆ་སྟོང་པ་ཡོད་པས།

How much is it per ...?	... ray-ray-la gong kâ-tsay ray	... རེ་རེ་ལ་ གོང་ག་ཚོད་རེད།
person	mi	མི
tent	gur	གུར
vehicle	mo-ta	མོ་ཊ

I want to hire a tent.
  nga gur-chig la-go-yö

ང་གུར་གཅིག་ལ་དགོས་ཡོད།

Where can I hire a tent?
  gur la-sa ka-bah yö-ray

གུར་ལ་ས་ག་བར་ཡོད་རེད།

Is it waterproof?
  chu thoob-ki re-bay

ཆུ་ཐུབ་ཀྱི་རེད་པས།

Are there shower facilities?
  tor-chü soog-po tu-sa
  yö re-bay

ཐོར་ཆུ་ཁྲུས་གཟུགས་པོ་འཁྲུས་ཡོད་རེད་པས།

Am I allowed to camp here?
  day gur gyâb-nay day
  cho-gi re-bay

འདིར་གུར་བརྒྱབ་ནས་སྡོད་ཆོག་གི་རེད་པས།

TREKKING

DON'T LIGHT UP!

You shouldn't light campfires while on a trek –
there's scant firewood available in Tibet and what
there is tends to be in high demand by the locals.

WEATHER གནམ་གཤིས

What's the weather like?
nâm-shi kân-day-du གནམ་གཤིས་གང་འདྲས་འདུག

The weather is	te-ring nâm-shi	དེ་རིང་གནམ་གཤིས
... today.	... du	... འདུག
Will it be ...	sa-nyin nâm-shi ...	སང་ཉིན་གནམ་གཤིས
tomorrow?	yö re-bay	... ཡོད་རེད་པས།
bad	dhuk-cha	སྡུག་ཆགས
cloudy	tin thib-	སྤྲིན་འཐིབས
cold	dâng-mo	གྲང་མོ
good	yâg-po	ཡག་པོ
hot (very)	tsa-po (shay-ta)	ཚ་པོ (ཞེ་དྲག)
warm	drö-po	དྲོད་པོ
windy	lhâg-pa tsa-po	རླུགས་པ་ཚ་པོ

It's humid (today).
(te-ring) sha-tsen chem-po du (དེ་རིང་)བཤར་ཚོན་ཆེན་པོ་འདུག

It's raining (today).
(te-ring) chah-pa bâb-ki-ray (དེ་རིང་)འཆར་པ་བབ་ཀྱི་རེད

It's snowing (today).
(te-ring) gâng bâb-ki-ray (དེ་རིང་)གངས་བབ་ཀྱི་རེད

It's raining heavily.
chah-shoog chem-po bâb-ki-ray འཆར་ཤུགས་ཆེན་པོ་བབ་ཀྱི་རེད

It's raining lightly.
chah-pa sib-sib bâb-ki-ray འཆར་པ་སིབ་སིབ་བབ་ཀྱི་རེད

It's flooding.
chu-lo gya-ki-ray ཆུ་ལོག་རྒྱག་ཀྱི་རེད

cloud	tin-pa	སྤྲིན་པ་
earth	sa	ས་
fog	moog-pa	སྨུག་པ་
frost	say/sil-wa/ba-mo	སད་/སིལ་བ་/བ་མོ་
ice	kyâg-pa	འཁྱགས་པ་
mud	dâm-pâg	འདམ་པ་
rain	chah-pa	འཆར་པ་
snow	gâng	གངས་
storm	loong-tsub dâng-wa	རླུང་འཚུབ་ལྡང་བ་
sun	nyi-ma	ཉི་མ་
thunderstorm	doo-kay gyâk-pa-dâng	འབྲུག་སྐད་རྒྱག་པ་དང་ཆར་
	cha-loong lâng-pa	རླུང་ལངས་པ་

TREKKING

SEASONS དུས་ཚིགས་

spring	chi-ka	དཔྱིད་ཀ་
summer	yar-ga	དབྱར་ཁ་
autumn	tön-ga	སྟོན་ཁ་
winter	gün-ga	དགུན་ཁ་
dry season	chah-chu may-pay	འཆར་ཆུ་
	dü-tsig	མེད་པའི་དུས་ཚིགས་
monsoon season	chah-shö dü-tsig	ཆར་ཤོད་དུས་ཚིགས་
rainy season	chah-du	འཆར་དུས་

WEATHERWISE

It's not uncommon to experience sudden temperature drops in Tibet, so make sure you're always well-equipped for a cold snap, even when it looks out of the question.

GEOGRAPHICAL TERMS ས་ཁམས་དང་འབྲེལ་བའི་མིང་ཚིག

agriculture	shing-lay	ཞིང་ལས་
beach	tsho-khay chay-tâng	མཚོའི་འགྲམ་བྱེ་ཐང་
border	sa-tsâm	ས་མཚམས་
bridge	sâm-pa	ཟམ་པ་
cave	dâg-phuk	བྲག་ཕུག
city	dong-kay	གྲོང་ཁྱེར་
desert	chay-tâng	བྱེ་ཐང་
earthquake	sa-yom	ས་ཡོམ་
farm	shing-ga	ཞིང་ཁ་
footpath	kâng-lâm	རྐང་ལམ་
forest	shing-nâg	ཤིང་ནགས་
gap; narrow pass	gâg dok-po	གགས་དོག་པོ་
grassy plains	tsa-kha sâng-pö-tâng	རྩ་ཁ་བཟང་པོའི་ཐང་
high plateau	sa thö tâng-shong	ས་མཐོའི་ཐང་གཤོངས་
hill	ri	རི་
hot spring	chu-tsen	ཆུ་ཚན་
island	tso-ling	མཚོ་གླིང་
jungle	shing-nâg	ཤིང་ནགས་
lake	tsho	མཚོ་
landslide	sa-rü	ས་རུད་
mountain	ri	རི་
mountain range	ri-gyü	རི་རྒྱུད་
national park	mi-mâng ling-ga	མི་དམངས་གླིང་ཁ་
ocean	gyâm-tsho	རྒྱ་མཚོ་
pass	la	ལ་
peak	tse-mo	རྩེ་མོ་
river	tsâng-po	གཙང་པོ་
scenery	yu-jong	ཡུལ་ལྗོངས་
sea	tsho	མཚོ་
valley	loong-shong	ལུང་གཤོངས་
village	dong-seb	གྲོང་གསེབ་
waterfall	bâb-chu	བབ་ཆུ་

FAUNA

ཟིར་ཡུལ་སྲོག་ཆགས།

What animal is that?
  sem-chen pha-gi kâ-ray ray

སེམས་ཅན་ཕ་གི་ག་རེ་རེད།

What's that animal called?
  sem-chen pha-gee ming-la
  kâ-ray-sa

སེམས་ཅན་ཕ་གིའི་མིང་ལ་ག་རེ་ཟ།

Domestic Creatures

ཁྱིམ་གསོས་སྲོག་ཆགས།

buffalo	ma-ye	མ་ཡེ
calf	bay-hu	བེའུ
cat	shi-mi	ཞི་མི
chicken	cha-te	བྱ་ཏེ
cow	ba-choog	བ་ཕྱུགས
dog	kyi	ཁྱི
domestic animal	go-choog	གོ་ཕྱུགས
donkey	boong-gu	བོང་བུ
duck	ngân-ba	ངང་པ
goat	ra	ར
hen	cha-mo	བྱ་མོ
horse	ta	རྟ
ox	lân-gok	གླང་གོག
pig	phâg-pa	ཕག་པ
rooster	cha-pho	བྱ་ཕོ
sheep	loog	ལུག

Wildlife རི་སྐྱེས་སྲོག་ཆགས།

ant	tog-ma	གྲོག་མ།
antelope	tsö	གཙོད།
bee	dâng-bu	སྦྲང་བུ།
bird	cha/chi-hu	བྱ།/བྱིའུ།
butterfly	chem chem ma; che-ma-leb	ཅེམ་ཅེམ་མ།/ཕྱེ་མ་ལེབ།
camel	nga-mong	རྔ་མོང་།
cockroach	shom-bu	ཤོམ་བུ།
crocodile	chu-sin	ཆུ་སྲིན།
fish	nya	ཉ།
fly	drâng-bu	སྦྲང་བུ།
frog	bag-pa	སྦལ་པ།
leech	pay-pa; bu bay-bay	པད་པ།/འབུ་སྦས་སྦས།
lion	sen-gay	སེང་གེ།
lynx	yi	གཡི།
marmot	chi-wa	འཕྱི་བ།
monkey	pi-oo	སྤྲེའུ།
mosquito	duk-drâng	དུག་སྦྲང་།
mouse	tsi-tsi	ཙི་ཙི།
snail	moog-pay bu-mo	སྒྲུག་པའི་བུ་མོ།
snake	drül	སྦྲུལ།
spider	dhom-tâg	སྡོམ་ཐག
squirrel	say-mong	སྲེ་མོང་།
toad	bag-pa chem-po-shig	སྦལ་པ་ཆེན་པོ་ཞིག
turtle	rü-bay	རུ་སྦལ།
wild animal	ri-dâg; nâg-nay sog-châg	རི་དྭགས།/ནགས་གནས་སྲོག་ཆགས།
wild ass	kyâng	རྐྱང་།
yak (male)	yâk	གཡག
yak (female)	dri	འབྲི།
yak (wild)	drong	འབྲོང་།

TREKKING

FLORA & AGRICULTURE ཆུ་ཤིང་དང་ཞིང་ལས།

What tree/plant/flower is that?
  shing-dong/tsi-shing/may-tog ཤིང་སྡོང་/ཚི་ཤིང་/མེ་ཏོག་
  pha-gi kâ-ray ray ཕ་གི་ག་རེ་རེད།
What is it used for?
  kâ-ray-la bay-chö yö-ray ག་རེ་ལ་བེད་སྤྱོད་ཡོད་རེད།
Can you eat the fruit?
  shing-day-te sa lo-gi re-bay ཤིང་འབྲས་དེ་ཟ་ལོ་གི་རེད་པས།

cactus	lhu-shing	ཀླུ་ཤིང་
eucalyptus	tsi-shing	ཚི་ཤིང་
oak	bay-shing/bay-doh	བེ་ཤིང་/བེ་དོ་
palm	ta-lay-shing	ད་ལའི་ཤིང་
coconut	bay-tay day-bu	བེ་ཏའི་འབྲས་བུ་
date	kha-sur	ཁ་ཟུར་
pine	tâng-shing	ཐང་ཤིང་
scrub	shing-ten	ཤིང་ཕྲན་
stick	gyuk-pa	རྒྱུག་པ་
tree	shing-dong	ཤིང་སྡོང་

TREKKING

Herbs, Flowers & Crops སྔན་རྩི་དང་ མེ་ཏོག་ ལོ་ཏོག

bougainvillea	til-shing ngo-doom-shig	འཇིལ་ཤིང་ངོ་སྡུམ་ཞིག
corn	ah-shom; ma-mö lo-tog	ཨ་ཤོམ་/མ་མོས་ལོ་ཏོག
crops	tön-tog	སྟོན་ཏོག
flower	may-tog	མེ་ཏོག
grapevine	gün-doom dong-po	རྒུན་འབྲུམ་སྡོང་བུ
harvest	tön-tog du-way-dü	སྟོན་ཏོག་བསྡུ་བའི་དུས
irrigation	shing-chu den-pa	ཞིང་ཆུ་འདྲེན་པ
jasmine	may-tog kun-ta	མེ་ཏོག་ཀུན་ད
lavender	shing-pö	ཤིང་སྤོས
leaf	lo-ma	ལོ་མ
lemon tree	lim-bu dong-po	ལིམ་བུ་སྡོང་པོ
orchard	shing-dong doom-ra	ཤིང་སྡོང་སྡུམ་ར
orange tree	tsa-lu-may dong-po	ཚ་ལུམ་མའི་སྡོང་པོ

planting/sowing	tsi-shing zook-pa; sa-bön deb-pa	རྩི་ཤིང་འཛུགས་པ།/ ས་བོན་འདེབས་པ།
rice field/paddy	day-shing; ma-ngay-pay day-shing	འབྲས་ཞིང་།/ མ་བཟས་པའི་འབྲས་ཞིང་
rose	gya-say may-tog	རྒྱ་སེ་མེ་ཏོག
rosemary	gyun-jâng dong-toong	རྒྱུན་ལྗང་སྡོང་སྦུང་
sunflower	nyi-ma may-tog	ཉི་མ་མེ་ཏོག
sugar cane	bur-shing	བུར་ཞིང་
terraced land	kay-shing	སྐས་ཞིང་
thyme	di-shim ngo-men-shig	དྲི་ཞིམ་སྔོ་སྨན་ཞིག
tobacco	doh-thâg	དོ་ཐག
vineyard	gün-doom shing-ra	རྒུན་འབྲུམ་ཞིང་ར་

SHOPPING

The Barkhor circuit in Lhasa offers the best souvenir shopping.
Lined with stalls, you'll find everything from jewellery and
handicrafts to prayer shawls and prayer wheels.

LOOKING FOR ...   ... འཚོལ་བ

How far is the ... from here?	di-nay ... ta ring-lö kâ-tsay yö-ray	འདི་ནས ... བར རིང་ལོས་ག་ཚོད་ཡོད་རེད།
Where's the nearest ...?	... nyay-shö ka-bah yö-ray	... ཉེ་ཤོས་ག་བར་ཡོད་རེད།
bank	ngü-khâng	དངུལ་ཁང
barber	ta sha-khâng	སྐྲ་བཤའ་ཁང
bookshop	teb tsong-khâng	དེབ་ཚོང་ཁང
camera shop	par tsong-khâng	པར་ཚོང་ཁང
clothing store	du-log tsong-khâng	དུག་ལོག་ཚོང་ཁང
craft shop	lâg-sö cha-lâg tsong-khâng	ལག་བཟོས་ཅ་ལག ཚོང་ཁང
department store	de-tsen tsong-khâng	སྡེ་ཚན་ཚོང་ཁང
general store	nay-zom tsong-khâng	སྣེ་འཛོམས་ཚོང་ཁང
laundry	du-log trü-khâng	དུག་ལོག་འཁྲུད་ཁང
market	trom	ཁྲོམ
newsagency	tsâg-sho tsong-khâng	ཚགས་ཤོག་ཚོང་ཁང
optician	mik-shay so-khen	མིག་ཤེལ་བཟོ་མཁན
pharmacy	men tsong-khâng	སྨན་ཚོང་ཁང
music shop	rö-ja tsong-khâng	རོལ་ཆ་ཚོང་ཁང
shoe shop	lhâm-ko tsong-khâng	ལྷམ་ཀོ་ཚོང་ཁང
souvenir shop	dren-ten cha-lâg tsong-khâng	དྲན་རྟེན་ཅ་ལག་ཚོང་ཁང
stationery shop	yig-chay tsong-khâng	ཡིག་ཆས་ཚོང་ཁང
supermarket	râng-kho râng-dem tsong-khâng	རང་མཁོ་རང་འཛེམས་ ཚོང་ཁང
Tibetan rug store	bö-ki room-den tsong-khâng	བོད་ཀྱི་ཁུམས་གདན་ཚོང་ཁང
travel agency	dim-drü-khâng	འགྲིམ་འགྲུལ་ཁང

MAKING A PURCHASE ཉོ་སྒྲུབ་བྱེད་པ།

I'm just looking.
nga ta-gâ-si mig-tâ-gi-yö ངད་གས་མིག་བལྟ་གི་ཡོད།

Excuse me Mr/Ms, please come here.
cho-la/ah-cha-la, day-chi ཇོ་ལགས/ཨ་ཅག་ལགས།
peb-dâng འདིར་ཕེབས་ཤེབས་དང་།

How much is this?
di gong kâ-tsay ray འདི་གོང་ག་ཚོད་རེད།

Can you write down the price?
gong shu-gu-tog dih nâng-da གོང་ཤོག་བུ་ཐོག་བྲིས་གནང་དང་།

I'd like to buy ...
nga ... chig nyo-dö yö ང ... གཅིག་ཉོ་འདོད་ཡོད།

Do you have any ...?
kay-râng-la ... tsong-ya yö-bay ཁྱེད་རང་ལ ... འཚོང་ཡག་ཡོད་པས།

We don't have any.
ngân-tsoh kyö-nay may ང་ཚོ་ཁྱོན་ནས་མེད།

Which one? This one?
ka-gi gö. di gö-bay ག་གི་དགོས། འདི་དགོས་པས།

Not that one. This one.
pha-gi man. di gö ཕ་གི་མན། འདི་དགོས།

Do you have any others?
shen-ta yö-bay གཞན་དག་ཡོད་པས།

Can you show me that?
pha-gi ngah mik tön-dâ ཕ་གི་ངར་མིག་སྟོན་དང་།

I don't like it.
te lo-la doh-ma-song དེ་བློ་ལ་འགྲོ་མ་སོང་།

Is this for sale?
di tsong-ya re-bay འདི་འཚོང་ཡག་རེད་པས།

How much is it?
gong kâ-tsay ray གོང་ག་ཚོད་རེད།

I'll buy this one.
nga di nyo-gi yin ང་འདི་ཉོ་གི་ཡིན།

Do you accept credit cards?
    bu-lön shog-jâng-tog བུ་ལོན་ཤོག་བྱང་ཏོག
    rim-pa tay-na di-gi re-bay རིན་པ་སྤྲད་ན་འགྲིག་གི་རེད་པས།
Could I have a receipt please?
    choong-zin nâng thoob-ki re-bay བྱུང་འཛིན་གནང་ཐུབ་ཀྱི་རེད་པས།
Does it have a guarantee?
    te-la gan-len gan-gya དེ་ལ་བགན་ལེན་བགན་རྒྱ
    tay-ki re-bay སྤྲད་ཀྱི་རེད་པས།
Can I have it sent overseas/abroad?
    te chi-gye-la tâng-nâng དེ་ཕྱི་རྒྱལ་ལ་གཏང་གནང
    thoob-ki re-bay ཐུབ་ཀྱི་རེད་པས།
Please wrap it.
    toom-sho gya-ro nâng བྱུམ་ཤོག་རྒྱག་རོགས་གནང་།

I'd like to return this please.
    ku-chi, di chi-log chay སྐུ་སྐྱིད། འདི་ཕྱིར་ལོག་བྱེད
    chu-rog-nâng བཅུག་རོགས་གནང་།
It's faulty.
    te kyön sho-sha དེ་སྐྱོན་ཤོར་ཤག
It's broken.
    te châg-sha དེ་ཆག་ཤག
I'd like my money back.
    ngay-ngü tsuh lo-ro-nâng ངའི་དངུལ་ཚུར་སློག་རོགས་གནང་།
What is this made of?
    dee gyoob-jâ kâ-ray ray འདིའི་རྒྱུབ་བྱ་ག་རེ་རེད།
Where does this come from?
    di loong-ba kâ-nay thön-ba ray འདི་ལུང་པ་ག་ནས་ཐོན་པ་རེད།

BARGAINING གོང་ཚོད་སྒྲིག་པ།

Bargaining at market stalls is the norm in Lhasa – you may initially be quoted a price up to 10 times the real value.

It's too expensive.
gong chay-ta-sha གོང་ཆེ་དྲགས་འདུག

What's your real price?
gong ngön-nay soong-dâ གོང་དངོས་གནས་གསུང་དང་།

Really?
ngön-nay དངོས་གནས།

It's too much.
gong chay-tah-sha གོང་ཆེ་དྲགས་འདུག

I don't have much money.
nga-la ngü shay-ta may ང་ར་དངུལ་ཤེ་དྲགས་མེད།

Could you give me a discount?
gong châg thoob-ki re-bay གོང་འཆག་ཐུབ་ཀྱི་རེད་པས།

Do you have something cheaper?
gong kay-pa yö-bay གོང་ཁེ་པ་ཡོད་པས།

I'll give you ...
ngay ... tay go ངས་ ... སྤྲད་དགོས།

No more than ...
...-lay mâng-wa tay-ki-man ...ལས་མང་བ་སྤྲད་ཀྱི་མིན།

SOUVENIRS དྲན་རྟེན་ཅ་ལག།

amber	pö-shay	སྤོས་ཤེལ།
carpets	room-den	རུམ་གདན།
earrings	ahm-cho gyen; na-gyen	ཨམ་ཅོག་རྒྱན་/རྣ་རྒྱན་
gold	say	གསེར།
handicraft	lag-sö	ལག་བཟོས།
necklace	ke-gyen/gü-gyen	སྐེ་རྒྱན་/མགུལ་རྒྱན་
pottery	za-chay	རྫ་ཆས།
ring	tsi-kok	ཚིགས་ཁེབས།
rug	khâ-den	ཁ་གདན།
silver	ngü	དངུལ།
turquoise	yu	གཡུ།

ESSENTIAL GROCERIES

དགོས་མཁོའི་ཉོ་ཆ

Where can I find (a) ...?	... ka-bah ra-gi ray	... གང་བར་རག་གི་རེད།
I'd like (a) ...	ngah ... gö	ང་ ... དགོས།
batteries	log-shu-men	གློག་ཤུ་སྨན
bread	bâk-lay	བག་ལེབ
butter	mâh	མར
candles	yâng-la	ཡང་ལ
cheese	chu-ra	ཕྱུར་ར
chocolate	chok-let	ཅོག་ལེཊ
eggs	go-nga	སྒོང་ང
flour (wholemeal)	dro-shib	གྲོ་ཞིབ
gas cyclinder	gas gâm	གེས་སྒམ

ham	phâg-sha dü-ma	ཕག་ཤ་དུས་མ
honey	dâng-tsi	སྦྲང་རྩི
margarine	mâh zü-ma	མར་བཟུས་མ
matches	tsâg-ta/mu-si	ཚག་ཏ/སུ་སེ
milk	oh-ma	འོ་མ
mosquito coil	du-dâng gog-ya-men	དུག་སྦྲང་འགོག་ཡག་སྨན
pepper	ey-ma	ཨེ་མ
salt	tsha	ཚ
sugar	chay-ma-ka-ra/chi-ni	བྱེ་མ་ཀ་ར/ཅི་ནི
water purification tablets	chu tsâng-ma sö-ya men	ཆུ་གཙང་མ་བཟོ་ཡག་སྨན
washing powder	du-log trü-ya po-ta	དུག་ལོག་འཁྲུད་ཡག་པོ་ཊར་ཞེ
yogurt	sho	ཞོ

CLOTHING

དྭགས་ལོགས

belt	kay-râ	སྐེད་རགས
blouse	wâng-ju	ཝོན་འཇུག
boots	ju-ta yu-ring	འཇུར་ཏུ་ཡུ་རིང
coat	ko-ti	གོ་ཏི
dress	mo-chay	མོ་ཆས
gloves	lâg-shoob	ལག་ཤུབས
hat	shah-mo	ཞྭ་མོ
jacket	ja-ke-ti	ཇ་ཀེ་ཏི
jeans	jeen	འཇིན
jumper	ba-len; o-mo-sü	སྦ་ལེན/འུ་མོ་སུད་སྟོད་སྒུང
(sweater)	tö-toong	
pants (trousers)	gö-toong/dho-ma	གོས་ཐུང/དོར་མ
raincoat	cha-keb	ཆར་ཁེབས
sandals	cha-pa-li	ཅ་པ་ལི
shirt	tö-toong/wâng-ju	སྟོད་ཐུང/ཝོན་འཇུག
shoes	lhâm-kok/ju-ta	ལྷམ་གོག/འཇུར་ཏ
shorts	ha-pan; gö-toong wog-dho	ཧ་པན/གོས་ཐུང་འོག་དོ
skirt	may-yog	སྨད་གཡོག
socks	u-su/o-mo-su	འུ་སུས/འུ་མོ་སུ
swimsuit	chu-kay gyön-chay	ཆུ་རྐྱལ་གྱོན་ཆས
T-shirt	gong-may tö-toong	གོང་མེད་སྟོད་ཐུང
	phu-che	ཕུ་ཆེད
underwear	nâng-gyön ha-pan	ནང་གྱོན་ཧ་པན

Can I try it on?
  tsö-ta-che gyön-na
  di-gi re-bay
  ཚོད་བལྟ་ཆེད་གྱོན་ན་འདི་གི་ཡིན་རེད་པས

My size is ...
  ngay-tsay ... ray
  ངའི་ཚད ... རེད

It doesn't fit.
  tâg-tâg ray min-du
  དག་དག་རེད་མིན་འདུག

Can it be altered?
  so-chö gya thoob-ki re-bay
  བཟོ་བཅོས་རྒྱག་ཐུབ་ཀྱི་རེད་པས

It's too ...	te ... tâg-sha	དེ་ ... དྲགས་ཤག
big	chay	ཆེ་
small	choong	ཆུང་
short	toong	ཐུང་
long	ring	རིང་
tight	dâm	དམ་
loose	lhö	ལྷོད་

COLOURS

ཚོས་གཞི་

black	nâg-po	ནག་པོ་
blue	ngön-po	སྔོན་པོ་
brown	gya-moog/mah-moog	རྒྱ་སྨུག/དམར་སྨུག
green	jâng-gu	ལྗང་གུ་
grey	kya-wo/ngön-kya	སྐྱ་བོ་/སྔོན་སྐྱ་
orange	mâ-say/li-wâng	དམར་སེར་/ལི་ཝང་
pink	sing-kya	ཟིང་སྐྱ་
purple	ngön-mah/mu-man	སྔོན་དམར་/སྨུ་མན་
red	mah-po	དམར་པོ་
white	ka-po	དཀར་པོ་
yellow	say-po	སེར་པོ་

I don't like this colour.

nga tsü-shi di-la gâ-bo min-du   ང་ཚོས་གཞི་འདི་ལ་དགའ་པོ་མིན་འདུག

Do you have another (colour)?

(tsü-shi) shen-da yö-bay   (ཚོས་གཞི་)གཞན་དག་ཡོད་པས།

TRUE COLOURS

To be more specific about colour, replace the second syllable of the relevant colour with **nâg** (ནག), 'dark', or **kya** (སྐྱ), 'light'. For example, 'blue' is **ngön-bo** (སྔོན་པོ་) but 'dark blue' is **ngön-nag** (སྔོན་ནག) and 'light blue' **ngön-kya** (སྔོན་སྐྱ).

MATERIALS

ཚོས་ཚོ་

brass	râg	རག
ceramic	za-sö	རྫ་བཟོའི་
corduroy	shur-mâ	ཤུར་མ་
cotton	tin-bay	སྲིན་བལ་
felt	ching-pâ	ཕྱིང་པ་
glass	shay	ཤེལ་
gold	say	གསེར་
leather	ko-wa	ཀོ་བ་
metal	châg	ལྕགས་
nylon	ni-len	ནི་ལེན་
plastic	pö-ka	པྲོས་ཀ་
silk	dru-zi	གྲུ་ཙི་
silver	ngü	དངུལ་
stainless steel	tsa mi-gya-pay si-tee	བཙའ་མི་རྒྱགས་པའི་སི་ཏིལ་
velvet	pu-mâ	སྤུ་མ་
wood	shing	ཤིང་
wool	bay	བལ་
handmade	lâg-sö	ལག་བཟོས་
synthetic	zay-jo sö-pay	རྫས་སྤྲོར་བཟོས་པའི་

Is this ...?	di ... re-bay	འདི་ ... རེད་པས་
amber	pö-shay	སྤོས་ཤེལ་
gold	say	གསེར་
jade	zü/yâng-ti	ཧྲེལ་/གཡང་ཏི་
silver	ngü	དངུལ་
turquoise	yu	གཡུ་

TOILETRIES ཁྲུས་ཁང་མོའི་ཆས།

Some toiletries are hard to find even in Lhasa, including shaving cream, decent razor blades, insect repellent and tampons.

aftershave	ka-bu sha-je ju-ya di-sång	ཁ་སྤུ་བཞར་རྗེས་སྦྱག་ཡག ། རྡི་བཟང་།
bath/shower gel	soog-po tru-dü ju-ya phik•phik•chi	གཟུགས་པོ་འཁྲུད་དུས་སྦྱག །ཡག་ཕིག་ཕིག་ཅིག
comb	gyook-shay	རྒྱུག་ཤས།
condoms	lig-shoob	ལིག་ཤུབས།
dental floss	so tsång-ma so-ya dar-kü	སོ་གཙང་མ་བཟོ་ཡག་དར་སྐུད།
deodorant	lü-di gok-men di-yo do-ren	ལུས་རྡི་འགོག་སྨན་རྡི་ཡོ་རོ་རེན།
face cream	shâb-sö	ཞབས་བསོས།
hairbrush	gyook-shay/pân-do	རྒྱུག་ཤས།/ཕག་མདོ།
hair dye	ta-tsö	སྐྲ་ཚོས།
insect repellent	bu-dång gok-men	འབུ་སྦྲང་འགོག་སྨན།
moisturiser	shâb-sö	ཞབས་བསོས།
razor (blades)	ta-di(-ka)	སྐྲ་རྡི་(ཁ)
sanitary napkins	tsång-day shu-gu	གཙང་སྦྲའི་ཤོག་གུ
shampoo	ta trü-ya shâm-bu	སྐྲ་འཁྲུད་ཡག་ཞམ་བུ།
shaving cream	ah-ra shar-dü ju-ya bhu-wa	ཨ་ར་བཞར་དུས་སྦྱག་ཡག་སྦུ་བ།
soap	yi-tsi	ཡི་ཙི།
sunblock	nyib-tâg gok-chay ju-ya men	ཉི་བཀག་འགོག་བྱེད། སྦྱག་ཡག་སྨན།
talcum powder	soog-por ju-ya tel-kâm po-tah	གཟུགས་པོར་སྦྱག་ཡག །ཏལ་ཀམ་པོ་ཏ།
tampons	ma-kha gok-chay sin-bay	སྨ་ཁ་འགོག་བྱེད་སྲིན་བལ།
tissues	lâg-chi shu-gu	ལག་ཕྱིས་ཤོག་གུ
toilet paper	sâng-chö shu-gu	གསང་སྤྱོད་ཤོག་གུ
toothbrush	so-trü	སོ་འཁྲུ།
toothpaste	so-men	སོ་སྨན།

SHOPPING

FOR THE BABY ཕྲུ་གུ་ལ་དགོས་ལས།

baby powder	pu-gü soog-po	ཕྲུ་གུའི་གཙག་ལས་པོ
	ju-ya po-tah	བྱུག་ལས་པོ་ཏ་ར
bib	ka-lâg tay-dü pu-gü	ཁ་ལག་སྟེར་དུས་ཕྲུག
	kay gyön-chay	གུའི་སྐེར་གྱོན་ཆས
disposable	bay-chö sin-jay	བེད་སྤྱོང་ཞིན་ཇེས་གཏུག
nappies	yu-roong pu-gü chu-den	རྡ་རུ་ཕྲུ་གུའི་ཆུ་གདན
dummy/pacifier	jib-ru	འཇིབ་རུ
feeding bottle	pu-gu o-ma tay-ya	ཕྲུ་གུའི་འོ་སྟེར་ལས་ཞེབ་དམ
	shay-tâm	
nappies	pu-gü chu-den	ཕྲུ་གུ་ཆུ་གདན
nappy rash cream	chu-den tor-sib	ཆུ་གདན་ཐོར་ཤིབ་འགོག་བྱེད
	gok-chay ju-ya-men	བྱུག་ལས་སྨན
powdered milk	o-tsâm	འོ་ཚམ
teat	jib-rü nu-ma	འཇིབ་རུ་ར་ནུ་མ
tinned baby food	pu-gu tay-ya	ཕྲུ་གུར་སྟེར་ལས
	châg-tin say	ལྕགས་ཏིན་ཟས

STATIONERY & PUBLICATIONS ཡིག་ཆས་དང་པར་སྐྲུན་དེབ

Is there an English-language
bookshop nearby?
    nye-dâm-la in-ji teb   ཉེ་འགྲམ་ལ་དབྱིན་ཇི་དེབ
    tsong-khâng yö re-bay   ཚོང་ཁང་ཡོད་རེད་པས།
Is there an English-language section?
    in-ji teb-ki de-tsen yö re-bay   དབྱིན་ཇི་དེབ་ཀྱི་སྡེ་ཚན་ཡོད་རེད་པས།
Is there a local entertainment
guide in English?
    sa-nay-la tay-mo gâng ta-gyu   ས་གནས་ལ་ལྟད་མོ་གང་ལ་བལྟ་རྒྱུ
    yö-may kyâb-ta-teb in-ji-tog   ཡོད་མེད་ཁྱབ་ལྟ་སྒྲགས་དེབ་དབྱིན་ཇི་ཐོག
    yö re-bay   ཡོད་རེད་པས།

SHOPPING

Do you have any books in
English by …?

| kay-râng-la …-nay | ཁྱེད་རང་ལ་…ནས་བརྩམས་པའི་དེབ་ |
| tsâm-pay-teb in-ji-tog yö-bay | དབྱིན་ཇི་ཐོག་ཡོད་པས། |

Do you sell …?   … tsong-ya yö-bay   … བཙོང་ཡ་ཡོད་པས།
  books   (in-ji)-teb   (དབྱིན་ཇི)དེབ་
    (in English)
  magazines   dü-teb   དུས་དེབ་
  newspapers   (in-ji) tsåg-ba   (དབྱིན་ཇི)ཚགས་པར་
    (in English)
  postcards   dåg-sho   སྒྲག་ཤོག་

(Tibetan-English)   (bö-in) tshing-dzö   (བོད་དབྱིན)ཚིག་མཛོད་
  dictionary
exercise book   jong-dah ti-teb   སྦྱོང་བརྡར་འབྲི་དེབ་
envelope   yi-gok   ཡིག་སྒྲོགས་
glue   jâr-tsi   སྦྱར་ཚི་
… map   … sâp-ta   … ས་བཀྲ་
  city   dong-kye   གྲོང་ཁྱེར་
  regional   sa-nay-ki   ས་གནས་ཀྱི་
  road   lâm-kay   ལམ་ཀའི་
  trekking   ri-loong do-ya   རི་ལུང་འགྲོ་ཡག་
notebook   di-teb   འབྲི་དེབ་
novel   doong-teb/nâm-thar སྒྲུང་དེབ/རྣམ་ཐར་
pad (letter   (tân-yig) ti-say-teb (གཏན་ཡིག)འབྲི་དེབ་
  writing)
paper   shu-gu   ཤོག་གུ་
pen   nyu-gu   སྙུ་གུ་
pencil   sha-nyoog/pen-see ཞ་སྙུག/པན་སིལ་
scissors   jâm-tse   ཇེམ་ཙེ་
writing paper   ti-shog   འབྲི་ཤོག་

SHOPPING

MUSIC རོལ་ཆ

I'm looking for a ... CD.

nga ... si-di ra-gi yö-may
ta-ki-yö ང་ ... སི་ཌི་རག་གི་ཡོད་མེད་ བལྟ་ཀྱི་ཡོད།

Do you have any ...?

kay-râng-la ... yö-bay ཁྱེད་རང་ལ་ ... ཡོད་པས།

What's his/her best recording?

kö/mö shay yâg-shö ka-re ray ཁོའི་/མོའི་གཞས་ཡག་ཤོས་ག་རེ་རེད།

I heard a band/singer called ...

ngay [rö-ja tsog-pa; shay
tong-khen] ... say-wa go
nyong-sha ངས་ [རོལ་ཆ་ཚོགས་པ་/གཞས་ གཏོང་མཁན་] ... ཟེར་བའི་སྐྱོང་ཉོག

Can I listen to this CD here?

si-di-di day nyen-na
di-gi re-bay སི་ཌི་འདི་འདིར་ཉན་ན་འགྲིག་གི་རེད་པས།

I need a blank tape.

ngah teb-tâg tong-ba-chig gö ངར་སྟོང་ཐག་བལྟ་གཏོང་བ་ཅིག་དགོས།

PHOTOGRAPHY པར

How much is it for developing?

phing-sho trü-la kâ-tsay ray པེང་ཤོག་བཀྲུ་ཀླུག་ག་ཚད་རེད།

When will it be ready?

kâ-dü tsha-gi ray ག་དུས་ཚར་གྱི་རེད།

I'd like a film for this camera.

par-chay di-la phing-sho chig gö པར་ཆས་འདི་ལ་པེང་ཤོག་གཅིག་དགོས།

Do you fix cameras?

par-chay so-chö gya-ki yö-bay པར་ཆས་བཟོ་བཅོས་རྒྱག་གི་ཡོད་པས།

battery	log-shu-men/bay-ti-ri	གློག་བཞུ་སྨན་/བྱེ་ཊི་རི
B&W film	phing-sho tshön-ta may-pa	པེང་ཤོག་ཚོན་ཁ་མེད་པ
camera	par-chay	པར་ཆས
colour film	phing-sho tshön-ta-chen	པེང་ཤོག་ཚོན་ཁ་ཅན

colour slide	sa-la-it phing-sho tshön-ta chen	ས་ལ་ཨིཊ་ཕིང་ཤོག་ཚོན་མདོག་ཅན
film	phing-sho	ཕིང་ཤོག
flash	par-chay-ki log	པར་ཆས་ཀྱི་གློག
flash bulb	par-chay-ki log shay-dok	པར་ཆས་ཀྱི་གློག་ཤེལ་དོག
lens	par-shay	པར་ཤེལ
light meter	wö-tshay gyab-ya	འོད་ཚད་བརྒྱབ་ཡག
slides	sa-la-it	ས་ལ་ཨིཊ
videotape	vi-do teb-tâg	ཝི་ཌོ་སྒྲིབ་ཐག

SMOKING ཐ་མག

A packet of ... cigarettes, please.
   ... tha-ma gâm-chig nâng-da ... ཐ་མག་སྒམ་གཅིག་གནང་དང
Are these cigarettes strong or mild?
   tha-ma din-tso gar-bo shay-ta ཐ་མག་འདི་ཚོ་གར་པོ་ཤེད་ལྡག
   yö-na, gar-la tsâm-bo yö-na འོད་ན་ གར་ལ་ཚམས་པོ་ཡོད་ན
Do you have a light?
   kay-râng-la may par-ya yö-bay ཁྱེད་རང་ལ་མེ་སྤར་ཡག་ཡོད་པས
Please don't smoke.
   tha-ma ma-ten-rog nâng ཐ་མག་མ་འཐེན་རོགས་གནང
Do you mind if I smoke?
   tha-ma ten-na dig-gi re-bay ཐ་མག་འཐེན་ན་འགྲིག་གི་རེད་པས
I'm trying to give up.
   nga tha-ma chö-yak tâb-shay ང་ཐ་མག་གཏོང་ཡག་ཐབས་ཤེས་བྱེད
   chay-ki yö ཀྱི་ཡོད

cigarettes	tha-ma	ཐ་མག
cigarette papers	tha-ma shu-gu	ཐ་མག་ཤོག་གུ
cigars	tha-ma si-gah	ཐ་མག་སི་སྒར
filtered	tsâg-gyâb-pa	འཚག་བརྒྱབ་པ
lighter	may par-ya	མེ་སྤར་ཡག
matches	tsâg-ta/mu-si	ཚག་ཏ/སྨུ་སི
pipe	tu-ten-dong	དུ་འཐེན་མདོང
tobacco	doh-tâg shib-shib	མདོ་ཐག་ཞིབ་ཞིབ

WEIGHTS & MEASURES हेद्-र्ळंद्-द्र-कु-द्विर्-र्ळंद्-

centimetre	sin-ti-mi-tar	སེན་ཏི་མི་ཊར
gram	ga-râm	གྲ་རམ
kilogram	ki-lo-ga-râm/chi-gya	གི་ལོ་གྲ་རམས/སྐྱི་རྒྱ
kilometre	ki-lo-mi-tar/ chi-lee/goong-li	གི་ལོ་མི་ཊར/ སྐྱི་ལི/གུང་ལི
litre	li-tar	ལི་ཊར
metre	mi-tar/chi-ti	མི་ཊར/སྐྱི་ཏི
millimetre	mi-li-mi-tar	མི་ལི་མི་ཊར
pound	pön	པརྦེན

SIZES & COMPARISONS ळे-ळुद-द्र-अळंद्रुब-ख्रु

big	chen-po	ཆེན་པོ
few	ka-shay	ཁ་ཤས
heavy	ji-bo	ལྗིད་པོ
less	nyoong-nga	ཉུང་ང
light	yâng-po	ཡང་པོ
long	ring-po	རིང་པོ
many	mâng-po	མང་པོ
more	mâng-wa	མང་བ
much	shay-tah	ཞེ་དྲགས
little (amount)	nyoong-nyoong	ཉུང་ཉུང
a little bit	tög-tsâm	ཏོག་ཙམ
short	toong-toong	ཐུང་ཐུང
small	choong-choong	ཆུང་ཆུང
some	ka-shay	ཁ་ཤས
tall	ring-bo/tho-po	རིང་པོ/མཐོ་པོ
too much/many	mâng tah-pa	མང་དྲགས་པ

(See page 181 for Useful Amounts.)

ཁ་ལག   # FOOD

In all of the main towns in Tibet, you'll find Tibetan, Muslim and Chinese restaurants. Tibetan cuisine centres around dumplings (mo-mo, ཨོག་ཨོག) and noodle soup (thuk-pa, ཐུག་པ), and Chinese dishes often include either noodles (gyâ-thuk, རྒྱ་ཐུག) or stir-fried vegetable dishes (tsay, ཚལ). In Lhasa, some restaurants serve Western food.

THROUGH THE DAY   ཉིན་རེ་བཞིན

Family members always eat together in Tibet. Usually they have a light breakfast and a big lunch and dinner. In addition, they drink a lot of butter tea (bö-ja; cha sü-ma, བོད་ཇ/ཇ་སུབ་མ), which is more like a tea soup made of butter, milk and salty black tea.

breakfast	shog-cha; shog-kay kha-la	ཞོགས་ཇ/ཞོགས་སྐད་ཁ་ལག
lunch	nyin-goong kha-la	ཉིན་གུང་ཁ་ལག
dinner	gong-da kha-la	དགོང་དག་ཁ་ལག

BREAKFAST   ཞོགས་སྐད་ཁ་ལག

Most people have breakfast between 7 and 8 am. The typical breakfast for Tibetans is either pâg (སྤགས), a dough made of roasted barley flour (tsâm-pa, རྩམ་པ), or kyo-ma (སྐྱོ་མ), a porridge-type mixture made with tsâm-pa. Both are served with butter tea. Although eaten by Tibetans at home, these dishes are rarely offered at guesthouses or hotels.

FOOD

bread	bâk-lay	བག་ལེབ
cereal	dru-say	འབྲུ་རས
... eggs	go-nga ...	སྒོ་ང་ ...
hard-boiled	dhog-tsö	རྡོག་བཙོས
soft-boiled	chay-tsö	ཤེད་བཙོས
fried	ngö-pâ	བཟོས་པ
jam	jam; shing-day mar	ཇེམ/ཤིང་འབྲས་མར
omelette	gong-dre ngö-pâ; om-let	སྒོང་འབྲས་བཟོས་པ/ཨོཾ་ལེཊ
rice porridge	day-thuk	འབྲས་ཐུག
toast	may-tâg bâk-lay	མེ་བཀྲག་བག་ལེབ

SNACKS

chu-ra kâm-po   ཕྱུར་སྐམ་པོ   **dried cheese**
small cubes of hardened dried cheese are popular in Tibet. They must be sucked at first, then chewed, and are often used as a thirst-quencher.

de-sil   འབྲས་སིལ   **sweet rice pudding**
regarded as an auspicious food, it's usually served at festivals and ceremonies, but only in small quantities

khâb-say   ཁབ་སེ   **deep-fried cookies**
always prepared for special occasions, such as weddings, parties and New Year, as well as offered to guests

tsâm-pa   རྩམ་པ   **roasted barley flour**
a staple food in Tibet, but rarely served to guests or found in restaurants. It's generally eaten as a snack or for breakfast – either on its own or with butter tea – but can also be eaten as a main meal, served with vegetables and meat.

FOOD

VEGETARIAN & SPECIAL MEALS

ཤ་མེད་དང་དམིགས་བསལ་ཁ་ལག

I'm vegetarian.
    nga sha mi-sa-ken yin   ང་ཤ་མི་ཟ་མཁན་ཡིན།

I don't eat meat.
    nga sha sa-gi may   ང་ཤ་ཟ་གྱི་མེད།

I don't eat chicken,
fish or ham.
    nga cha-sha-dâng, nya-sha,   ང་བྱ་ཤ་དང་ ཉ་ཤ་ཕག་ཤ་དུས་མ་ཟ་གྱི་མེད།
    phâg-sha dü-ma sa-gi-may

I can't eat dairy products.
    ngah kar-chu-rig trö-ki may   ངར་དཀར་ཆུ་རིགས་འཕྲོད་ཀྱི་མེད།

Do you have any dishes
without meat?
    sha may-pay kha-la gay yö-bay   ཤ་མེད་པའི་ཁ་ལག་གང་ཡོད་པས།

Does this dish have meat?
    kha-la di-la sha yö re-bay   ཁ་ལག་འདི་ལ་ཤ་ཡོད་རེད་པས།

Can I get this without meat?
    di sha may-pa ra-gi re-bay   འདི་ཤ་མེད་པ་རག་གི་རེད་པས།

Does it contain eggs?
    di-la go-nga yö re-bay   འདི་ལ་སྒོ་ང་ཡོད་རེད་པས།

I'm allergic to (peanuts).
    ngah (ba-tâm) pho-gi-yö   ངར་(བུ་རམ)་ཕོག་གི་ཡོད།

EATING OUT

ཟ་ཁང་ནང་ཁ་ལག་ཟ་བ

A table for ... please.
    mi ...-la chog-tse-chig nang-ro   མི་...་ལ་ཅོག་ཙེ་གཅིག་གནང་རོགས།

Can I see the menu please?
    ngah kha-la-gi-tho tön nang-da   ངར་ཁ་ལག་གི་ཐོ་སྟོན་གནང་དང་།

Do you have a menu
in English?
    kha-la-gi-tho in-ji kay-tog   ཁ་ལག་གི་ཐོ་དབྱིན་ཇི་སྐད་ཐོག་ཡོད་པས།
    yö-bay

FOOD

What's this/that?

    diy/pha-gi kâ-ray ray   འདི་/ཕ་གི་ག་རེ་རེད།

What do you recommend?

    kay-râng chay-na kâ-ray   ཁྱེད་རང་བྱེད་ན་ག་རེ་ལགས་གི་རེད།
    yâ-gi-ray

I'll have what they're having.

    khong-tsö chö-ya-te na-shin   ཁོང་ཚོས་མཆོད་ཡག་དེ་ན་བཞིན་ང་ལ་དགོས།
    nga-la gö

What's in that dish?

    kha-la pha-gi-nâng kâ-ray   ཁ་ལག་ཕ་གིའི་ནང་ག་རེ་ཡོད་རེད།
    yö-ray

Please bring me ...

    nga-la ...-chig tay-ro-nâng   ང་ལ་ ...ཅིག་སྟེར་རོགས་གནང་།

I'd like the set lunch, please.

    nga-la nyin-goong   ང་ལ་ཉིན་གུང་གསོལ་སྟོན་
    sö-tön nâng-ro   གནང་རོགས།

What does it include?

    tay nyâm-tu kha-la   དེའི་མཉམ་དུ་ཁ་ལག
    kâ-ray kâ-ray sa-ya yö-ray   ག་རེ་ག་རེ་ཟ་ཡག་ཡོད་རེད།

Not too spicy, please.

    men-na shay-ta   སྨན་སྣ་ཞེ་དྲགས་
    ma-gyâ-ro-nâng   མ་རྒྱག་རོགས་གནང་།

Do I get it myself or do they bring it to us?

    nga-râng râng-gi len-gah   ང་རང་རང་གིས་ལེན་གྱི་འགྲོ་དགོས་རེད།
    do-gö-ray, khong-tsö kye   ཁོང་ཚོས་འཁྱེར་ཡོང་གི་རེད།
    yong-gi-ray

TO TIP OR NOT TO TIP?

Traditionally, people neither tip nor expect to be tipped in Tibet, but it's changing ...

Please bring a/an/the ...   ...-chig nâng-da   ...ཅིག་གནང་དང་།

ashtray	tha-ma dâb-sa-nö	ཐ་མ་འདབ་ས་སྣོད་
bill	kha-la-gi zihn	ཁ་ལག་གི་འཛིན་
fork	kâng-ta	ཀང་ཏ་
glass of water	chu ga-la-si	ཆུ་གེ་ལ་སེ་
with ice	kyâk-pa yö-pa	འཁྱགས་པ་ཡོད་པ་
without ice	kyâk-pa may-pa	འཁྱགས་པ་མེད་པ་
knife	di	གྲི་
plate	tha-pa	ཐབ་

Another ... please.
   da-toong ... nang-da   དདུང་ ... གནང་དང་།

Nothing more?
   ta dig-song   ད་འགྲིགས་སོང་།

Anything else?
   shen-da-gay gö-bay   གཞན་དག་གི་དགོས་པས།

No ice in my drink, please.
   ngay toong-ya nyâm-tu   ངའི་བཏུང་ཡག་དེ་མཉམ་དུ་བཞུགས་པས
   kyâk-pa ma-loog-ro nâng   འཁྱགས་རོགས་གནང་།

Is service included in the bill?
   ngü-tsi-nang lay-la tsi   དངུལ་རྩིས་ནང་ལས་ཀ་བཙི་ཡོད་
   yö re-bay   རེད་པས།

I love this dish.
   nga kha-la di-la ka-bo yö   ང་ཁ་ལག་འདི་ལ་དགའ་པོ་ཡོད།

We love the local cuisine.
   ngân-tso sa-nay-ki   ང་ཚོ་ས་གནས་ཀྱི་ཁ་ལག་ལ་དགའ་པོ་ཡོད།
   kha-la-la ka-bo yö

The meal was delicious!
   kha-la shim-bu shay-ta choong   ཁ་ལག་ཞིམ་པོ་ཞེ་དྲགས་བྱུང་།

FOOD

TYPICAL DISHES   མཚན་མོང་ལ་ཡིན་པའི་ཁ་ལག

bâk-thuk   བག་ཐུག
  a variety of Tibetan soup
  (like ten-thuk but with hand made
  shell-shaped noodles)

day-thuk   འབྲས་ཐུག
  rice soup

gya-thuk   རྒྱ་ཐུག
  Tibetan noodle soup

kö-den/châng-kö   སྐོལ་ལྡན་/ཆང་འཁོལ
  hot châng soup with tsâm-pa

rhü cho-tse   རུས་ཅོ་ཙེ
  meat dumplings in soup

rü-tâng   རུ་ཐང
  clear bone soup

sog-thuk   སོག་ཐུག
  Mongolian-style Tibetan soup

ten-thuk   ཐེན་ཐུག
  traditional Tibetan soup,
  with meat, vegetables and
  hand made noodles

chi-may mo-mo   ཆི་སྨྱུན་མོག་མོག
  steamed yeast meat dumplings

mo-mo   མོག་མོག
  steamed meat dumplings

mo-mo ngö-pa   མོག་མོག་འཛོས་པ
  fried meat dumplings

tsay mo-mo   ཚལ་མོག་མོག
  vegetable dumplings

cha-sha (ngö-pa/tâg-pa)   བྱ་ཤ་(འཛོས་པ་/བཀྲགས་པ)
  chicken (fried/roasted)

dâng-tsay   གྱང་ཚལ
  salad

day ngö-pa   འབྲས་འཛོས་པ
  fried rice

FOOD

do-fu dâng tsay ཌོཕུ་དང་ཚལ
  sauteed bean curd with
  peppers/vegetables
phing-sha ཕིང་ཤ
  beef/chicken/pork with bean
  thread and red pepper (capsicum)
sham-day ཤ་འབྲས
  plain/fried rice with meat and
  bean thread/mokroe/vegetables
(cha-sha/phâg-sha/loog-sha/ (བྱ་ཤ/ཕག་ཤ/ལུག་ཤ/
yâk-sha/lâng-sha) tsay གཡག་ཤ/གླང་ཤ)དང་ཚལ
  (chicken/pork/lamb/yak meat/
  beef) and stir-fried vegetables
tsib-sha རྩིབ་ཤ
  pork spare ribs

ahm-dho bâk-lay ཨ་མཆོ་བག་ལེབ
  roasted pancake (bread)
bâk-cha ma-ku བག་ཚ་མར་ཁུ
  small tubes of wheat flour
  dough fried in ghee with molasses
lo-ko mo-mo ལོ་སྐོར་མོག་མོག
  boiled bread
sha bâk-lay ཤ་བག་ལེབ
  fried pancake (bread)
  stuffed with meat
ting mo-mo སྒྱིའི་མོག་མོག
  steamed bread
yu-shâng ཡུ་ཤང
  deep fried bread (puree)

sho dâng shing-toh ཞོ་དང་ཤིང་ཏོག
  fruit with yogurt
shing-toh dâng o-ti ཤིང་ཏོག་དང་འོ་སྦྲི
  fruit with cream

SELF-CATERING ཁ་ལག་རང་རང་གིས་བཟོན
Making Your Own Meals ཁ་ལག་རང་རང་གིས་བཟོ་བ

Where can I find the ...?	... nyo-sa ka-bah yö-ray	... ཉོ་ས་གང་ན་ཡོད་རེད།
I'd like some ...	nga ... gö	ང་ ... དགོས།
bread	bâk-lay	བག་ལེབ
butter	mâh	མར
cereal	dru-say	འབྲུ་རིགས
cheese	chu-ra	ཆུར
chocolate	chok-let	ཅོག་ལེད
eggs	go-nga	སྒོང་ང
flour		
plain	may-da	མེ་ད
roasted barley	tsâm-pa	ཙམ་པ
wholemeal	dro-shib	གྲོ་ཞིབ
ghee	mâh-ku	མར་ཁུ
ham	phâg-sha dü-ma	ཕག་ཤ་དུད་མ
honey	dâng-tsi	སྦྲང་རྩི
marmalade	tsa-lu-may jam	ཚ་ལུ་མའི་ཇེམ
milk	oh-ma	འོ་མ
molasses	bu-râm	བུ་རམ
noodles	gyâ-thuk	རྒྱ་ཐུག
olive oil	o-lib-noom	ཨོ་ལིབ་སྣུམ
pepper	ey-ma	ཝ་ཕེར་མ
powdered milk	oh-tsâm	འོ་ཚམ
salt	tsha	ཚ
sugar	chay-ma ka-ra; chi-ni	ཞེ་མ་ཀ་ར/ཅི་ནི
vermicelli (bean thread noodles)	phing	ཕིང
yeast	chay-men	ཕེ་སྨན
yogurt	sho	ཞོ

FOOD

AT THE MARKET

བཙོང་ཁང་ནས་

How much is (a kilo of cheese)?
    (chu-ra ki-lo-ray)-la gong
    kâ-tsay ray
    (ཕྱུར་ཀི་ལོ་རེ་)ལ་གོང་ག་ཚོད་རེད།

Do you have anything cheaper?
    gong kay-wa gay yö-bay
    གོང་ཁེ་བ་གའི་ཡོད་པས།

What's the local speciality?
    sa-nay-ki sa-chay mig-say
    ས་གནས་ཀྱི་བཟའ་ཆས་དམིགས་བསལ་
    kâ-ray kâ-ray tsong-ya yö-ray
    ག་རེ་ག་རེ་བཙོང་ཡ་ཡོད་རེད།

Give me (half) a kilo please.
    ngah ki-lo (chay-ka) nâng-da
    ངར་ཀི་ལོ་(ཕྱེད་ཀ)་གནང་དང་།

I'd like (six slices of ham).
    ngah (phâg-sha dü-ma
    lheb-lheb doog) nâng-da
    ངར་(ཕག་ཤ་འདུད་མ་ལྟེབ་ལྟེབ་དྲུག)་
    གནང་དང་།

Can I taste it?
    toh-wa mik ta-na di-gi re-bay
    ཏྟོ་བ་མིག་བལྟ་ན་འགྲིག་གི་རེད་པས།

Do you have any ... to sell?
    kay-râng-lâ ... tsong-ya yö-bay
    ཁྱེད་རང་ལ་ ... བཙོང་ཡ་ཡོད་པས།

How much does the ... cost?
    ...-la gong kâ-tsay ray
    ...ལ་གོང་ག་ཚོད་རེད།

I'll buy ... kilos.
    ngay ki-lo ... nyo-gi-yin
    ངས་ཀི་ལོ་ ... ཉོ་གི་ཡིན།

TAKING A DIP!

Impress the locals with your knowledge of this **châng** (see page 147) drinking ritual:

Raise your cup to eyelevel with your left hand. Dip in your right ring finger, then take it out and flick it. Repeat three times to show respect to heaven, earth and the gods.

FOOD

MEAT & POULTRY

beef	lâng-sha	གླང་ཤ
chicken	cha-sha	བྱ་ཤ
fish	nya-sha	ཉ་ཤ
goat meat	ra-sha	ར་ཤ
ham	phâg-sha dü-ma	ཕག་ཤ་དུད་མ
lamb	loog-sha	ལུག་ཤ
liver	chin-pa	མཆིན་པ
meat	sha	ཤ
boiled	sha tsö-bâ	ཤ་བཙོས་པ
dried	sha kâm-po	ཤ་སྐམ་པོ
roast	shâp-ta	ཤ་བརྒྱག
pork	phâg-sha	ཕག་ཤ
sausage	gyu-ma	རྒྱུ་མ
yak meat	yâk-sha	གཡག་ཤ

FRUIT & NUTS

ཤིང་ཏོག

apple	ku-shu	ཀུ་ཤུ
apricot	ngâ-ri khâm-bu	མངའ་རིས་ཁམ་བུ
banana	kye-la	གི་ལ
berry	say-hu	སེ་བུ
date	kha-su	ཁ་སུར
fruit	shing-tog	ཤིང་ཏོག
grape	chu gün-doom	རྒུན་འབྲུམ
lemon	lim-bu	ལིམ་བུ
mango	shing-tog-âhm	ཤིང་ཏོག་ཨམ
orange/tangerine	tsâ-lu-mâ	ཚ་ལུ་མ
peach	lo-soom khâm-bu	ལོ་གསུམ་ཁམ་བུ
peanut	ba-tâm	སྤ་དམ
pear	li	ལི
pomegranate	sin-dru	སེན་འབྲུ
rhubarb	chu-chu/chu-lo	ཆུ་རྩི/ཆུ་ལོ
walnut	tar-ka	སྟར་ཀ

FOOD

VEGETABLES ཚོ་ཚལ

bamboo shoots	nyug-tsa	སྨྱུག་ཚ
beans	tray-ma	སྲན་མ
cabbage (Chinese-style)	lo-koh pay-tsay	ལོ་ཀོང་པད་ཚལ
capsicum (pepper)	ey-ma	གཡེར་མ
carrot	gong lâ-bu	སྒོང་ལ་ཕུག
cauliflower	pool go-bi	ཕུལ་གོ་འབེ
celery	jin-tsay	ཇིན་ཚལ
cucumber	kâng-ra	གང་ར
eggplant (aubergine)	chay-tsay	ཆེ་ཚལ
onion	tsong	ཙོང
peas	tray-ma	སྲན་མ
potato	sho-gok	ཞོག་ཁོག
radish	lâ-buk	ལ་ཕུག
pickled radish	sön lâ-buk	སོན་ལ་ཕུག
spinach	po-tsay	པོ་ཚལ
spring onion	tsong ngön-po	ཙོང་སྔོན་པོ
tomato	to-ma-to	ཏོ་མ་ཏོ
turnip	nyoong-mâ	ཉུང་མ

GRAINS & PULSES འབྲུ་རིགས

barley	nay/dru	ནས་/འབྲུ
popped barley	nay-yö	ནས་ཡོས
buckwheat (sweet)	gya-da	རྒྱ་བྲ
corn	ah-shom; ma-mö lo-tog	ཨ་ཤོམ་/ མ་མོས་ལོ་ཏོག
millet	mön-châg	མོན་ཆག
plain flour	may-da	མེ་དྲ
rice	day	འབྲས
popped rice	day-yö	འབྲས་ཡོས
wholemeal flour	dro-shib/ah-ta	གྲོ་ཞིབ་/ཨ་ཀྲ

FOOD

SPICES & CONDIMENTS ﾠ སྐོན་སྣ་རེ་གས་

chilli (ground)	si-pan (shib-shib)	སི་པན་ (ཤིབ་ཤིབ་)
chilli (with water)	si-pan mah-du	སི་པན་དཀར་འདུར་
coriander	so-nam pay-zom	བསོད་ནམས་པད་འཛོམ་
garlic	gok-pa	སྒོག་པ་
ginger	ga-moog	ག་སྨུག་
pepper	ey-ma	གཡེར་མ་
salt	tsha	ཚྭ་
soy sauce	jâng-yü	བྱང་ཡུལ་
turmeric	ga-say	གུ་སེ་
vinegar	tsuh	ཚུར་

DRINKS ﾠ བཏུང་བ་
Nonalcoholic ﾠ ཆང་རག་མིན་པའི་བཏུང་བ་

coffee	cha ka-bi; tsig-cha	ཇ་ཀོ་ཕི་ / ཚིག་ཇ་
black	cha ka-bi oh-ma may-pa	ཇ་ཀོ་ཕི་འོ་མ་མེད་པ་
juice	shin-tog khu-wa	ཞིང་ཏོག་ཁུ་བ་
orange	tsâ-lu-may khu-wa	ཚ་ལུ་མའི་ཁུ་བ་
milk	oh-ma	འོ་མ་
soda	chu nga-mo	ཆུ་མངར་མོ་
orange	tsâ-lu-may chu nga-mo	ཚ་ལུ་མའི་ཆུ་མངར་མོ་
tea	cha	ཇ་
black	cha-tâng	ཇ་ཐང་
butter	bö-ja; cha sü-ma	བོད་ཇ་ / ཇ་སྲུབ་མ་
Chinese-style	chin-drâng	ཆིན་ཐང་
with sugar	cha nga-mo	ཇ་མངར་མོ་
water	chu	ཆུ་
boiled	chu khö-ma	ཆུ་འཁོལ་མ་
mineral	bu-tog-chu	བྲག་ཏོག་ཆུ་

FOOD

Alcoholic ཆང་རིགས།

Home-brewed **chârng** (ཆང་), made from fermented barley, wheat, rice and millet, is very popular in Tibet.

beer (home-brew)	chârng	ཆང་
beer (bottled)	bee-yar	སྦྱིར་ཡར་/ཤེལ་ཆུ
Chinese brandy	gya-mee ah-râk	རྒྱ་མིའི་ཨ་རག
liquor	ah-râk	ཨ་རག
wine	gün-doom chârng-râk	རྒུན་འབྲུམ་ཆང་རག

IN THE BAR ཆང་ཁང་ནང་

Excuse me!
    ku-chi (inf); gong-ge   སྐུ་སྐྱིད།/དགོངས་འགལ་མེད་པ་ཤི
    may-pa-chi (pol)
I'm next.
    ta ngay ray-mö ray   ད་ངའི་རེ་མོས་རེད
I'll buy you a drink.
    toong-ya-chig ngay nyo-go   འཐུང་ཡག་ཅིག་ངས་ཉོ་གི
What would you like?
    kay-râng kâ-ray gö   ཁྱེད་རང་ག་རེ་དགོས
I'll have ...
    nga ... gö   ང་ ... དགོས

THE LESSER OF TWO EVILS

chârng toong-na go-na,	ཆང་བཏུང་ན་མགོ་ན།
ma-toong-na nying-na	མ་བཏུང་ན་སྙིང་ན།

If you drink **chârng**, you'll get a headache;
if you don't, you'll get heartache.

FOOD

No ice please.
  kyâk-pa ma-loog-ro nâng

བཁྱག་པ་མ་ལུག་རོགས་གནང་།

You can get the next one.
  je-ma-te ngâg cho-gi ray

རྗེས་མ་དེ་ཨང་ཚོག་གི་རེད།

Same again, please.
  yâng-kya te na-shin-chig
  nâng-da

ཡང་བསྐྱར་དེ་ན་བཞིན་གཅིག་གནང་དང་།

How much is that?
  te-la gong kâ-tsay ray

དེ་ལ་གོང་ག་ཚད་རེད།

�འཕྲོད་བསྟེན།   # HEALTH

Should you require medical attention in any of Tibet's main towns, you'll generally have a choice of Tibetan or Western medicine. Doctors are well trained, but it's unlikely they'll speak English. At Tibetan hospitals (men-tsi-khâng, སྨན་རྩིས་ཁང་, or bö-bay men-khâng, བོད་པའི་སྨན་ཁང་), where Tibetan medicine is practised, staff generally speak Tibetan. At People's or Chinese hospitals, (mi-mâng men-khâng, མི་དམངས་སྨན་ཁང་, or gyâ-mee men-khâng, རྒྱ་མིའི་སྨན་ཁང་), where Western medicine is practised, staff speak either Chinese or Tibetan (more commonly Chinese).

Outside of the main towns, there's little choice of medical care and it tends to be of a lower standard.

AT THE DOCTOR   ཨེམ་ཆི་འི་སར།

I'm sick.
  nga na-gi-du   ང་ན་གི་འདུག

My friend is sick.
  ngay rog-pa na-gi-du   ངའི་རོགས་པ་ན་གི་འདུག

Is there a doctor who speaks English?
  in-ji-kay shin-khen ahm-chi   དབྱིན་ཇི་སྐད་ཤེས་མཁན་ཨེམ་ཆི་ཡོད་རེད་པས།
  yö re-bay

Could the doctor come here?
  ahm-chi-la day pheb thoob-ki   ཨེམ་ཆི་ལགས་འདིར་ཕེབས་ཐུབ་ཀྱི་རེད་པས།
  re-bay

I need a doctor.
  nga ahm-chi-chig ten gö yö   ང་ཨེམ་ཆི་ཅིག་བསྟེན་དགོས་ཡོད།

Where's the   ... tâg nye-shö   ... ཐག་ཉེ་ཤོས་
nearest ...?   ka-bah yö-ray   ག་བར་ཡོད་རེད།
  chemist   men tsong-khâng   སྨན་ཚོང་ཁང་
  dentist   so men-khâng   སོ་སྨན་ཁང་
  doctor   ahm-chi   ཨེམ་ཆི་
  hospital   men-khâng   སྨན་ཁང་

HEALTH

THE DOCTOR MAY SAY ...

kay-râng kâ-ray na-gi-du ཁྱེད་རང་ག་རེ་ན་གྱི་འདུག
What's the matter?

na-tsa tâng-gi du-gay ན་ཚ་གཏོང་གི་འདུག་གས
Do you feel any pain?

na-tsa ka-bah tâng-gi-du ན་ཚ་ག་པར་གཏོང་གི་འདུག
Where does it hurt?

tsha-wa ba-gi du-gay ཚ་བ་འབར་གྱི་འདུག་གས
Do you have a temperature?

**kay-râng na-nay gyün
ring-lö chin-song** ཁྱེད་རང་ན་ནས་རྒྱུན་
རིང་ལོས་ཕྱིན་སོང་།
How long have you been ill?

din-ta ngön-ma na nyong-ngay འདི་འད་སྔོན་མ་ན་མྱོང་ངས
Have you had this before?

kay-râng men sa-gi yö-bay ཁྱེད་རང་སྨན་ཟ་གྱི་ཡོད་པས།
Are you on medication?

tha-ma ten-gi yö-bay ཐ་མག་འཐེན་གྱི་ཡོད་པས།
Do you smoke?

châng-râg toong-gi yö-bay ཆང་རག་འཐུང་གི་ཡོད་པས།
Do you drink?

si-men sa-gi yö-bay གཟི་སྨན་ཟ་གི་ཡོད་པས།
Do you take drugs?

**kay-râng-gi lü-la phog-khen-ri
gay yö-bay** ཁྱེད་རང་གི་ལུས་ལ་ཕོགས་མཁན་
རི་གས་གང་ཡོད་པས།
Are you allergic to anything?

ngay kay-râng-gi	དས་ཁྱེད་རང་གི་	I'll take your/a ...
... ta-gi-yin	... ལྟ་གི་ཡིན།	
tâg	ཁྲག	blood sample
tâg-shay chay-chung	ཁྲག་ཤེད་ཆེ་ཆུང་	blood pressure
tsa	རྩ	pulse
châp-chen	ཆབ་ཆེན	stool sample
tsha-wa	ཚ་བ	temperature
chin-pâ/châp-sâng	གཅིན་པ/ཆབ་སང་	urine sample

HEALTH

THE DOCTOR MAY SAY ...

kha dhong-dâ   ཁ་གདངས་དང༌།
  Open your mouth.
oog shoog-chay ya ten-dâ   དབུགས་ཤུགས་ཆེ་ཡར་ཐེན་དང༌།
  Take a deep breath.
lo gyön-da   གློ་བརྒྱབ་དང༌།
  Please cough.
ngay kâp gyâ-gi-yin   ངས་ཁབ་རྒྱག་གི་ཡིན།
  I'll give you an injection.
ngay men tay-gi-yin   ངས་སྨན་སྟེར་གི་ཡིན།
  I'll give you medicine.
kay-râng-gi na-tsa   ཁྱེད་རང་གི་ན་ཚ་ཚུག་ཆགས
dhuk-cha min-du   མིན་འདུག
  Your illness is not serious.

AILMENTS   ན་ཚུལ

I've been ill for ... days.
  nga na-nay nyi-ma ... chin-song   ང་ནས་ཉིན་མ ... ཕྱིན་སོང་།
I've been vomiting.
  nga kyoog-pa kyu-gi-du   ང་སྐྱུགས་པ་སྐྱུག་གི་འདུག
I can't sleep.
  nga nyi ku-gi min-du   ང་གཉིད་ཁུག་གི་མིན་འདུག

I feel ...   nga ...-gi   ང ...གི།
  dizzy   gu-yu kho   མགོ་འཁྱུར་འཁོར
  nauseous   kyong-may lâng   སྐྱུག་མེར་ལངས
  shivery   dâr   འདར

I feel feverish.   ngah tsha-wa gye-sha   ངར་ཚ་བ་རྒྱས་ཤག
I feel weak.   ngay tob-shay   ངའི་སྟོབས་ཤེད་ཉམས་ཤག
               nyâm-sha

HEALTH

I'm having trouble breathing.
nga oog tong-ya kâg-po
chay-ki-du

ད་དབུགས་གཏོང་ལ་ཁལ་པོ་བྱེད་ཀྱི་འདུག

It hurts here.
day na-tsa gya-gi

འདིར་ན་ཚ་རྒྱག་གི་ས

I have (a/an) ...	ngah ... yö	ངར་ ... ཡོད།
I've had (a/an) ...	nga ... na-nyong	ང་ ... ན་མྱོང།
allergy	phog-nay	ཕོགས་ནད།
cancer	can-sah; ten-nay na-tsa	གེན་སར་/སྐྲན་ནད་ན་ཚ
chickenpox	sib-bi na-tsa	ཤིབ་པི་ན་ཚ
diabetes	chay-ma ka-ray na-tsa	བྱེ་མ་ཀ་རའི་ན་ཚ
glandular fever	men-bü tsay-nay	མྗེན་བུའི་ཚད་ནད།
hay fever	mig-na-nay chu zâg-pay phog-nay	མིག་སྣ་ནས་ཆུ་འཛག་པའི་ཕོགས་ནད།
heart condition	nying-khâm ma-de-wa	སྙིང་ཁམས་མ་བདེ་བ
hepatitis	chim-ba na-tsa	མཆིན་པ་ན་ཚ
indigestion	say-ju ma-thoob-pay nay	ཟས་འཇུ་མ་ཐུབ་པའི་ནད།
infection	gö-nay/rim-nay	འགོས་ནད་/རིམས་ནད།
malaria	ma-le-ri-ya rim-nay	མ་ལེ་རི་ཡ་རིམས་ནད།
migraine	go-se gya-gyu na-tsa-shig	མགོ་གཅིག་རྒྱག །རྒྱུ་ཚ་ཚ་ཤིག
rheumatism	doom-nay	གྲུམ་ནད།
typhoid	ta-ye-pho gö-nay	གཏའ་ཡེ་ཕོ་འགོས་ནད།
venereal disease	tig-joh-lay choong-way gö-nay	འབྲིག་ལ་སྐྱོན་ལས་འབྱུང་ འབའི་འགོས་ནད།

HEALTH

I have (a/an) ...	ngah ...-sha	ང་ ...ཤ
I've had ...	ngah ... nyong	ང་ ... མྱོང་
anaemia	trâg-shay nyâm	ཁྲག་ཤེད་ཉམས
blister	chu-gâng dön	ཆུ་གང་དོན
boil	nyem-bu dön	གཉེན་འབུར་དོན
conjunctivitis	mig-nâng nyen-ga bâh	མིག་ནང་གཉན་ག་བ་འབར
cramp (in calf)	nya gyur	ཉ་འགྱུར
dehydration	lü-nâng shâ-lön kâm	ལུས་ནང་ཤ་ལོན་སྐམས
food poisoning	say-doog phog	ཟས་དུག་ཕོག
frostbite	khyâg-bö teb	འཁྱག་སྦོར་ཐེབ
gastroenteritis	pho-wa-dâng	ཕོ་བ་དང་རྒྱུ་མ་ཕྲང་
	gyu-ma trâng	
inflammation	lü-la nyen-ga bâh	ལུས་ལ་གཉན་ག་འབར
lice	shig	ཤིག
lump	boor-tog dön	འབུར་ཏོག་དོན
rash	tho-mâh sib-sib	ཐོར་དམར་སིབ་སིབ་དོན
sore throat	mik-pay-nâng ma châg	མིད་པ་ནང་མ་ཆགས
sprain	tsig chü	ཚིགས་འཆུས
sunburn	nyib-ta teb	ཉི་བརྒྱབ་འཐེབས
swollen foot	kâng-ba trâng	རྐང་པ་སྐྲངས
urinary infection	chin-lâm-la	གཅིན་ལམ་ལ་འགོས་
	gö-nay-chi phog	ནད་ཅིག་ཕོག

HEALTH

I have (a/an) ...	nga ...-gi	ང་ ...གིས།
I've had ...	ngah ... nyong	ང་ ... མྱོང།
altitude sickness	lâ-du na	ལ་དུག་ན།
bronchitis	lo-yü tsa-nay na	གློ་ཡུའི་ཚ་ནད་ན།
cold	châm-ba na	ཆམ་པ་ན།
cystic fibrosis	sis-tik fa-ye bor-sis-shay	སིས་ཊིག་ཕ་ཡེ་བོར་སིས།
	mi-gyü-nay yong-way	མིས་མི་རྒྱུད་ནས་ཡོང་བའི།
	men-bü nay-chig na	ནེན་བུའི་ནད་ཅིག
dysentery	di-sen-ti-ri na-tsa	ཌི་སེན་ཊི་རི་ནད་ཚ་ལོག
	drö-kog mâ-shay gya	དམར་བཤལ་རྒྱ།
fever	tsha-wa na	ཚ་བ་ན།
flu	châm-rim	ཆམ་རིམས་དགར་པོ་བཞི་ན།
	dâg-po-shi na	
headache	go na	མགོ་ན།
itch	sâb-ra lâng	ཟ་འབྲ་ལང་།
pain	na-soog gya	ན་ཟུག་རྒྱག
stomachache	drö-kog na	གྲོད་ཁོག་ན།
sunstroke	tsa-doog na	ཚ་དུག་ན།
toothache	so na	སོ་ན།
travel sickness	dim-drü-la tan-nay	འགྲིམ་འགྲུལ་ལ་བརྟེན།
	go-yom-dâng	མགོ་ཡོམ་དང་།
	kyook-may lâng	དང་སྐྱུག་མེར་ལང་།

I'm constipated.
    nga tsog-pa bâb-kee min-du   ང་བཙོག་པ་འབབ་ཀྱི་མིན་འདུག
I have diarrhoea.
    nga drö-kog shay-gi   ང་གྲོད་ཁོག་བཤལ་གིས།
I have a cut.
    ngah ma sö-song   ངར་རྨ་བཟོས་སོང་།
My foot's swollen.
    ngay kâng-pa bö-sha   ངའི་རྐང་པ་སྦོས་ཤག
I have a temperature.
    ngah tsha-wa gye-sha   ངར་ཚ་བ་རྒྱས་ཤག

I have worms.
  ngay khog-pay nâng bu du   འདི་ཁོག་པའི་ནང་འབུ་འདུག
I feel better/worse.
  nga dâg-tu/dhuk-tu chin-sha   ང་དགའ་ཏུ/སྡུག་ཏུ་ཕྱིན་ཤག
This is my usual medicine.
  di ngay dü-gyün sa-ya men ray   འདི་ངའི་དུས་རྒྱུན་ཟ་ཡ་སྨན་རེད
I don't want a blood transfusion.
  ngah tâg tay mi-gö   ངར་ཁྲག་སྟེར་མི་དགོས
Can I have a receipt for my insurance?
  in-shu-ren gan-gyay-chay   ཨིན་ཤུ་རེན་གན་རྒྱའི་ཆེད་བྱང་
  choong-zin-chi nâng thoob-ki   འཆོང་ཛིན་ཅིག་གནང་ཐུབ་ཀྱི་རེད་པས
  re-bay

HEALTH

WOMEN'S HEALTH   བུད་མེད་ཀྱི་འཕྲོད་བསྟེན

I'd like to see a female doctor.
  nga kye-man ahm-chi-chig   ང་སྐྱེ་དམན་ཨེམ་ཆི་ཞིག་བསྟེན
  ten-dö yö   འདོད་ཡོད
I want to see a gynaecologist.
  nga mo-nay ahm-chi kay-pa-chi   ང་མོ་ནད་ཨེམ་ཆི་མཁས་པ་ཞིག་བསྟེན
  ten-dö yö   འདོད་ཡོད
I'm pregnant.
  nga-la pu-gu kye-ya-yö   ང་ལ་ཕྲུ་གུ་སྐྱེ་ཡ་ཡོད
I think I'm pregnant.
  ngah pu-gu châg yö-sa-ray   ངར་ཕྲུ་གུ་ཆགས་ཡོད་ས་རེད
I'm on the Pill.
  nga kye-gok-men sa-gi-yö   ང་སྐྱེ་འགོག་སྨན་ཟ་གྱི་ཡོད

THE DOCTOR MAY SAY ...

kay-râng-la pu-gu   ཁྱེད་རང་ལ་ཕྲུ་གུ
kye-ya yö-bay   སྐྱེ་ཡག་ཡོད་པས
  Are you pregnant?
kay-râng dha-tsen   ཁྱེད་རང་ཟླ་མཚན
bâb-ki du-gay   འབབ་ཀྱི་འདུག་གས
  Are you menstruating?

HEALTH

I haven't had my period for ... months.
  nga-la dha-tsen ma-bâb-nay
  da-wa ... chin-song
I'd like to get the morning-after pill.
  nga chu-tsö so-doog tsâm-ring
  kye-gok thoob-ya men nyon-dö yö
I'd like to use contraception.
  nga kye-gok bay-chö
  tong-ya dö-pa yö
I'd like to have a pregnancy test.
  nga pu-gu châg yö-may
  tâg-chay chay-dö yö

abortion	pu-gu ngel-nay dön-pa	
cystitis	chin-nö gâng-bu-nâng	
	nyen-ga châg-pa	
diaphragm	ngel-ka-la jog-ya	
	kye-gok lâg-ja-shig	
mammogram	log-pah-shig	
maternity hospital	pu-gu kay-say men-khâng	
menstruation	dha-tsen/dha-trâg	
miscarriage	pu-gu nge-nay shor-wa	
pap smear	chay-shay-tog tâg-chay chay-ya zay	
period pain	dha-tsen bâb-kâb na-soog	
the Pill	kye-gok-men	
pregnancy test kit	pu-gu châg-man ta-ya yo-chay	
thrush	thor-kya sib-sib dön-pay gö-nay-chig	
ultrasound	öl-dra-sa-wong-shay tso-o kog-pay-nâng pu-gu châg yö-may ta-ya log-pah trü-cha-shig	

SPECIAL HEALTH NEEDS

འཕྲོད་བསྟེན་ཆེད་དགོས་གལ་
གནད་འགག་སྐབས་པ

HEALTH

I'm ...	nga ... chog-chog yin	ང་ ... ཆོག་ཆོག་ཡིན།
anaemic	trâg-shay nyâm	ཁྲག་ཤེད་ཉུངས།
asthmatic	oog-tsâng-nay na	དབུགས་འཚང་ནད་ན།
diabetic	chay-ma ka-ray na-tsa na	ཆེ་མ་ཀ་རའི་ན་ཚན།
epileptic	sa-dib na	གཟའ་གྲིབ་ན།

I'm allergic to ...	... nga-la phog-gi yö	... ང་ལ་ཕོག་གིས་ཡོད།
antibiotics	nay-bu gok-men an-ti ba-ye o-tik	ནད་འབུ་འགོག་སྨན། ཨེན་ཏི་བྱའི་ཨོ་ཊིག
aspirin	nyen-jom-men es-pi-rin	མཉེན་འཇོམས། སྨན་ཨེ་སི་པི་རིན།
bees	dâng-bu	སྦྲང་བུ།
dairy products	kar-chu	དཀར་ཆུ།
penicillin	nyen-jom-men pe-ni-si-lin	མཉེན་འཇོམས། སྨན་པེ་ནི་སི་ལིན།
pollen	may-tog-gi sen-drü-dü	མེ་ཏོག་གི་ཟེའི་འབུའི་རྡུལ།

I have a skin allergy.
   ngay sha pâg-pa-la nyen-ga
   lâng chog-chog yin
ངའི་ཤ་ལྤགས་པ་ལ་མཉེན།
ག་ལང་ཆོག་ཆོག་ཡིན།

I have high/low blood pressure.
   ngay tâg-shay tho-po/ma-po ray
ངའི་ཁྲག་ཤེད་མཐོ་པོ་/དམའ་པོ་རེད།

I have a heart condition.
   ngay nying-kâm de-po-may
ངའི་སྙིང་ཁམས་བདེ་པོ་མེད།

I've been vaccinated.
   ngah nay-rim ngön-gok-gi
   men-khâb gyâb-tsa yin
ང་ནད་རིམས་སྔོན་འགོག་གི་སྨན།
ཁབ་བརྒྱབ་ཚར་ཡིན།

Is that a new syringe you're using?
   kay-râng-gi bay-chö chay-ya
   men-khâb-te sa-pa re-bay
ཁྱེད་རང་གི་བེད་སྤྱོད་བྱེད་ཡག
སྨན་ཁབ་དེ་གསར་པ་རེད་པས།

HEALTH

I have my own syringe.
    nga-râng râng-gi men-khâb yö   ང་རང་རང་གི་སྨན་ཁབ་ཡོད།

I'm on medication for ...
    nga men sa-nay nyin-ma   ང་སྨན་ཟ་ནས་ཉིན་མ ... ཕྱིན་སོང་།
    ... chin-song

I'm on a special diet.
    nga trö-ten-chay kha-la sa-tsö   ང་འཕྲོད་བསྟེན་ཆེད་ཁ་ལག་ལ
    kay-pa chay-ki yö   ཟ་ཚོད་མཁས་ལས་བྱེད་ཀྱི་ཡོད།

I need a new pair of glasses.
    ngah mik-shay   ང་ར་མིག་ཤེལ
    sa-pa-shig go-ki du   གསར་པ་ཞིག་དགོས་ཀྱི་འདུག

PARTS OF THE BODY   ལུས་ཀྱི་ཆ་ཤས

My ... hurts.
    ngay ... na-soog gya-gi   ངའི ... ན་ཟུག་རྒྱག་གིས།

I have a pain in my ...
    ngay ...-la na-soog gya-gi   ངའི ...ལ་ན་ཟུག་རྒྱག་གིས།

I can't move my ...
    ngay ... gü-kyok gya   ངའི ... འགུལ་སྐྱོད་རྒྱག
    thoob-ki min-du   ཐུབ་ཀྱི་མིན་འདུག

ankle	kâng-tsig	རྐང་ཚིགས
appendix	gyu-lhâg	རྒྱུ་ལྷག
arm	lâg-pa	ལག་པ
back	gyâb	རྒྱབ
bladder	chin-nö gâng-bu	གཅིན་སྣོད་སྒང་བུ
blood	tâg	ཁྲག
body	soog-po	གཟུགས་པོ

HEALTH

bone	rü-gok	རུས་གོག
chest	bang-go	བང་ཁོག
chin	ma-lay/og-ma	མ་ལེ/འོག་མ
ear	ahm-chog	ཨམ་ཅོག
elbow	dru-mo	གྲུ་མོ
eye	mig	མིག
face	dong	གདོང
finger	zu-gu	མཛུབ་གུ
foot	kâng-pa	རྐང་པ
hand	lâg-pa	ལག་པ
head	goh	མགོ
heart	nying	སྙིང
hip	chi-go	དཔྱི་མགོ
jaw	dâm-pa	འགྲམ་པ
kidney	kay-ma	མཁལ་མ
knee	pü-mo	པུས་མོ
leg	kâng-pa	རྐང་པ
liver	chin-pa	མཆིན་པ
lungs	lo-wa	གློ་བ
mouth	kha	ཁ
muscle	sha-gyü	ཤ་རྒྱུས
nose	na-khoog	སྣ་ཁུག
ribs	tsib-ma	རྩིབ་མ
shoulder	poong-pa/trâg-pa	དཔུང་པ/ཕྲག་པ
skin	sha pâg-pa	ཤ་པགས་པ
spine	gay-tsig	སྒལ་ཚིགས
stomach	drö-kog	གྲོད་ཁོག
teeth	so	སོ
throat	mik-pa	མིད་པ
tongue	chay	ལྕེ
tonsils	chay-tsay men-bu	ལྕེ་ཚེར་སྨན་བུ
vein	tâg-tsa	ཁྲག་རྩ

HEALTH

AT THE CHEMIST   སྨན་ཚོང་ཁང་

Is there an (all-night) chemist
nearby?

    day (tsen-gâng) go-chay-khen men   འདིར་(མཚན་གང་)སྐྱོ་བྱི་མཁན་སྨན་
    tsong-khâng yö re-bay   ཚོང་ཁང་ཡོད་རེད་པས།

Do I need a prescription for ...?

    ... nyo-wa-la ahm-chi men-tho   ... ཉོ་བ་ལ་ཨེམ་ཆིའི་སྨན་ཐོ་
    go-gi re-bay   དགོས་ཀྱི་རེད་པས།

I have a prescription.

    ngah men-tho yö   ངར་སྨན་ཐོ་ཡོད།

How many should I take a day?

    nyin-ma re-ray-la teng   ཉིན་མ་རེ་རེ་ལ་ཐེང་
    kâ-tsay sa-gö-ray   ག་ཚོད་ཟ་དགོས་རེད།

Take this ... a day.	di nyin-mâ re-ray-la	འདི་ཉི་མ་རེ་རེ་ལ་ཐེང་ ...
	teng ... chö-nâng	མཆོད་གནང་།
twice	nyi-ray	གཉིས་རེ་
three times	soom-ray	གསུམ་རེ་
four times	shi-ray	བཞི་རེ་

Take ... pill(s)	teng re-ray ri-bu ...	ཐེང་རེ་རེར་རི་ལ་བུ་ ...
each time	(kha-la nyâm-tu)	(ཁ་ལག་མཉམ་དུ་)
(with food).	chö-gö	མཆོད་དགོས།
one	re-ray	རེ་རེ་
two	nyi-ray	གཉིས་རེ་
three	soom-ray	གསུམ་རེ་

Can I drive on this medication?

    men-di sa-shin-khâb mo-ta   སྨན་འདི་ཟ་བཞིན་སྐབས་མོ་ཊ་གཏང་
    tâng-na di-gi re-bay   ན་འགྲིག་གི་རེད་པས།

Will it make me drowsy?

    tey nyi doh chu-ki ma-re-bay   དེའི་གཉིད་དྲོ་བཅུག་གི་མ་རེད་པས།

HEALTH

antibiotics	nay-bu gok-men	ནད་འབུ་འགོག་སྨན་ཡེན་ཏི་
	an-ti ba-ye o-tik	བུ་ལེ་འོ་ཏིག
anti-diarrhoeal drug	drö-gok shay-gok men	གྲོད་ཁོག་འཕལ་འགོག་སྨན་
antiseptic	nyen-ka gok-chay men	མཚན་ཀ་འགོག་བྱེད་སྨན་
aspirin	nyen-jom-men as-pi-rin	མཚན་འཇོམས་སྨན་ཨེས་པི་རིན་
bandage	ma-ti/ma-ray	སྨ་དཀྲི་/སྨ་རས་
Band-Aid	ko-yö	ཀོ་ཡོལ་
cold/flu medicine	châm-bay-men	ཆམ་པའི་སྨན་

condoms	lig-shoob	ལིག་ཤུབས་
contraceptives	kye-go gok-men	སྐྱེ་སྒོ་འགོག་སྨན་
cotton balls	tin-bay du-gu	སྤྲིན་པའི་གུ་གུ
cough medicine	lo-men	གློ་སྨན་
eye medicine	mik-men	མིག་སྨན་
gauze	sâng-ray	སང་རས་
iodine	nyen-chog ba-tsha ah-ey-o-din	མཚན་གཙོག་བ་ཚ་ཨེ་ཨོ་ཌིན་
laxatives	tsog-pa bâb chu-ya-men lek-sa-tiv	བཙོག་པ་འབབ་བཅུག་ཡ་ལེགས་སྨན་ལེགས་ས་ཏིཝ་
painkillers	nay-soog cha-ya-men	ནད་གཟུག་གཅོག་ཡ་ལ་སྨན་
sleeping pills	nyi-men	གཉིད་སྨན་
throat medicine	mik-pay-men	མིད་པའི་སྨན་
vitamins	tob-kye-men	སྟོབས་བསྐྱེད་སྨན་
worm medicine	bu-men	འབུ་སྨན་

See the Shopping chapter, page 129, for general toiletries.

HEALTH

AT THE DENTIST

སོ་ཨེམ་རྗེ་མར་

I have a toothache.
    nga so na-gi   ང་སོ་ན་གིས།

I have a cavity.
    ngah so kog-tong yö   ངར་སོ་ཁོག་སྟོང་ཡོད།

I've lost a filling.
    ngay so-koong-nâng gyong-zay   ངའི་སོ་ཁུང་ནང་སྐྱོན་ཟུག་མེད་པ་ཆགས་ཤག
    may-pa châg-sha

I've broken my tooth.
    ngay so châg-sha   ངའི་སོ་ཆག་ཤག

My gums hurt.
    ngay so-nyil-nâng soog gya-gi   ངའི་སོ་རྙིལ་ནང་ཟུག་རྒྱག་གིས།

I don't want it extracted.
    nga so chi-log dön-dö may   ང་སོ་ཕྱིར་འདོན་འདོད་མེད།

Please give me an anaesthetic.
    nga-la bee-men gya nâng-dâng   ང་ལ་སྦྱིར་སྨན་རྒྱག་གནང་དང་།

| Ouch! | âh-tsa-tsa | ཨ་ཚ་ཚ། |

DISABLED TRAVELLERS

འགྲུལ་པ་དབང་པོ་སྐྱོན་ཅན

I'm ...	nga ... yin	ང ... ཡིན།
blind	long-wa	ལོང་བ
deaf	wön-ba	འོན་པ
disabled	wâng-po kyön-chen	དབང་པོ་སྐྱོན་ཅན

I need assistance.
  nga ... rog gö-ki-du   ང ... རོགས་དགོས་ཀྱི་འདུག

What services do you have for
disabled people?
  mi wâng-po kyön-chen-la   མི་དབང་པོ་སྐྱོན་ཅན་ལ་ཆ
  cha-kyen kâ-ray kâ-ray yö   སྐྱེན་ག་རེ་ག་རེ་ཡོད།

Is there wheelchair access?
  kho-lö koob-gya do-sa yö re-bay   འཁོར་ལོའི་ཀྲུབ་ཀྱག་འགྲོ་ས་ཡོད་རེད་པས།

I have a hearing aid.
  nga ahm-cho go-ya-gi   ང་ཨམ་ཆོ་གོ་ཡག་གི་
  trü-ja gyön-yö   འཕྲུལ་ཆ་སྒྱོན་ཡོད།

Speak more loudly, please.
  soong-kay chay-tsâm   གསུང་སྐད་ཆེ་ཙམ་བསྒྱུན
  kyön nâng-da   གནང་དང་།

Are guide dogs permitted?
  long-wa ti-khen-gi kyi tih   ལོང་བ་འཁྲིད་མཁན་གྱི་འཁྱིས་
  cho-gi re-bay   ཆོག་གི་རེད་པས།

braille library	long-yi pen-zö-khâng	ལོང་ཡིག་དཔེ་མཛོད་ཁང་
disabled person	mi wâng-po kyön-chen	མི་དབང་པོ་སྐྱོན་ཅན
guide dog	long-wa ti-khen-kyi	ལོང་བ་འཁྲིད་མཁན་ཁྱི་
wheelchair	kho-lö koob-gya	འཁོར་ལོའི་ཀྲུབ་ཀྱག

TRAVELLING WITH THE FAMILY

Children are welcome visitors in Tibet, generally receiving a lot of attention, and travelling with children poses no more of a challenge than it would elsewhere.

Are there facilities for babies?
  pu-gu mah-ja-la gö-ya
  kho-chay du-gay
                                        ཕུ་གུ་སྨད་འབུར་ལ་དགོས་ལས་ལ
                                        མཁོ་ཆས་འདུག་གས།
Do you have a child-minding service?
  pu-gu ta-khen yö re-bay   ཕུ་གུ་བལྟ་མཁན་ཡོད་རེད་པས།
Where can I find a/an
(English-speaking) babysitter?
  (in-ji-kay shin-khen) bu-zi-chi   (དབྱིན་ཇི་སྐད་ཤེས་མཁན་)བུ་ཇི་
  ka-bah ra-gi-ray   གཅིག་ག་བར་རག་གི་རེད།
Can you put a/an (extra)
bed in the room?
  khâng-pay-nâng nye-ti   ཁང་པའི་ནང་ཉལ་ཁྲི
  (tö-pa)-chig shâg nâng-da   (ཙོལ་པ་)ཅིག་བཞག་གནང་དང་།
I need a car with a child seat.
  ngah pu-gu dö-say koob-gya   ངར་ཕུ་གུ་སྡོད་སའི་ཀྲུབ་རྒྱ་ཡོད་པའི་མོ་
  yö-pay mo-ta-chi gö   ཊ་གཅིག་དགོས།
Is it suitable for children?
  te pu-gu-la ren-gi re-bay   དེ་ཕུ་གུ་ལ་རན་གྱི་རེད་པས།
Is there a family discount?
  kyim-tsâng-la chay-cha   ཁྱིམ་ཚང་ལ་ཕྱེད་ཆ
  yö re-bay   ཡོད་རེད་པས།
Are children allowed?
  pu-gu ti-na di-gi re-bay   ཕུ་གུ་འཁྲིན་ན་འགྲིག་གི་རེད་པས།
Do you have a children's menu?
  pu-gu-la ka-la ming-to yö-bay   ཕུ་གུ་ལ་ཁ་ལག་མིང་ཐོ་ཡོད་པས།
Is there a playground nearby?
  tih-la pu-gü tse-tâng yö re-bay   འཁྲིས་ལ་ཕུ་གུའི་རྩེད་ཐང་ཡོད་རེད་པས།

ON BUSINESS   ཚོང་དོན

We're attending a ...	ngân-tso ... tsog-gi yö	ངཚོ ... འཚོགས་གྱི་ཡོད།
conference	dö-leng tsong-du	གྲོས་སྤྲེང་ཚོངས་འདུ
meeting	tsong-du	ཚོགས་འདུ
trade fair	tsong-sog dem-tön	ཚོང་ཆོག་འགྲེམས་སྟོན

I'm on a course.
  nga lob-jong chay-ki yö   ང་སློབ་སྦྱོང་བྱེད་ཀྱི་ཡོད།
I have an appointment with ...
  nga ... thoog-gyü dü-kâg gyâb-yö   ང་ ... ཐུག་རྒྱུའི་དུས་བཀག་བརྒྱབ་ཡོད།
Here's my business card.
  di ngay tsong-gi ka-châng ray .   འདི་ངའི་ཚོང་གི་ཀ་བྱང་རེད།
I need an interpreter.
  ngah kay-gyu gö-ki-du   ང་ར་སྐད་སྒྱུར་དགོས་ཀྱི་འདུག
I'd like to use a computer.
  nga câm-pu-tah bay-chö   ང་ཀམ་པུ་ཊར་བེད་སྤྱོད་བྱེད་དགོས་ཡོད།
  chay-gö yö
I'd like to send a/an fax/email.
  nga faks/ee-mel tâng-gö yö   ང་ཕེག་སི་/ཨི་མེལ་གཏང་དགོས་ཡོད།

mobile/cell	mo-ba-yel/po-kay	མོ་བྱེལ/སྤོ་བྱེར
phone	kha-pah	ཁ་པར
client	tsong-sha	ཚོང་ཤག
colleague	lay-rog	ལས་རོགས
distributor	tsong-so dem-pay	ཚོག་ཚོག་འགྲེམས
	chay-ken	སྤེལ་བྱེད་མཁན
email	ee-mel	ཨི་མེལ
exhibition	dem-tön	འགྲེམས་སྟོན
manager	oo-zin	དབུ་འཛིན
profit	keb-sâng	ཁེ་བཟང
proposal	sâm-chah/dö-shi	བསམ་འཆར/གྲོས་གཞི

PILGRIMAGE & RELIGION གནས་མཇལ་དང་ཆོས་ལུགས་སྐོར་

In Tibet, it's considered very important to untertake a pilgrimage at least once to each of the major Buddhist sites in the country, as well as those in India and Nepal. Tibetans believe that the sacred sites are blessed with positive energy and that simply being there brings hope, vision and clarity to their lives.

What's your religion?
kay-râng-gi chö-loog kâ-ray yin ཁྱེད་རང་གི་ཆོས་ལུགས་ག་རེ་ཡིན།

I'm ...	nga ... yin	ང་ ... ཡིན།
Buddhist	nâng-pa	ནང་པ།
Catholic	yig-su cay-tho-li	ཡེ་ཤུ་ཀེ་ཐོ་ལི་
Christian	yig-shu	ཡེ་ཤུ་
Hindu	hin-du	ཧིན་དུ།
Jewish	ji-u	ཇིཡུ།
Muslim	kha-che	ཁ་ཆེ།

I'm not religious.
nga chö-la yi-chay may ང་ཆོས་ལ་ཡིད་ཆེས་མེད།

I'm (Catholic), but not practising.
nga (yig-su cay-tho-li) yin-yâng ང་(ཡེ་ཤུ་ཀེ་ཐོ་ལི་)ཡིན་ཡང་ཉམས།
nyâm-len chay-khen men ལེན་བྱེད་མཁན་མིན།

DIVINE INTERVENTION

The practice of divination (**mo**, མོ) is very common in Tibet and is relied on when making decisions about marriage, farming, travelling, health etc. People who practise divination generally consult a specific deity with whom they have formed a bond through meditation. Popular methods of divination involve rosaries, mirrors, dice or dough balls.

I think I believe in God.

nga kön-chog-la yi-chay yö
sâm-gi-du ང་དགོན་མཆོག་ལ་ཡིད་ཆེས་ཡོད་
བསམ་གྱི་འདུག

I believe in destiny/fate.

nga len-day-la yi-chay-yö ང་ལས་འབྲས་ལ་ཡིད་ཆེས་ཡོད།

I'm interested in
astrology/philosophy.

nga ka-tsi/doob-ta-la ying yö ང་སྐར་རྩིས་/གྲུབ་མཐའ་ལ་དབྱིངས་ཡོད།

I'm agnostic.

nga kön-chog sog yö-may
sü-kyâng tog mi-nü shay
ma-ken yin ང་དགོན་མཆོག་སོགས་ཡོད་མེད་སུས་
ཀྱང་རྟོགས་མི་ནུས་ཞེས་སྨྲ་མཁན་ཡིན།

Can I attend this service?

tsog-la yong-na di-gi re-bay ཚོགས་ལ་ཡོང་ན་འགྲིག་གི་རེད་པས།

Can I pray here?

day ka-dön chay-na di-gi re-bay འདིར་ཁ་འདོན་བྱེད་ན་འགྲིག་གི་རེད་པས།

Where can I pray/worship?

ka-dön/cha-chö nyâm-len
ka-bah chay-gö-ray ཁ་འདོན་/ཕྱག་མཆོད་ཉམས་ལེན་
ག་བར་བྱེད་དགོས་རེད།

SPECIFIC NEEDS

SPECIFIC NEEDS

OCEAN OF WISDOM

The Dalai Lama is considered to be a reincarnation of Avalokiteshvara, the patron saint of Tibet. The honorific title means 'Ocean of Wisdom'.

Tibetans use three additional titles for his Holiness the Dalai Lama – The Presence, The Wish-fulfilling Jewel and The Precious Refuge Protector.

Much as Tibetans enjoy talking about His Holiness the Dalai Lama, remember religion and politics are sensitive and risky issues in Tibet.

His Holiness the Dalai Lama	kün-dün/ye-shin nor-bu/kyâb-gön rin-po-che	སྐུ་མདུན་/ཡིད་བཞིན་ནོར་བུ་/ སྐྱབས་མགོན་རིན་པོ་ཆེ་
funeral	ro-phoong kye-way cho-ga	རོ་ཕུང་སྐྱེ་བའི་ཆོ་ག
god	kön-chog	དཀོན་མཆོག
monastery	gom-pa	དགོན་པ་
monk	ta-pa	གྲྭ་པ་
nun	ah-ni	ཨ་ནེ་
prayer	shay-dön/mön-lâm	ཞལ་འདོན་/སྨོན་ལམ་
priest	la-ma	བླ་མ་
reincarnation	kye-wa nga-chi	སྐྱེ་བ་སྔ་ཕྱི་
relic	ring-say	རིང་བསྲེལ་
saint	kye-bu dâm-pa	སྐྱེས་བུ་དམ་པ་
shrine	chö-khâng/chö-ten	མཆོད་ཁང་/མཆོད་རྟེན་
temple	lha-khâng	ལྷ་ཁང་

TIME, DATES & FESTIVALS

TELLING THE TIME   ཆུ་ཚོད་གཅོད

Telling the time is very straightforward in Tibetan – just remember to use ordinal numbers (see Numbers & Amounts, page 180) in your sentences.

What time is it?
  tân-da chu-tsö kâ-tsay-ray?   ད་ལྟ་ཆུ་ཚོད་ག་ཚོད་རེད

It's two o'clock.
  chu-tsö nyi-pa ray   ཆུ་ཚོད་གཉིས་པ་རེད
  (lit: hour second is)

It's five o'clock.
  chu-tsö nga-pa ray   ཆུ་ཚོད་ལྔ་པ་རེད
  (lit: hour fifth is)

Quarter to three.
  soom-pa sin-ba ka-ma cho-nga   གསུམ་པ་ཟིན་པར་སྐར་མ་བཅོ་ལྔ
  (lit: third to minutes fifteen)

Twenty to six.
  doog-pa sin-ba ka-ma nyi-shu   ལྦུག་པ་ཟིན་པར་སྐར་མ་ཉི་ཤུ
  (lit: sixth to minutes twenty)

There are some unusual expressions, however, which must be learnt separately:

It's midnight.
  gong-da chu-tsö chu-nyi ray   དགོང་དག་ཆུ་ཚོད་བཅུ་གཉིས་རེད

It's noon.
  nyin-goong chu-tsö chu-nyi ray   ཉིན་གུང་ཆུ་ཚོད་བཅུ་གཉིས་རེད

The term for 'half past' is **chay-ka** (ཕྱེད་ཀ), literally meaning 'half', and for 'quarter past' is **ka-ma chö-nga** (སྐར་མ་བཅོ་ལྔ), literally meaning 'minutes fifteen':

It's two thirty.
 chu-tsö nyi-dâng chay-ka ray   ཆུ་ཚོད་གཉིས་དང་ཕྱེད་ཀ་རེད།
 (lit: hour two-and half is)
It's quarter past six.
 chu-tsö doog-dâng ka-ma   ཆུ་ཚོད་དྲུག་དང་སྐར་མ་བཅོ་ལྔ་རེད།
 chö-nga ray
 (lit: hour six-and minutes fifteen is)

DAYS OF THE WEEK   གཟའ་བདུན

Monday	sa da-wa	གཟའ་ཟླ་བ
Tuesday	sa mig-ma	གཟའ་མིག་དམར
Wednesday	sa lhâg-bâ	གཟའ་ལྷག་པ
Thursday	sa phu-bu	གཟའ་ཕུར་བུ
Friday	sa pa-sâng	གཟའ་པ་སངས
Saturday	sa pem-pa	གཟའ་སྤེན་པ
Sunday	sa nyi-mâ	གཟའ་ཉི་མ

MONTHS   ཟླ་བ
Tibet uses both the traditional lunar calendar, where each month has 30 days, and the Gregorian calendar, as used in the West. There are 12 months in each, which are simply referred to as the '1st month', the '2nd month' etc. However, the Lunar New Year is about six weeks after the Western New Year.

1st month	da-wa dâng-po	ཟླ་བ་དང་པོ
2nd month	da-wa nyi-pa	ཟླ་བ་གཉིས་པ
3rd month	da-wa soom-pa	ཟླ་བ་གསུམ་པ
4th month	da-wa shi-pa	ཟླ་བ་བཞི་པ
5th month	da-wa nga-pa	ཟླ་བ་ལྔ་པ
6th month	da-wa doog-pa	ཟླ་བ་དྲུག་པ

7th month	da-wa dün-pa	ཟླ་བ་བདུན་པ་
8th month	da-wa gye-pa	ཟླ་བ་བརྒྱད་པ་
9th month	da-wa gu-pa	ཟླ་བ་དགུ་པ་
10th month	da-wa chu-pa	ཟླ་བ་བཅུ་པ་
11th month	da-wa chu-chig-pa	ཟླ་བ་བཅུ་གཅིག་པ་
12th month	da-wa chu-nyi-pa	ཟླ་བ་བཅུ་གཉིས་པ་

To be more precise, you can substitute chin-da (ཕྱི་ཟླ), 'Western month', or bön-da (བོད་ཟླ), 'Tibetan month', for da-wa (ཟླ་བ) 'month'. February, for example, would be either chin-da nyi-pa (ཕྱི་ཟླ་གཉིས་པ) or bön-da nyi-pa (བོད་ཟླ་གཉིས་པ).

DATES   ཚེས་པ་

What date is it today? (Western calendar)
  te-ring chi-tsay kâ-tsö ray?   དེ་རིང་ཕྱི་ཚེས་ག་ཚོད་རེད།
It's 28 June.
  te-ring chin-da doog-bay tsay   དེ་རིང་ཕྱི་ཟླ་དྲུག་པའི་ཚེས་
  nyi-shu tsâb-gye ray   ཉི་ཤུ་རྩ་བརྒྱད་རེད།
  (lit: today Western-month sixth
    of-date twenty eight is)
It's 1 April.
  te-ring chin-da shi-bay tsay   དེ་རིང་ཕྱི་ཟླ་བཞི་པའི་ཚེས་གཅིག་རེད།
  chig ray
  (lit: today Western-month fourth
    of-date one is)

PRESENT   ད་ལྟ་

today	te-ring	དེ་རིང་
this morning	te-ring shoh-gay	དེ་རིང་ཞོགས་གས་
this afternoon	te-ring chi-toh	དེ་རིང་ཕྱི་དྲོ་
this evening	dho-gong	དགོང་
tonight	dho-gong-tshen	དགོང་མཚན་
this week	dün-tâ di; sa-koh-di	བདུན་ཕྲག་འདི་/གཟའ་འཁོར་འདི་
this month	da-wa di	ཟླ་བ་འདི་
this year	tâ-lo/lo-di	ད་ལོ་/ལོ་འདི་

TIME, DATES & FESTIVALS

PAST བདས་པ་

yesterday	kay-sa	ཁ་ས་
day before yesterday	kay nyin-mo	ཁེ་ཉིན་མོ་
yesterday morning	kay-sa shoh-gay	ཁ་ས་ཞོགས་སྐར་
yesterday afternoon	kay-sa chi-toh	ཁ་ས་ཕྱི་དྲོ་
yesterday evening	dång-gong	མདང་དགོང་
last night	kay-sa gong-ta	ཁ་ས་དགོང་དག་
last week	dün-ta ngön-ma; sa-koh ngön-ma	བདུན་ཕྲག་སྔོན་མ་/ གཟའ་འཁོར་སྔོན་མ་
last month	da-wa ngön-ma	ཟླ་བ་སྔོན་མ་
last year	da-nyi/lo ngön-ma	ཟླ་ཉིད་/ལོ་སྔོན་མ་
(half an hour) ago	(chu-tsö chay-ka) ngön-la	(ཆུ་ཚོད་ཕྱེད་ཀ)སྔོན་ལ་
(three) days ago	nyin-(soom) ngön-la	ཉིན་(གསུམ་)སྔོན་ལ་
(five) years ago	lo (nga) ngön-la	ལོ་(ལྔ་)སྔོན་ལ་
since (May)	(chin-da nga-pa) nay soong	(ཕྱི་ཟླ་ལྔ་པ་)ནས་བཟུང་

FUTURE མ་འོངས་པ་

tomorrow	sa-nyin	སང་ཉིན་
day after tomorrow	nång-nyin	གནངས་ཉིན་
tomorrow morning	sång-shoh	སང་ཞོག་
tomorrow afternoon	sång chi-toh	སང་ཕྱི་དྲོ་
tomorrow evening	sång-nyi gong-da; sång-noob	སང་ཉིན་དགོང་དག/སང་ནུབ་
next week	dün-ta je-ma; sa-koh je-ma	བདུན་ཕྲག་རྗེས་མ་/ གཟའ་འཁོར་རྗེས་མ་
next month	da-wa je-ma	ཟླ་བ་རྗེས་མ་
next year	lo je-ma/tü-sång	ལོ་རྗེས་མ་/སང་ལོ་/དུས་སང་
in (five) minutes	ka-ma (ngay) nång	སྐར་མ་(ལྔའི་)ནང་
in (six) days	nyin-ma (doog) nång	ཉིན་མ་(དྲུག)ནང་
within an hour/ month	chu-tsö/da-wa chig nång	ཆུ་ཚོད་/ཟླ་བ་ གཅིག་ནང་
until (June)	(chin-da doog-pa) bah-tu	(ཕྱི་ཟླ་དྲུག་པ)་ བར་དུ་

DURING THE DAY ཉིན་དུས།

It's early.	nga-po ray-sha	ས྄་པོ་རེད་ཤག
It's late.	chi-po ray	ཕྱི་པོ་རེད།
afternoon	chi-toh	ཕྱི་དྲོ
dawn	toh-reng/kya-reng	ཐོ་རེངས་/སྐྱ་རེངས་
day(time)	nyin-mo	ཉིན་མོ
early	nga-po	ས྄་པོ
evening	gong-da	དགོང་དག
late	chi-po	ཕྱི་པོ
lunchtime	nyin-goong kha-la dü-tsö	ཉིན་གུང་ཁ་ལག་དུས་ཚོད
midday	nyin-goong	ཉིན་གུང
midnight	nâm-chay	ནམ་ཕྱེ
morning	shoh-gay	ཞོགས་སྐད
night	tsen-mo	མཚན་མོ
noon	nyin-goong	ཉིན་གུང
sunset	nyin-ma noob-dü	ཉི་མ་ནུབ་དུས
sunrise	nyin-ma shar-dü	ཉི་མ་ཤར་དུས

USEFUL WORDS ཕན་འབྱོར་བའི་མིང་ཚིག

a while ago	dü-yün-kay ngön-la	དུས་ཡུན་ཤག་འགའི་སྔོན་ལ
after	jay-la	རྗེས་ལ
always	tâg-pa/châr-chen	རྟག་པར་/འཆར་ཅན
before	ngön-la	སྔོན་ལ
every day	nyin-tar	ཉིན་ལྟར
forever	tâg-tu	རྟག་ཏུ
immediately	tân-ta-râng	དལྟ་རང
long ago	nga-mo nga-mo	སྔ་མོ་སྔ་མོ
never	nâm-yang	ནམ་ཡང
not any more	yâng-kya-min/ chin-chay-min	ཡང་སྐྱར་མིན་/ ཕྱིན་ཆད་མིན
not yet	tân-da-yâng may	དལྟ་ཡང་མེད
now	tân-da	དལྟ
recently	nye-char	ཉེ་ཆར
sometimes	tshâm tshâm	མཚམས་མཚམས
soon	gyok-po/lâm-sâng	མགྱོགས་པོ་/ལམ་སང

FESTIVALS & HOLIDAYS དུས་ཆེན་དང་གུང་སེང་

If your trip coincides with a Tibetan festival, there's a good chance you'll see a **châm** performance. Châm is a ritual dance performed by monks and lamas and held over several days. The performers wear colourful masks and each movement has special significance.

All festivals are held according to the Tibetan lunar calendar (see page 170).

lo-sar ལོ་གསར་ (བོད་ཟླ་ ༡ ཚེས་ ༡)

This is the New Year Festival, and so begins on the first day of the first lunar month.

mön-lâm chen-mo སྨོན་ལམ་ཆེན་མོ་ (བོད་ཟླ་ ༡ ཚེས་ ༡༥)

The Great Prayer Festival runs from the 1st to 15th of the first lunar month and celebrates Buddha's miracles and victory over the six non-Buddhist masters at Sravasti in India.

sa-ga da-wa ས་གཱ་ཟླ་བ་ (བོད་ཟླ་ ༤ ཚེས་ ༡༥)

The anniversary of Buddha's birth, death and enlightenment is celebrated on the 15th day of the fourth lunar month. Outdoor operas (see page 176) take place and throngs of pilgrims follow the Barkhor circuit.

zâm-ling chi-sâng འཛམ་གླིང་སྤྱི་བསངས་ (བོད་ཟླ་ ༥ ཚེས་ ༡༥)

Occuring on the 15th day of the fifth lunar month, this festival marks the successful completion of the first Tibetan monastery – the Samye Monastery. Incense is burned and prayer flags are strung up for world peace.

lha-sa sho-ton ལྷ་ས་ཞོ་སྟོན་ (བོད་ཟླ་ ༧ ཚེས་ ༣)

Held on the 2nd day of the seventh lunar month. Operas and masked dances take place and locals enjoy picnics.

lha-sa wong-koh ལྷ་ས་འོང་བསྐོར་ (བོད་ཟླ་ ༧)

The Lhasa Farmer Festival generally occurs during the seventh lunar month. Farmers around Lhasa burn incense and string up prayer flags to honour the local deities who control the region's peace and stability, as well as the fertility of the soil.

TIME, DATES & FESTIVALS

toong-kah dü-chen   བཙུགས་སྐར་དུས་ཆེན (ཟླ་བ 7 ཚེས 6)
His Holiness the Dalai Lama's birthday is celebrated on 6 July. It commemorates the birth of the 14th Dalai Lama in Amdo, Eastern Tibet, in 1935.

cho-kor dü-chen   ཆོས་འཁོར་དུས་ཆེན (བོད་ཟླ 6 ཚེས 4)
The remembrance of Buddha's first discourse, when he taught the Four Holy Truths to his five disciples, takes place on the 4th day of the sixth lunar month.

lha-bâb dü-chen   ལྷ་བབས་དུས་ཆེན (བོད་ཟླ 9 ཚེས 22)
Held on the 22nd day of the ninth lunar month, this celebration commemorates Buddha's descent from heaven. You'll find many pilgrims in Lhasa on this day.

gân-den ngâm-chö   དགའ་ལྡན་སྔ་མཆོད (བོད་ཟླ 10 ཚེས 25)
Sometimes referred to as the Tsong Khapa anniversary, this event is held on the 25th day of the tenth lunar month. Tsong Khapa (1357-1419) was a renowned Tibetan lama, scholar and meditator who founded the Gelugpa School of Tibetan Buddhism.

TIME, DATES & FESTIVALS

ngan-pa gu-zom   དགཔདགུའཛོམས་(བོདཟླ་༡༡ཚེས་༦)

The 6th day of the eleventh lunar month is considered a day of nine inauspicious signs – a very bad day to start a trip or any projects.

sang-po chu-zom   བཟངཔོབཅུའཛོམས་(བོདཟླ་༡༡ཚེས་༡)

The 7th day of the eleventh lunar month is a day of 10 auspicious signs – a good day for picnicking and generally having fun.

tse gu-tor   ཚེདགུགཏོར་(བོདཟླ་༡༢ཚེས་༢༩)

This is a festival to banish evil spirits and takes place on the 29th day of the twelfth lunar month.

LEGENDARY LHAMO!

Lha-mo (ལྷམོ) is Tibetan opera and is very popular at festival times. It recounts historical events and ancient legends and tells of heroes and villains.

NEW YEAR   ལོགསར་

The Year End Festival, **nyi-shu-gu** (ཉིཤུདགུ) is held on the 29th day of the twelfth lunar month. People go to watch the spiritual dance associated with a ritual to banish the evil forces.

In the evening, families make a special porridge soup, **gu-thuk** (དགུཐུག), into which they put balls of dough, each containing a roll of paper with a message. The messages are supposed to be humourous, as well as revealing of the individual personalities.

On New Year's Day, everyone gets up as early as possible to try to get the first of the water for good luck. For the rest of the day, however, people stay home as it's believed that too much socialising and spending money on the first day will decrease good fortune. From the second day onwards, people attend public celebrations, socialise and party!

Day before New Year's Eve (29th of the twelfth Tibetan month)	nyi-shu-gu	ཉི་ཤུ་དགུ
Tibetan New Year's Eve	nâm-gâng	གནམ་གང
New Year's Day	lo-sar	ལོ་གསར
New Year 1st Day	lo-sar tse-chig	ལོ་གསར་ཚེས་གཅིག
New Year 2nd Day	lo-sar tse-nyi	ལོ་གསར་ཚེས་གཉིས
New Year 3rd Day	lo-sar tse-soom	ལོ་གསར་ཚེས་གསུམ

Happy New Year! lo-sar ta-shi de-lek ལོ་གསར་བཀྲ་ཤིས་བདེ་ལེགས

BIRTHDAYS སྐྱེས་སྐར

When's your birthday?
kay-râng-gi kye-tsay
ka-dü ray? ཁྱེད་རང་གི་སྐྱེ་ཚེས་ག་དུས་རེད

My birthday is on (25 January).
ngay kye-tsay (chin-da tâng-pö ངའི་སྐྱེ་ཚེས་ (ཕྱི་ཟླ་དང་པོའི་ཚེས་ཉེར་ལྔ)
tse nye-nga) la ray ལ་རེད

Happy birthday!
kye-kah-nyin ta-shi de-lek སྐྱེ་སྐར་ཉིན་བཀྲ་ཤིས་བདེ་ལེགས

birthday cake	kye-kah kek	སྐྱེ་སྐར་ཀེག
candles	yân-lah	ཡང་ལ

TIME, DATES & FESTIVALS

SEVEN WEEKS IN TIBET

When people are cremated in Tibet, the day of the cremation is organised in accordance with astrological charts. In order to rest the spirit and help it find a better rebirth, people make offerings to the temple and give charity to the needy. Once a week for seven weeks following the death, a special religious service is held. Seven weeks is believed to be the maximum amount of time needed for the spirit to find its rebirth.

WEDDINGS
བག་སྟོན

Traditional Tibetan weddings begin with a one-day celebration at the bride's home, with her family and friends. The actual wedding then takes place at the groom's home, with lots of singing and all the guests offering ka-ta (see page 42). The partying and celebrating may continue for three or more days!

Congratulations!		
ta-shi de-lek		བཀྲ་ཤིས་བདེ་ལེགས།
To the bride and groom!		
bâg-ma dâng mâg-ba nyi-la		བག་མ་དང་མགཔ་གཉིས་ལ

engagement	long-châng tong-wa	སློང་ཆང་གཏོང་བ
honeymoon	châng-sa gyâb-jay-ki toh-seng	ཆང་ས་བརྒྱབ་རྗེས་ཀྱི་སྤྲོ་གསེང
wedding	châng-sa	ཆང་ས

གྲངས་ཀ་དང་ཕྱོན་འབོར་

CARDINAL NUMBERS

གྲངས་གྲངས་

The Tibetan counting system is quite logical – as long as you follow the pattern below, you won't have a problem.

0	০	lay-koh	ཀླད་ཀོར་
1	༡	chig	གཅིག
2	༢	nyi	གཉིས
3	༣	soom	གསུམ
4	༤	shi	བཞི
5	༥	nga	ལྔ
6	༦	doog	དྲུག
7	༧	dün	བདུན
8	༨	gye	བརྒྱད
9	༩	gu	དགུ
10	༡༠	chu/chu-tâm-pa	བཅུ/བཅུ་ཐམ་པ
11	༡༡	chu-chig	བཅུ་གཅིག
12	༡༢	chu-nyi	བཅུ་གཉིས
13	༡༣	chu-soom	བཅུ་གསུམ
14	༡༤	chu-shi	བཅུ་བཞི
15	༡༥	chö-nga	བཅོ་ལྔ
16	༡༦	chu-doog	བཅུ་དྲུག
17	༡༧	chu-dün	བཅུ་བདུན
18	༡༨	chö-gye	བཅོ་བརྒྱད
19	༡༩	chu-gu	བཅུ་དགུ
20	༢༠	nyi-shu;	ཉི་ཤུ/
		nyi-shu tâm-pa	ཉི་ཤུ་ཐམ་པ
21	༢༡	nyi-shu tsa-chig	ཉི་ཤུ་རྩ་གཅིག
22	༢༢	nyi-shu tsa-nyi	ཉི་ཤུ་རྩ་གཉིས
30	༣༠	soom-chu;	སུམ་ཅུ/
		soom-chu tâm-pa	སུམ་ཅུ་ཐམ་པ
31	༣༡	soom-chu so-chig	སུམ་ཅུ་སོ་གཅིག

40	༤༠	shib-chu; shib-chu tâm-pa	བཞི་བཅུ/བཞི་བཅུ་ཐམ་པ
41	༤༡	shib-chu shay-chig	བཞི་བཅུ་ཞེ་གཅིག
50	༥༠	ngâb-chu; ngâb-chu tâm-pa	ལྔ་བཅུ/ལྔ་བཅུ་ཐམ་པ
51	༥༡	ngâb-chu ngay-chig	ལྔ་བཅུ་ང་གཅིག
60	༦༠	doog-chu; doog-chu tâm-pa	དྲུག་བཅུ/དྲུག་བཅུ་ཐམ་པ
61	༦༡	doog-chu re-chig	དྲུག་བཅུ་རེ་གཅིག
70	༧༠	dün-chu; dün-chu tâm-pa	བདུན་ཅུ/བདུན་ཅུ་ཐམ་པ
71	༧༡	dün-chu dön-chig	བདུན་ཅུ་དོན་གཅིག
80	༨༠	gyay-chu; gyay-chu tâm-pa	བརྒྱད་བཅུ/བརྒྱད་བཅུ་ཐམ་པ
81	༨༡	gyay-chu gya-chig	བརྒྱད་ཅུ་གྱ་གཅིག
90	༩༠	goob-chu; goob-chu tâm-pa	དགུ་བཅུ/དགུ་བཅུ་ཐམ་པ
91	༩༡	goob-chu go-chig	དགུ་བཅུ་དོན་གཅིག
100	༡༠༠	gya; gya tâm-pa	བརྒྱ/བརྒྱ་ཐམ་པ
101	༡༠༡	gya dâng chig	བརྒྱ་དང་གཅིག
155	༡༥༥	gya dâng ngâb-chu ngay-nga	བརྒྱ་དང་ལྔ་བཅུ་ང་ལྔ
1000	༡༠༠༠	chig-tong; chig-tong tâm-pa	ཆིག་སྟོང / ཆིག་སྟོང་ཐམ་པ
10,000	༡༠༠༠༠	chig-ti/tong-tâg-chu	ཆིག་ཁྲི/སྟོང་ཕྲག་བཅུ
100,000	༡༠༠༠༠༠	chig-boom/ boom-tâg-chig	ཆིག་འབུམ/ འབུམ་ཕྲག་གཅིག

one million	༡༠༠༠༠༠༠	sa-ya-chig/boom-chu	ས་ཡ་གཅིག/འབུམ་བཅུ
ten million	༡༠༠༠༠༠༠༠	chay-wa-chig	བྱེ་བ་གཅིག
one hundred million	༡༠༠༠༠༠༠༠༠	doong-chu-chig	དུང་ཕྱུར་གཅིག

ORDINAL NUMBERS རིམ་གྲངས

Ordinal numbers are easy to form in Tibetan – just add the suffix -pa (པ) to the relevant cardinal number. The only exception is with chig (གཅིག), 'one', which becomes dâng-po (དང་པོ), 'first'.

1st	dâng-po	དང་པོ
2nd	nyi-pa	གཉིས་པ
3rd	soom-pa	གསུམ་པ
4th	shi-pa	བཞི་པ
5th	nga-pa	ལྔ་པ

FRACTIONS

ཆ་གྲངས།

a quarter	shi-cha-chig	བཞི་ཆ་གཅིག
a half	chay-ka	ཕྱེད་ཀ
a third	soom-cha-chig	གསུམ་ཆ་གཅིག
three-quarters	shi-cha-soom	བཞི་ཆ་གསུམ

DIGITAL COUNTING

When using their fingers to count, Tibetans touch the tip of their thumb to each finger or the joint lines of each finger, so each can be used three times.

USEFUL AMOUNTS

ཁུན་མཁོའི་གྲངས་འབོར

How much?	gong kâ-tsay	གོང་ག་ཚད།
How many?	kâ-tsö	ག་ཚོད
Could you please give me ...?	ngah ... nâng-da	ང་ ... གནང་དང་།
I need ...	ngah ... gö	ང་ ... དགོས།
all	tsâng-ma	ཚང་མ
a bottle	shay-tâm-chig	ཤེལ་དམ་གཅིག
a bottle of water	chu shay-tâm chig	ཆུ་ཤེལ་དམ་གཅིག
double	nyi-tsâg	ཉི་ཚེག
a dozen	dha-tsen-chig	དར་ཚན་གཅིག
half a dozen	dha-tsen chay-ka	བདར་ཚན་ཕྱེད་ཀ
half a dozen eggs	go-nga dha-tsen chay-ka	སྒོང་ང་བདར་ཚན་ཕྱེད་ཀ
enough	dâng-ngay/dâng-pa	འདང་ངེས/འདང་བས
a few	nyoong-nyoong	ཉུང་ཉུང
few	ka-shay/te-si	ཁ་ཤས/�hེག་ཙམ
gram	ga-râm	གྲ་རམ
100 grams	ga-râm gya	གྲ་རམ་བརྒྱ
a kilogram	ki-lo chig	ཀི་ལོ་གཅིག
a kilogram of rice	day ki-lo chig	འབྲས་ཀི་ལོ་གཅིག
half a kilogram	ki-lo chay-ka	ཀི་ལོ་ཕྱེད་ཀ

NUMBERS & AMOUNTS

less	nyoong-wa	ཉུང་བ།
litre	li-tar	ལི་ཏར།
two litres of oil	noom li-tar nyi	སྣུམ་ལི་ཏར་གཉིས།
half a litre	li-tar chay-ka	ལི་ཏར་ཕྱེད་ཀ།
a little	te-si	དོག་ཙམ།
many; much; a lot	mâng-po	མང་པོ།
more	mâng-wa	མང་བ།
none	tsa-nay may-pa	རྩ་ནས་མེད་པ།
once	teng-chig	ཐེངས་གཅིག
a packet	châg-pa chig;	ཚག་པ་གཅིག/
	gâm-chig	སྒམ་གཅིག
a packet of cigarettes	tha-ma gâm-chig	ཐ་མག་སྒམ་གཅིག
a packet of	tsong ngön-po	ཙོང་སྔོན་པོ་ཚག་པ་གཅིག
green onions	châg-pa chig	
a pair	cha-chig	ཆ་གཅིག
a slice	lheb-chig	ལྔེབ་གཅིག
some	ka-shay	ཁ་ཤས།
a tin	tin-chig	ཏིན་གཅིག
too many/much	mâng-dâg-pa	མང་དྲགས་པ།
twice	teng-nyi	ཐེངས་གཉིས།

ཇོ་དྲག EMERGENCIES

GENERAL

སྤྱིར་བཏང་

Help!	rog nâng-da	རོགས་གནང་དང་།
Stop!	kha kâg-dâng	ཁ་བཀག་དང་།
Go away!	phâh gyook	ཕར་རྒྱུགས།
Thief!	ku-ma du	རྐུ་མ་འདུག
Fire!	may bâh-gee	མེ་འབར་གྱིས།
Watch out!	sâb sâb nâng	གཟབ་གཟབ་གནང་།
Wait!	gu nâng-da	སྒུག་གནང་དང་།
Don't move!	gü-kyog ma-tâng	འགུལ་སྐྱོད་མ་གཏང་།

Does anyone speak English?
  in-ji-kay shay-khen yö ray-bay   དབྱིན་ཇི་སྐད་ཤེས་མཁན་ཡོད་རེད་པས།
It's an emergency.
  za dâg-po ray   ཇོ་དྲག་པོ་རེད།
There's been an accident!
  phâ-gay kye-ngen choong sha   ཕ་གིར་སྐྱེན་ངན་བྱུང་ཤག
Please help me.
  ngah ro nâng-dâ   ང་ལ་རོགས་གནང་དང་།
Could I please use the telephone?
  kha-pah bay-chö chay-na   ཁ་པར་བེད་སྤྱོད་བྱེད་ན་འགྲིག་གི་རེད་པས།
  di-gi re-bay
I'm lost.
  nga lâm-ga la-sha   ང་ལམ་ཀ་བརྫུགས་ཤག
Where are the toilets?
  sâng-chö ka-bah yö-ray   གསང་སྤྱོད་ག་པར་ཡོད་རེད།

183

EMERGENCIES

POLICE ࿐་སྲུང་བ།

Call the police!

    kor-soong-wa kay tong-da ࿐་སྲུང་བ་སྐད་གཏོང་དང་།

I'll get the police!

    ngay kor-soong-wa kay tâng-go ངས་࿐ོར་སྲུང་བ་སྐད་གཏང་གོ།

Where's the police station?

    kor-soong-way le-koong ࿐ར་སྲུང་བའི་ལས་ཁུངས་ག་པར་ཡོད་རེད།
    ka-bah yö-ray

We want to report an offence.

    ngân-tsö chay-nyen nye-sâng ང་ཚོས་བྱས་ཉེས་སྙན་ཞུ་གྱི་ཡིན།
    shu-gi yin

I've been raped.

    nga-la tsen-wâng-tog ང་ལ་བཙན་དབང་ཐོག་ཆགས་པ་བྱས་སོང་།
    châg-pa chay-song

I've been assaulted.

    ngah gö-zing chay-choong ངར་རྐྱོལ་འཛིངས་བྱས་བྱུང་།

I've been robbed.

    nga ku-may chom-song ང་རྐུ་མས་བཙོམས་སོང་།

My ... was/were stolen.	ngay ... ku-ma shoh-song	ངའི་ ... རྐུ་མ་ཤོར་སོང་།
I've lost my ...	ngay ... lâg-song	ངའི་ ... བརླགས་སོང་།
backpack	gya-phay	རྒྱབ་ཁད་
bags	bag-la/jo-la	འབེག་ལག/འཇོ་ལག
handbag	lâg-kye bag-la	ལག་འཁྱེར་འབེགལག
money	ngü	དངུལ་
papers	yig-cha	ཡིག་ཆ་
passport	pa-se-pot; chi-kyö lâg-teb	པ་སེ་པོང་/ ཕྱིར་བསྐྱོད་ལག་དེབ་
travellers cheques	drü-shü ngü-zin	འགྲུལ་བཞུད་དངུལ་འཛིན་
wallet	bâh-koog	སྒུ་ཁུག

EMERGENCIES

My possessions are insured.

**ngay cha-lâg-la in-shu-ren
gan-gya sö-yö**

ངའི་ཅ་ལག་ལ་ཨིན་ཤུ་རན་བརྒྱབ་ནས་རྒྱ་
བཙོས་ཡོད།

I'm sorry; I apologise.

gong-da

དགོངས་དག

I didn't realise I was doing
anything wrong.

**ngay nön-trü chay yö-pa
ha-ko-ma-song**

ངས་ནོར་འཁྲུལ་བྱས་ཡོད་པ་ཧ་གོ་མ་སོང་།

I didn't do it.

ngay chay-gyu ma-choong

ངས་བྱེད་རྒྱུ་མ་བྱུང་།

We're innocent.

ngân-tsoh nâg-nye may

ང་ཚོར་ནག་ཉེས་མེད།

We're foreigners.

ngân-tso chi-gye-wa yin

ང་ཚོ་ཕྱི་རྒྱལ་བ་ཡིན།

I want to contact my
embassy/consulate.

**ngân-tsö shoong-tsab/dön-chö
khâng-la day-wa chay-gö-yö**

ང་ཚོའི་གཞུང་ཚབ/དོན་གཅོད་ཁང་ལ་འབྲེལ་བ་
བྱེད་དགོས་ཡོད།

Can I call someone?

ngay chig-la kha-pah tâng-ga

ངས་གཅིག་ལ་ཁ་པར་གཏང་ག

Can I have a lawyer
who speaks English?

**ngah in-ji-kay shin-khen
tim-tsö-pa-chi râg thoob-ki
re-bay**

ངར་དབྱིན་ཇི་སྐད་ཤེས་མཁན་ཁྲིམས་རྩོད་
པ་གཅིག་རག་ཐུབ་ཀྱི་རེད་པས།

EMERGENCIES

Is there a fine we can pay to clear this?
　nye-chay-di ngü tay-nay ཉེས་ཆད་འདི་དངུལ་སྤྲད་ནས་འཛབ་
　ja-ya yö re-bay ཡག་ཡོད་རེད་པས།
Can we pay an on-the-spot fine?
　nye-chay ngü-bâb da-ta-râng ཉེས་ཆད་དངུལ་འབབ་ད་ལྟ་རང་
　tay-na di-gi re-bay སྤྲད་ན་འགྲིག་གི་རེད་པས།
I understand.
　ha go-song ཧ་གོ་སོང་།
I don't understand.
　ha go-ma-song ཧ་གོ་མ་སོང་།
I know my rights.
　ngay nga-râng-gi thob-tâng ངས་ང་རང་གི་ཐོབ་ཐང་ཧ་གོ་གི་ཡོད།
　ha go-gi-yö

arrested	zin-soong chay-pa	འཛིན་བཟུང་བྱས་པ
cell	tsön-khâng nâng-gi khâng-choong	བཙོན་ཁང་ནང་གི་ཁང་ཆུང་
consulate	dön-chö-khâng	དོན་གཅོད་ཁང་
embassy	shoong-tsâb-khâng	གཞུང་ཚབ་ཁང་
fine	nye-chay	ཉེས་ཆད་
guilty	nâg-nye yö-pa	ནག་ཉེས་ཡོད་པ
not guilty	nâg-nye may-pa	ནག་ཉེས་མེད་པ
lawyer	tim-tsö-pa	ཁྲིམས་རྩོད་པ
police officer	kor-soong-wa	སྐོར་སྲུང་བ
police station	kor-soong lay-koong	སྐོར་སྲུང་ལས་ཁུངས
prison	tsön-khâng	བཙོན་ཁང་
trial	tim-chö	ཁྲིམས་གཅོད་

What am I accused of?	ngah nâg-nye kâ-ray gay yö-ray	ངར་ནག་ཉེས་ག་རེ་ བགལ་ཡོད་རེད།
You'll be charged with ...	kay-râng-la ... nye-chay gay-gi-ray	ཁྱེད་རང་ལ ... ཉེས་ཆད་ བགོལ་གྱི་རེད།
He'll/She'll be charged with ...	kho/mo-la ... nye-chay gay-gi-ray	ཁོ/མོ ... ཉེས་ཆད་ བགོལ་གྱི་རེད།
anti-government activity	shoong-la ngo-lo-gi lay-gü tsâm-pa	གཞུང་ལ་ངོ་ལོག་གི་ལས་ བགལ་བརྩམས་པ
assault	gö-zing chay-pa	ཀྲོལ་འཛིང་བྱེད་པ
disturbing the peace	shi-de toog-pa	ཞི་བདེ་དཀྲུགས་པ
possession (of illegal substances)	(trim-gay-gi ngö-zay) kye-wa	(ཁྲིམས་འགལ་གྱི་དངོས་ རྫས་)འཁྱེར་བ
illegal entry	trim-gay-gi gya-kâb-nâng zü-ba	ཁྲིམས་འགལ་གྱིས་ རྒྱལ་ཁབ་ནང་འཛུལ་བ
murder	mi sö-pa	མི་གསོད་པ
not having a visa	vi-za may-pa	ཝི་ཛ་མེད་པ
overstaying your/his/her visa	kay-râng-gi/ khö/mö vi-zay dü-tsö-lay gay-te dhö-pa	ཁྱེད་རང་གི/ ཁོའི/མོའི ཝི་ཛའི་དུས་ཚོད་ ལས་བརྒལ་ཏེ་སྡོད་པ
rape	tsen-yem chay-pa	བཙན་གཡེམ་བྱེད་པ
robbery/theft	tog-chom chay-pa; ku-ma kü-pa	འཕྲོག་བཅོམ་བྱེད་པ/ རྐུ་མ་རྐུ་བ
shoplifting	tsong-so jâb-kü chay-pa	ཚོང་ཁོ་ཇབ་འབཙལ་རྐུ་བྱེད་པ
traffic violation	lâm-gay-trim gay-wa	ལམ་ཀའི་ཁྲིམས་འགལ་བ
working without a permit	chog-chen may-pah lay-ga chay-pa	ཆོག་འཆན་མེད་པར་ལས་ ཀ་བྱེད་པ

EMERGENCIES

HEALTH

འཕྲོད་བསྟེན།

Call a doctor!

ahm-chi kay tong-da

ཨེམ་ཆི་སྐད་གཏོང་དང་།

Call an ambulance!

**nay-pa or-khen mo-ta
kay tong-da**

ནད་པ་འབོར་མཁན་མོ་ཊ་སྐད་གཏོང་དང་།

I'm ill.

nga na-gi-du

ང་ན་གི་འདུག

My friend is ill.

ngay rog-pa na-gi-du

ངའི་རོགས་པ་ན་གི་འདུག

I have medical insurance.

**nga-la trö-ten-chay in-shu-ren
gan-gya sö-yö**

ང་ལ་འཕྲོད་བསྟེན་ཆེད་ཨིན་ཤུ་རན་འབགས་རྒྱ་བཙལ་ཡོད།

My blood group is (A/B/O/AB)
positive/negative.

ngay tâg-rig (e/bi/o/e-bi)

ངའི་ཁྲག་རིགས་(ཨེ/བི/ཨོ/ཨེ་བི)

po-si-ti-yu/ne-ge-ti-yu ray

པོ་སི་ཏི་ཡུ/ནེ་གེ་ཏི་ཡུ་རེད།

Contact number (next of kin).

**de-thoog chay-sa
(pün-tâg-nye-shö)
kha-pah ahng-dâng**

འབྲེལ་ཐུག་བྱེད་ས་(སྤུན་ཐག་ཉེ་ཤོས་)
ཁ་པར་ཨང་གྲངས།

A

| able, to be (can) | thoob-pa • nü-pa | ཐུབ་པ་ • ནུས་པ་ |

Can I take a photo (of you)?
(kay-rǎng) par-chig gyǎb-na (ཁྱེད་རང་)པར་ཅིག་རྒྱབ་ན་
di-giy ray-bay འདྲི་གི་ཡི་རེད་པས།
Can you show me (on the map)?
(sâp-ta di-nâng) tön nâng-da (ས་བཀྲ་འདི་ནང་)སྟོན་གནང་དང་།

aboard	du-sing dâng nâm-du	གྲུ་གཟིངས་དང་གནམ་གྲུ་
	sog nâng shoog-pa	སོགས་ནང་ཤུགས་པ་
abortion	pu-gu ngay-nay	ཕྲུག་གུ་ངལ་ནས་ཕྱིར་འདོན་པ་
	chi dön-pa	
above	gâng-la	སྒང་ལ་
abroad	chi-gye	ཕྱི་རྒྱལ་
to accept	ngö-len chay-pa	ངོས་ལེན་བྱེད་པ་
accident (collision)	dhong-tu gyâb-pa	གདོང་ཐུག་རྒྱབ་པ་
accommodation	dhö-nay	སྡོད་གནས་
across	tay-la	འཁྱོང་ལ་
activist	hoor-tsön-chen	ཧུར་བརྩོན་ཅན་
adaptor	log-shoog cho-ya	གློག་ཤུགས་གཅོག་ཡག
addiction	kya-lâng sho-wa	རྒྱུན་ལྭ་ཤོར་བ་
address	ka-châng	ཁ་བྱང་
to admire	tö-pa	བསྟོད་པ་
admission	nâng zü	ནང་འཇུག་
to admit	ngö len-pa	ངོས་ལེན་པ་
adult	na-so lön-pa	ན་སོ་ལོན་པ་
advantage	kay-pen	ཁེ་ཕན་
advice	lâb-ja	བསླབ་བྱ་
aeroplane	nâm-du	གནམ་གྲུ་
afraid, to be	shay-nâng kye-wa	ཞེད་སྣང་སྐྱེ་བ་
after	je-la	རྗེས་ལ་
(in the) afternoon	chi-toh(-la)	ཕྱི་དྲོ(་ལ)
this afternoon	te-ring chi-toh	དེ་རིང་ཕྱི་དྲོ་
again	yâng-kya	ཡང་སྐྱར་
against	khâ-te-tu	ཁ་གཏད་དུ་
age	lo	ལོ་
aggressive	tsen-po wâng-yö	བཙན་པོ་དབང་ཡོད་

A

(a while) ago	(dü gay) ngön-tu	(དུས་ལ་གཤི)སྔོན་དུ
(half an hour) ago	(chu-tsö chay-ka) ngön-tu	(ཆུ་ཚོད་ཕྱེད་ཀ)སྔོན་དུ
(three days) ago	(nyin soom) ngön-tu	(ཉིན་གསུམ)སྔོན་དུ
to agree	mö-thün chay-pa	མོས་མཐུན་བྱེད་པ

I don't agree.
nga mö-thün may ང་མོས་མཐུན་མེད

Agreed!
mö-thün yö མོས་མཐུན་ཡོད

agriculture	shing-lay	ཞིང་ལས
ahead	dün-la	མདུན་ལ
aid (help)	rog-râm	རོགས་རམ
air	loong	རླུང
air-conditioned	dâng-log	གྲང་ལྟོག
air mail	nâm-dâg	གནམ་སྒྲུག
airport	nâm-tâng	གནམ་ཐང
airport tax	nâm-tâng tel	གནམ་ཐང་ཁྲལ
alarm clock	lâng-da tong-ya chu-tsö	ལང་འད་གཏོང་ཡག་ཆུ་ཚོད
all	tshâng-ma	ཚང་མ
allergy	phog-nay	ཕོག་ནད
to allow	chay chog-pa	བྱེད་ཆོག་པ

It's allowed.
cho-gi ray ཆོག་གི་རེད

It's not allowed.
cho-gi ma-ray ཆོག་གི་མ་རེད

almost	phay-chay	ཕལ་ཆེར
alone	chig-po	གཅིག་པོ
already	tsar-wa	ཚར་བ
also	yâng	ཡང
altitude	gyâm-tsö ngö-nay	རྒྱ་མཚོ་ངོས་ནས་འཛིན
	tsi-pay tho-tsay	བརྩི་པའི་མཐོ་ཚད
always	tâg-pah	རྟག་པར
amateur	lay-sho-la ka-lay	ལས་ཤོར་ལ་བཀག་ལས
	gya-khen	རྒྱག་མཁན
ambassador	shoong-tsâp	གཞུང་ཚབ

190

A

among	nâng-nay	བརྣགས
anarchist	si-shoong may-pay ring-loog	སྲིད་གནོན་མེད་པའི་རིང་ལུགས
ancient	na nga-mo	གནའ་སྔོན
and	dâng	དང
angry	loong lâng-po	ཀྲོང་ལང་པོ
animals	dü-do • sem-chen	དུད་འགྲོ • སེམས་ཅན
annual	lo-ray	ལོ་རེར
answer	len	ལན
ant	(bu) tog-ma	(འབུ)གྲོག་མ
antibiotics	nay-bu gok-men	ནད་འབུ་འགོག་སྨན
	an-ti ba-ye ot-ik	ཨེན་ཊི་བ་ཡེ་འོཊིག
antiques	na-nga-mö	གནའ་སྔ་མོ
antiseptic	nyen-ka gok-chay-men	མཉེན་ཀ་འགོག་བྱེད་སྨན
any	kâ-ray yi-nay	གར་ཡིན་ནས
apartment	dö-khâng cha-tsâng-chi	སྡོད་ཁང་ཚོ་ཚང་གཅིག
appointment	dü-kâg thoog-tay	དུས་ཀག་ཐུག་འཛད
archaeological	na ngo-la tâg-pay	གནའ་རྡོ་ལ་བལྟག་པའི
	rig-nay	རིག་གནས
architect	ahr-lay cha-gö-pa	འར་ལས་ཆ་འགོད་པ
architecture	ahr-lay lâg-tsay	འར་ལས་ལག་རྩལ
to argue	tsö-pa gyâk-pa	རྩོད་པ་རྒྱག་པ
arm	lâg-nga • lâg-pa	ལག་ང • ལག་པ
to arrive	lep-pa • jor-wa	སྙེབས་པ • འབྱོར་བ
art	lâg-tsay	ལག་རྩལ
art gallery	lâg-tsay dem-tön-khâng	ལག་རྩལ་འགྲེམ་སྟོན་ཁང
artist	ri-mo kay-pa • gyu-tsay-wa	རི་མོ་མཁས་པ • རྒྱུ་རྩལ་པ
artwork	ri-mo • lâg-sö	རི་མོ • ལག་བཟོས
ashtray	tha-ma dâb-sa-nö	ཐ་མ་འདབ་ས་སྣོད
to ask (for something)	ray-kü shu-wa	རེ་སྐུལ་ཞུབ
to ask (a question)	di pa	འདྲི
aspirin	nyen-jom-men es-pi-rin	མཉེན་འཇོམས་སྨན་ཨེས་པི་རིན
asthmatic	oog-tsâng-nay na chog-cho	དབུགས་འཚང་ནད་ན་ཚོག་ཆོག
atmosphere	ba-nâng loong	བར་སྣང་རླུང
aunt	su-mo	སུ་མོ
autumn (fall)	tön-ga	སྟོན་ཀ
awful	shay-nâng-chen	ཞེ་སྣང་ཅན

D I C T I O N A R Y

B

baby	pu-gu	ཕྲུ་གུ
baby food	pu-gü kha-la	ཕྲུ་གུའི་ཁ་ལག
baby powder	pu-gü soog-poh	ཕྲུ་གུའི་གཟུགས་པོའི
	chu-ya po-tah	ཕྱག་ལྱ་པོ་ཏར
babysitter	pu-gu ta-khen • bu-zi	ཕྲུ་གུ་བལྟ་མཁན • བུ་ཛི
back (body)	gyâb	རྒྱབ
at the back (behind)	gyâb-la	རྒྱབ་ལ
backpack	gya-phay	རྒྱབ་ཕད
bad	dhuk-cha	སྡུག་ཆགས
bag	bag-la • jo-la	འབག་ལག • ཇོ་ལ
baggage	tog-tay	དོག་ཁྱེར
baggage claim	tog-tay len-sa	དོག་ཁྱེར་ལེན་ས
bakery	bâg-leb tsong-khâng	བག་ལེབ་ཚོང་ཁང
balcony	tsom-chen	ཚོམས་ཆེན
ball (sport)	po-lo	པོ་ལོ
bank	ngü-khâng	དངུལ་ཁང
banknotes	ngü-shog	དངུལ་ཤོག
bar	châng-khâng	ཆང་ཁང
bath	soog-po tru-wa	གཟུགས་པོ་འཁྲུད
bathing suit	chu-kay gyön-chay	ཆུ་ཁྲུས་གྱོན་ཆས
bathroom	trü-khâng	ཁྲུས་ཁང
battery	log-shu-men • bay-ti-ri	གློག་ཤུ་མན • བྱེ་ཊི་རི
to be	yin/ray • yö/du •	ཡིན/རེད • ཡོད/འདུག •
	yö-ray	ཡོད་རེད
beach	tsho-khay chay-tâng	མཚོ་ཁའི་བྱེ་ཐང
beautiful	nying je-po	སྙིང་རྗེ་པོ
because	gâng-yin say-na	གང་ཡིན་ཟེར་ན
bed	nye-ti	ཉལ་ཁྲི
bedroom	nye-khâng	ཉལ་ཁང
before	ngön-la	སྔོན་ལ
beggar	trâng-po	སྤྲང་པོ
to begin	gon-zoog	འགོ་འཛུགས
behind	gyâb-la	རྒྱབ་ལ
below	wog-la	འོག་ལ
beside	tih-la	འགྲིགས་ལ
best	yâg-shö	ཡག་ཤོས

English	Tibetan	
bet	gyen jog-pa	རྒྱན་འཇོག་པ
better	yâg-pa	ཡག་པ
bicycle	kâng-ga-ri	ཀང་ག་རི
big	chen-po	ཆེན་པོ
bill (account)	ngü-tsi	དངུལ་རྩིས
binoculars	gyâng-shay	རྒྱང་ཤེལ
biography	nâm-tar	རྣམ་ཐར
bird	chi-hu	བྱིའུ
birth certificate	kye-tse lâg-kay	སྐྱེ་ཚེས་ལག་འཁྱེར
birthday	kye-kah-nyin	སྐྱེ་སྐར་ཉིན
bite	so gyâb-pa	སོ་བརྒྱབ་པ
black	nâg-po	ནག་པོ
B&W (film)	(phing-sho)	(ཕིང་ཤོག)
	tshön-ta may-pa	ཚོན་མདངས་མེད
blanket	nye-chay • kâm-ba-li	ཉལ་ཆས • ཀམ་པ་ལི
to bleed	tâg zâg-pa	ཁྲག་འཛག་པ
to bless	jin-gi lâb-pa	བྱིན་གྱིས་བརླབས་པ
blind	long-wa • shar-wa	ལོང་བ • ཞར་བ
blood	tâg	ཁྲག
blood group	tâg-rig	ཁྲག་རིགས
blood pressure	tâg-shay	ཁྲག་ཤེད
blood test	tâg tâg-chay	ཁྲག་བརྟག་དཔྱད
blue	ngön-po	སྔོན་པོ
to board (ship etc)	nâng shoog-pa	ནང་ཞུགས་པ
boarding pass	dhö-say pa-say	སྡོད་སའི་པ་སེ
boat	dru • dru-zing	གྲུ • གྲུ་གཟིངས
body	soog-po • lü	གཟུགས་པོ • ལུས

> Bon appetit!
> shay-la nye-bo nâng
> བཞེས་ལ་སྙིང་པོར་གནང
>
> Bon voyage!
> toh-bo-chay peb-nâng
> སྟོབ་པོ་ཆེར་ཕེབས་གནང

bone	rü-gok	རུས་གོག
book	teb	དེབ
to book	ngön-ngâg chay-pa	སྔོན་མངགས་བྱེད་པ
bookshop	teb tsong-khâng	དེབ་ཚོང་ཁང
boots	lhâm-gok yün-ring •	ལྷམ་གོག་ཡུ་རིང •
	ju-ta yu-ring	འཇུ་ཏ་དུ་ཡུ་རིང

border	sa-tsâm	ས་མཚམས།
bored	nyob-pa	ཉོབ་པ།
boring	nyob-to	ཉོབ་ཏོ།
to borrow	yâr-wa	གཡར་བ།
both	nyi-ga	གཉིས་ཀ
bottle	shay-tâm	ཤེལ་དམ།
bottle opener	shay-tâm kha che-yâk	ཤེལ་དམ་ཁ་ཕྱེ་ཡག
(at the) bottom	thih(-la)	མཐིལ་(ལ)
box	gâm	སྒམ།
boy	bu	བུ
boyfriend	tok-po	གྲོགས་པོ།
branch	ye-ga • yen-la	ཡལ་ག • ཡན་ལག
brave	pah-o	དཔའ་བོ།
bread	bâk-lay	བག་ལེབ།
to break	chog-pa	གཅོག་པ།
breakfast	shog-cha •	ཞོགས་ཇ •
	shog-kay kha-la	ཞོགས་ཀའི་ཁ་ལག
to breathe	oog tong-wa	དབུགས་གཏོང་བ།
bribe	kog-ngan	སྒོག་ངན།
to bribe	kog-ngan tö-pa	སྒོག་ངན་སྟེར་བ།
bridge	sâm-pa	ཟམ་པ།
brilliant	kay-tu phâg-pa	ཁྱད་དུ་འཕགས་པ།
to bring	kay yong-wa	འཁྱེར་ཡོང་བ།
broken	châg-pa	ཆག་པ།
brother	pün-kya-bu	སྤུན་སྐྱ་བུ
brown	moog-po	སྨུག་པོ།
bruise	moog-tig	སྨུག་ཐིག
Buddhist	nâng-pa	ནང་པ།
bug	de-shig	འབུ་ཞིག
to build	soh-wa	བཟོ་བ།
building	khâng-pa	ཁང་པ།
bus (city)	(dong-kay)	(གྲོང་ཁྱེར་)
	chi-chö lâng-kho	སྤྱི་སྤྱོད་རླངས་འཁོར་
bus (intercity)	(dong-kay nâng-ku)	(གྲོང་ཁྱེར་ནང་ཁུལ་)
	do-khen	འགྲོ་མཁན
	chi-chö lâng-kho	སྤྱི་སྤྱོད་རླངས་འཁོར་

bus station	chi-chö lâng-kho bâb-tsoog	སྤྱི་སྤྱོད་ལྡང་འཁོར་ འབབ་ཚུགས་
bus stop	chi-chö lâng-kho kâg-sa	སྤྱི་སྤྱོད་ལྡང་འཁོར་བཀག་ས་
business	tsong	ཚོང་
businessperson	tsong-pa	ཚོང་པ་
busy	tay-wa	ཏེལ་བ་
but	yin-ma-yâng • yin-nay	ཡིན་ན་ཡང་
butterfly	chay-ma-leb	ཕྱེ་མ་ལེབ་
buttons	teb-ji	ཏེབ་ཇི་
to buy	nyo-wa	ཉོ་བ་

I'd like to buy ...
nga ... nyon-dhö yö   ང་ ... ཉོ་འདོད་ཡོད།
Where can I buy a ticket?
ti-ka-si nyo-sa ka-bah yö-ray   ཏི་ཀ་སི་ཉོ་ས་ག་བར་ཡོད་རེད།

C

cafe	cha (tsong-)khâng	ཇ་(ཚོང་)ཁང་
calendar	lo-tho	ལོ་ཐོ་
camera	par-chay	པར་ཆས་
camera operator	par gya-khen	པར་རྒྱག་མཁན་
camera shop	par (tsong-)khâng	པར་(ཚོང་)ཁང་
to camp	gur gyâb-nay dö-pa	གུར་བརྒྱབ་ནས་སྡོད་པ་

Can we camp here?
day gur gyâb-nay   འདིར་གུར་བརྒྱབ་ནས་བསྡད་
de-na di-gi re-bay   ན་འགྲིག་གི་རེད་པས།

campsite	gur gyâb-sa sa-cha	གུར་རྒྱབ་ས་ས་ཆ་
can (to be able)	thoob-pa • nü-pa	ཐུབ་པ་ • ནུས་པ་

We can do it.
nga-tsö thoob-ki ray   ང་ཚོས་ཐུབ་ཀྱི་རེད །
I can't do it.
ngay thoob-sa ma-ray   ངས་ཐུབ་ས་མ་རེད།

can (aluminium)	châg-tin	ལྕགས་ཏིན་
can opener	châg-tin kha che-yak	ལྕགས་ཏིན་ཁ་ཕྱེ་ཡག
to cancel	chi-ten chay-pa	ཕྱིར་འཐེན་བྱེད་པ་
candle	yân-lah	ཡང་ལ་

car	mo-ta	ཨོ་ཊ
car owner's title	mo-ta dâg-pö ming	ཨོ་ཊ་བདག་པོའི་མིང
car registration	mo-tay teb-kye	ཨོ་ཊའི་དེབ་སྐྱེ
to care (about)	sâb-sâb chay	གཟབ་གཟབ་བྱེད
to care (for someone)	tse-doong chay-pa	བརྩེ་གདུང་བྱེད་པ

Careful!
sâb-sâb nâng — གཟབ་གཟབ་གནང

caring	tse-doong-chen	བརྩེ་གདུང་ཅན
to carry	kay-wa	འཁྱེར་བ
carton	sho-gâm	ཤོག་སྒམ
cashier	ngü-nyay	དངུལ་གཉེར
cassette	teb-tâg	ཊེབ་ཐག
castle	khâr-zong	མཁར་རྫོང
cat	shi-mi	ཞི་མི
cathedral	ye-shu lha-khâng	ཡེ་ཤུ་ལྷ་ཁང
cave	dâg-phuk	བྲག་ཕུག
CD	si-di	སི་ཌི
to celebrate	ten-del chay	རྟེན་འབྲེལ་བྱེད
centimetre	sin-ti-mi-tar	སིན་ཊི་མི་ཊར
ceramic	za-sö	རྫ་བཟོས
certificate	lâg-kay	ལག་ཁྱེར
chair	koob-kyâg	ཀུབ་ཀྱག
chance (opportunity)	go-kâb	གོ་སྐབས
to change	je-wa • gyur-wa	བརྗེ་བ • འགྱུར་བ
change (coins)	ngü sil-ma je-wa	དངུལ་སིལ་མ་བརྗེ
changing rooms	khâng-pa je-wa	ཁང་པ་བརྗེ
charming	sem goog-pa	སེམས་དགུག་པ
to chat up	kay-cha shö-pa	སྐད་ཆ་ཤོད་པ
cheap	kay-po	ཁེ་པོ
to cheat	go-kor tong-wa	མགོ་སྐོར་གཏོང་བ

Cheat!
go kor-sha — མགོ་སྐོར་ཤ

to check	shib-shay chay-pa	ཞིབ་བཤེར་བྱེད་པ
checkpoint	gâ-go	བག་སྒོ
cheese	chu-ra	ཕྱུར་བ

chemist	men tsong-khâng	སྨན་ཚོང་ཁང་
chest	bâng-go	བྲང་ཁོག
chewing gum	gyik chi-ri	འགྱིག་ཅི་རིས
chicken	cha-te	བྱ་ཕྲུག
child/children	pu-gu	ཕྲུ་གུ
childminding	pu-gu ta-khen	ཕྲུ་གུ་བལྟ་མཁན
chocolate	chok-let	ཅོག་ལེཏ
to choose	dem-pa	འདེམས་པ
Christian	yig-shu	ཡེ་ཤུ
church	lha-khâng	ལྷ་ཁང
cigarettes	tha-ma	ཐ་མག
cigarette papers	tha-ma shu-gu	ཐ་མའི་ཤོག་གུ
cinema	lo-nyen	གློག་བརྙན
citizenship	mi-say	མི་སེར
city	dong-kay	གྲོང་ཁྱེར
city centre	dong-kay-kyil	གྲོང་ཁྱེར་དཀྱིལ
civil rights	mi-say thob-tâng	མི་སེར་ཐོབ་ཐང
class	de-rim	གྲལ་རིམ
clean	tsâng-ma	གཙང་མ
client	tsong-shah	ཚོང་ཤག
cliff	yang sah-po	གཡང་ས་བརྫར་པོ
to climb	zeg-pa	འཛེག་པ
clock	chu-tsö	ཆུ་ཚོད
closed	go gyâb-pa	སྒོ་རྒྱབ་པ
clothing	du-log	དུགས་ལོག
clothing store	du-log tsong-khâng	དུགས་ལོག་ཚོང་ཁང
cloud	tin-pa	སྤྲིན་པ
cloudy	tin thib-pa	སྤྲིན་པ་འཐིབས་པ
coins	pay-sha sil-ma	དོ་ལ་གསིལ་མ
cold (n)	châm-pa	ཆམ་པ
to have a cold	châm-pa gyâ-pa	ཆམ་པ་རྒྱག་པ
cold (adj)	dâng-mo	གྲང་མོ
cold water	chu dâng-mo	ཆུ་གྲང་མོ

It's cold.		
dâng-mo du		གྲང་མོ་འདུག

colleague	lay-rog	ལས་རོགས
college	tho-lob	མཐོ་སློབ

C

colour	tsön-dog	ཚོན་མདོག
comb	gyook-shay	ཀྲུགས་ཤད
to come	yong-wa	ཡོང་བ
comfortable	kyi-po • de-po	སྐྱིད་པོ • བདེ་པོ
communion	thun-mong-gi long-chö	ཐུན་མོང་གི་ལོངས་སྤྱོད
communist	goong-ten ring-loog	གུང་ཁྲན་རིང་ལུགས
companion	rog-pa	རོགས་པ
company	so-tsong khâng	བཟོ་ཚོང་ཁང
compass	chog-tön khor-lo	ཕྱོགས་སྟོན་འཁོར་ལོ
computer	câm-pu-tah	ཀམ་པུ་ཊར
computer games	câm-pu-tah tse-mo	ཀམ་པུ་ཊར་རྩེད་མོ
concert	ro-yâng to-tön	རོལ་དབྱངས་སྟོན
confession (religious)	shag-pa	བཤགས་པ
to confirm (a booking)	ra-tö	ར་འཕྲོད

Congratulations!
ta-shi de-lek   བཀྲ་ཤིས་བདེ་ལེགས

conservative	lay-pa nying-pa	ལུགས་པ་རྙིང་པ
to be constipated	tsog-pa mi-bâb-pa	བཙོག་པ་མི་འབབ་པ
construction work	so-lay	བཟོ་ལས
consulate	dön-chö	དོན་གཅོད
contraception	kye-go gok-pa	སྐྱེ་སྒོ་འགོག་པ
contraceptives	kye-go gok-chay	སྐྱེ་སྒོ་འགོག་བྱེད
contract	gan-gya	གན་རྒྱ
convent	tsong-du kong-wa	ཚོགས་འདུ་ཀོང་བ
to cook	kha-la so-wa	ཁ་ལག་བཟོ་བ
cool (colloquial)	tsâb-tsoob may-pa	འཚབ་ཚུབ་མེད་པ
corner	sur	ཟུར
corrupt	lhay sho-wa	ལྷད་ཤོར་བ
to cost	gong gyâb-pa	གོང་རྒྱབ་པ

How much does it cost to go to ...?
... doh-wa-la gong kâ-tsay   ...འགྲོ་བ་ལ་གོང་ག་ཚོད
nay-ki ray   གནས་ཀྱི་རེད
It costs a lot.
gong chen-po nay-ki ray   གོང་ཆེན་པོ་གནས་ཀྱི་རེད

cotton	tin-bay	སྲིན་བལ
country	dong-seb	གྲོང་གསེབ

198

ENGLISH – TIBETAN

countryside	dong-seb-kü	�གྲོང་གསེབ་ཀྱི་
cough	lo	གློ་
to count	dâng-ga tsi-pa	གྲངས་ཀ་རྩི་པ་
court (legal)	tim-khâng	ཁྲིམས་ཁང་
cow	ba-choog	བ་ཕྱུགས་
crafts	lâg-shay	ལག་ཤེས་
crafty	yo-gyu tsa-po	གཡོ་སྒྱུ་ཚ་པོ་
crag	dâg-rong	བྲག་རོང་
crazy	nyön-pa	སྨྱོན་པ་
credit card	bu-lön shog-jâng	བུ་ལོན་ཤོག་བྱང་

> **Do you accept credit cards?**
> bu-lön shog-jâng-tog | བུ་ལོན་ཤོག་བྱང་ཏོག་རིན་པ་
> rim-pa tay-na di-gi re-bay | སྤྲད་ན་འགྲིག་གི་རེད་པས།

cross (angry)	loong lâng-wa	ལུང་ལངས་བ་
cup	ka-yö	དཀར་ཡོལ་
current affairs	sân-gyur	གསར་འགྱུར་
customs	gom-söl	གོམས་སྲོལ་
to cut	toob-pa	གཏུབ་པ་
to cycle	kâng ga-ri shön-pa	རྐང་རི་འི་བཞོན་པ་
cyclist	kâng ga-ri tong-khen	རྐང་རི་འི་གཏོང་མཁན་

D

dad	pa-la	པ་ལགས་
daily	nyin-tah	ཉིན་ལྟར་
dairy products	kar-chu	དཀར་ཆུ་
to dance	shay tâb-pa	གཞས་འཐབ་པ་
dangerous	nyan-ga	ཉེན་ག་
dark	nâ-goong	ནག་ཁུང་
date (appointment)	dü-kâg	དུས་ཚོད་
date (time)	tshe-pa	ཚེས་པ་
date of birth	kye-tse	སྐྱེ་ཚེས་
to date (someone)	dü-kâg gya-pa	དུས་ཚོད་རྒྱག་པ་
daughter	bu-mo	བུ་མོ་
dawn	nâm lâng-dü	ནམ་ལངས་དུས་
day	nyin-ma	ཉིན་
day after tomorrow	nâng-nyin	གནངས་ཉིན་
day before yesterday	kay nyin-mo	ཁེ་ཉིན་མོ་
in (six) days	nyin (doog) nâng	ཉིན་（དྲུག་）ནང་

D I C T I O N A R Y

199

dead	shi-wa	ཤི་བ
deaf	wön-ba	འོན་པ
to deal	de-wa chay-pa	འབྲེལ་བ་བྱེད་པ
death	chi-wa	འཆི་བ
to decide	tâg-chö chay-pa	ཐག་ཆོད་བྱེད་པ
deep	ting	གཏིང
deforestation	shing-na may-pa so-wa	ཤིང་ནགས་མེད་པ་བཟོ་བ
delay	gyâng-wa	འགྱང་བ
delirious	sem-toog chem-po	སེམས་ཁ་འཁྲུགས་ཆེན་པོ
democracy	mâng-tso ring-loog	དམངས་གཙོའི་རིང་ལུགས
demonstration	ngâm-tön	ངམ་སྟོན
dental floss	so-trü dar-kü	སོ་ཁྲུད་དར་བཀུད
dentist	so ahm-chi	སོ་ཨེམ་ཆི
to deny	kay-len mi-chay-pa	ཁས་ལེན་མི་བྱེད་པ
deodorant	lü-di gok-men	ལུས་དྲི་བཀག་སྨན་ཉི་པོ་དོ་རེན
	di-yo do-ren	
to depart (leave)	chi thön-pa	ཕྱིར་ཐོན་པ
department store	de-tsen tsong-khâng	སྡེ་ཚན་ཚོང་ཁང
departure	thön-yak	ཐོན་ཡག
descendant	mi-gyü	མི་རྒྱུད
desert	chay-tâng	བྱེ་ཐང
design	cha-shi ding-wa	བཀར་གཞི་འདིང་བ
destination	leb-sa	སླེབས་ས
to destroy	tor-shi tong-wa	གཏོར་བཤིག་གཏོང་བ
detail	shib-ta	ཞིབ་ཕྲ
diabetic	chay-ma ka-ray na-tsa	བྱེ་མ་ཀ་རེའི་ན་ཚ
diaper (nappy)	pu-gü chu-den	ཕྲུ་གུའི་ཆུ་གདན
diarrhoea	nyâng-shay	རྒྱུ་བཤལ
diary	nyin-to gö-teb	དཀར་ཆ
dice/die	sho	ཤོ
dictionary	tshing-dzö	ཚིག་མཛོད
different	mi-da-wa	མི་འདྲ་བ
difficult	khâg-po	དཀའ་པོ
dinner	gong-da kha-la	དགོང་དགའ་ཁ་ལག
direct	ka-thoog	ཀ་ཐུག
director	wu-zin	དབུ་འཛིན
dirty	tsog-ba-chen	བཙོག་པ་ཅན
disabled	wâng-po kyön-chen	དབང་པོ་སྐྱོན་ཅན

D

disadvantage	kyön	སྐྱོན་
discount	gong châg-pa	གོང་ཆག་པ
to discover	tsay-wa	བཙལ་བ
discrimination	ten-kye • yen-je	བསྟེན་བཀྱེ • དབྱེ་འབྱེད
disease	nay	ནད་
diving	chu-ting do-wa	ཆུ་གཏིང་འགྲོ་བ
dizzy	goh-yu kho-wa	མགོ་ཡུ་འཁོར་བ
to do	chay-ya	བྱེད་ཡག

> **What are you doing?**
> kâ-ray chay-ki yö
> ག་རེ་བྱེད་ཀྱི་ཡོད
>
> **I didn't do it.**
> ngay chay-gyu ma-choong
> ངས་བྱེད་རྒྱུ་མ་བྱུང

doctor	ahm-chi	ཨེམ་ཆི
dog	kyi	ཁྱི
dole	lay-may-phog	ལས་མེད་ཕོགས
(unemployment benefits)		
door	go	སྒོ
dope (drugs)	si-men • nye-tha	བསི་སྨན • ཉེ་ཐག
double	nyi-tsâg • nyi-dâb	ཉིས་ཚེགས • ཉིས་ལྡབ
double bed	mi-nyi shong-say nye-ti	མི་གཉིས་ཤོང་སའི་ཉལ་ཁྲི
double room	mi-nyi dö-say khâng-mi	མི་གཉིས་སྡོད་སའི་ཁང་མིག
downhill	too	ཐུར
dozen	dar-tsen	བདར་ཚན
drama	tâb-shoong • dhö-gar	བཏབ་གཤུང • སྟོས་གར
dramatic	dhö-ga tâb-pa tar	སྟོས་གར་བཏབ་པ་ལྟར
to dream	mi-lâm tong-wa	རྨི་ལམ་གཏོང་བ
dress	mo-chay	མོ་ཆས
drink	toong-ya	འཐུང་ཡག
to drink	toong-wa	འཐུང་བ
to drive	mo-ta tong-wa	མོ་ཊ་གཏོང་བ
drivers licence	mo-ta tong-ya lâg-kay	མོ་ཊ་གཏོང་ཡག་ལག་ཁྱེར
drug(s)	si-men	བསི་སྨན
drug addiction	si-men sa-ya kya-lâng sho-wa	བསི་སྨན་ཟ་ཡག་སྐྱ་ལངས་ཤོར་བ
drug dealer	nye-tha dem-pay chay-khen	ཉེ་ཐག་འགྲེམས་པའི་བྱེད་མཁན

D I C T I O N A R Y

drums	nga	≅
to be drunk	ra si-wa	ར་བཟིབ
to dry (clothes)	(du-log) kâm-po so-wa	(དུག་ལོག)སྐམ་པོ་བཟོ་བ
dummy (pacifier)	jib-ru	ཞིབ་རུ

E

each	re-re	རེ་རེ
ear	ahm-chog	ཨམ་ཆོག
early	nga-po	སྔ་པོ

> It's early.
> nga-po ray-sha   སྔ་པོ་རེད་ཤག

earrings	ahm-cho-gyen	ཨམ་ཆོག་རྒྱན
ears	ahm-chog	ཨམ་ཆོག
Earth	sa	ས
earth (soil)	sa	ས
earthquake	sa-yom	ས་ཡོམ
east	shâr	ཤར
easy	lay-la-po	ལས་སླ་པོ
to eat	sa-wa	ཟ་བ
economy	pay-jor	དཔལ་འབྱོར
education	shay-yön • lob-jong	ཤེས་ཡོན • སློབ་སྦྱོང
elections	wö-dem	འོས་འདེམས
electricity	log	གློག
elevator (lift)	log ken-za	གློག་སྐས་འཛེགས
embarrassed	ka kyeng-pa	ཁ་སྐྱེངས་པ
embassy	shoong-tsab	གཞུང་ཚབ
emergency	za-dâg	ཛ་དྲག
employee	lay-chay-pa	ལས་བྱེད་པ
employer	lay-ka trö-khen	ལས་ཀ་སྤྲོད་མཁན
empty	tong-pa	སྟོང་པ
end	ta-joog	མཐའ་འཇུག
to end	ta-joog dil-wa	མཐའ་འཇུག་དིལ་བ
endangered species	tsa-tong do-way nyen-ga leb-pay sem-chen	རྩ་སྟོང་འགྲོ་བའི་ཉེན་ཁ་ལེབ་པའི་སེམས་ཅན
engine	trü-kho ah-ma	འཕྲུལ་འཁོར་ཨ་མ
English	in-ji	དབྱིན་ཇི
to enjoy (oneself)	(rang-râng) kyi-po tong-wa	(རང་རང)སྐྱིད་པོ་གཏོང་བ

| enough | dig-pa | འགྲིགས་པ |

Enough!
dig-song འགྲིགས་སོང་

to enter	zü-pa	འཛུལ་བ
entertaining	nâng-wa kyi-kyi	སྣང་བ་སྐྱིད་སྐྱིད
envelope	yi-gok	ཡི་གོགས
environment	khor-yoog	ཁོར་ཡུག
epileptic	sa-dib	གཟའ་གྲིབ
equal opportunity	thob-tâng da-nyâm	ཐོབ་ཐང་འདྲ་མཉམ
equality	da-nyâm	འདྲ་མཉམ
equipment	lâg-cha	ལག་ཆ
European	eu-rop-mi	ཡུ་རོབ་མི
euthanasia	jâm-sö • jâm-shi	འཇམ་གསོད་ • འཇམ་ཤི
evening	gong-da	དགོང་དག
every day	nyin-tar	ཉིན་ལྟར
example	pay	དཔེ

For example ...
pay sha-na ... དཔེ་བཤད་ན ...

excellent	pay-mi-si yâk-po	དཔེ་མི་སྲིད་ཡག་པོ
exchange	je-len	འཇེ་ལེན
to exchange	je-len gya-pa	འཇེ་ལེན་རྒྱག་པ
exchange rate	ngü-je-gong	དངུལ་འཇེ་གོང
excluded	khong-nay bü-pa	ཁོངས་ནས་བཅུག་པ

Excuse me.
gong-da དགོངས་དག

to exhibit	dem-tön chay-pa	འགྲེམས་སྟོན་བྱེད་པ
exhibition	dem-tön	འགྲེམས་སྟོན
exit	dön-sa	དོན་ས
expensive	gong chen-po	གོང་ཆེན་པོ
to express (one's view)	tön-pa	སྟོན་པ
express mail	nyur-kye-dâg	མྱུར་སྐྱེལ་སྒྲག
eye	mig	མིག

F

face	dong	གདོང་
face cloth (flannel)	dong chi-ray	གདོང་ཕྱིས་རས་
factory	so-ta	བཟོ་གྲྭ
factory worker	so-ta lay-ka chay-khen	བཟོ་གྲྭ་ལས་ཀ་བྱེད་མཁན་
fall (autumn)	tön-ga	སྟོན་ཀ
family	mi-tshâng	མི་ཚང་
famous	kay-ta chem-po	སྐད་གྲགས་ཆེན་པོ་
fan (hand-held)	loong-yâb	རླུང་གཡབ
fan (machine)	loong-khoh	རླུང་འཁོར་
fans (of a team)	ga-po chay-khen	དགའ་པོ་བྱེད་མཁན་
far	ta ring-po	ཐག་རིང་པོ་
farm	shing-ga	ཞིང་ག
farmer	shing-pa	ཞིང་པ
fast	gyok-po	མགྱོགས་པོ་
fat	gyâk-pa	རྒྱགས་པ
father	pa-pha	པཕ
fault (someone's)	non-trü	ནོར་འཁྲུལ་
faulty	kyön sho-wa	སྐྱོན་ཤོར་བ
fear	shay-nâng	ཞེད་སྣང་
to feel	tsor-wa • nyong-wa	ཚོར་བ • མྱོང་བ
feelings	tsor-wa	ཚོར་བ
fence	châg-ri	ལྕགས་རི་
fencing	ti-tse tse-wa	གྲི་རྩེད་རྩེ་བ
festival	dü-chen	དུས་ཆེན
fever	tsha-wa	ཚ་བ
few	nyoong-shay	ཉུང་ཤས
fiance(e)	long-châng sin-pay	ལོང་ཚང་བྱིན་པའི་
	na-ma • mâg-pa	མནའ་མ • མགཔ
fiction	tog-sö	རྟོག་བཟོ
field	shing-ga	ཞིང་ག
fight	gyâk-re	རྒྱག་རེས
to fight	gyâk-re gyâk-pa	རྒྱག་རེས་རྒྱག་པ
to fill	gyong-wa	སྐྱོང་བ
film (camera)	phing-sho	ཕིང་ཤོག
film (cinema)	log-nyen	གློག་བརྙན
filtered	tsâg gyâk-pa	འཚག་གྱག་པ
to find	tsay-wa	བཙལ་བ

fine (money)	chay-pa	ཆད་པ
finger	zu-gu	མཛུབ་གུ
fire	may	མེ
firewood	may-shing	མེ་ཤིང
first	tâng-po	དང་པོ
first-aid kit	ka-toog bay-chö chay-ya	ཁ་ཐུག་བྱེད་ཆོག་བྱེད་ཡག
	men-chö yo-chay	སྨན་བཅོས་ཡོ་བྱད
fish (alive)	nya	ཉ
fish (as food)	nya-sha	ཉ་ཤ
fish shop	nya thong-khâng	ཉ་ཚོང་ཁང
flag	dar-chog	དར་ཆོག
flannel (face cloth)	dong chi-ray	གདོང་ཕྱིས་རས
flat (land etc)	sa thay-thay	ས་མཐེ་མཐེ
flea	kyi-shig	ཁྱི་ཤིག
flashlight (torch)	log-shu	གློག་འཆུ
flight	nâm-du do-ya	གནམ་གྲུ་འགྲོ་ཡག
floor	shay-la • pâng-chay	གཞལ་ལ • པང་བཅལ
floor (storey)	khâng-tog	ཁང་ཐོག
flour (wholemeal)	dro-shib	གྲོ་ཞིབ
flower	may-tog	མེ་ཏོག
fly	dâng-bu	སྦྲང་བུ

> It's foggy.
> moog-pa tig-sha — སྨུག་པ་འཐིབས་ཤ

to follow	je-su dâng-wa	རྗེས་སུ་འབྲང་བ
food	kha-la	ཁ་ལག
foot	kâng-pa	རྐང་པ
football (soccer)	kâng-pol	རྐང་པོལ
footpath	kâng-lâm	རྐང་ལམ
foreign	chi-gye	ཕྱི་རྒྱལ
forest	shing-nâg	ཤིང་ནགས
forever	tâg-tu	རྟག་ཏུ
to forget	jay-pa	བརྗེད་པ

> I forget.
> ngay jay-sha — ངས་བརྗེད་ཤ
>
> Forget about it; Don't worry!
> kay chay-kiy ma-ray • — གལ་བྱེད་ཀྱི་མ་རེད •
> sem-tel ma-chay — སེམས་འཚབ་མ་བྱེད

to forgive	nying-je tâ-wa	སྙིང་རྗེ་བཏང་བ
fortnight	dün-ta nyi-re	བདུན་ཕྲག་གཉིས་རེས
fortune teller	ngön-shay shö-ken	མངོན་ཤེས་ཤོད་མཁན
free (not bound)	râng-wâng thob-pa	རང་དབང་འཐོབ་པ
free (of charge)	rin may-pa	རིན་མེད་པ
to freeze	kyâg choog-pa	འཁྱགས་བཅུགས་པ
friend	tok-po/tok-mo (m/f)	གྲོགས་པོ/གྲོགས་མོ
in front of	dün-lâ	མདུན་ལ
frozen foods	kyák-teb kha-la	འཁྱགས་ཐེབ་ཁ་ལག
full	kheng-pa	ཁེངས་པ
fun	nâng-wa kyi-kyi	སྣང་བ་སྐྱིད་སྐྱིད
for fun	nâng-wa kyi-kyi-chay	སྣང་བ་སྐྱིད་སྐྱིད་ཆེད
to have fun	ten-shig long-wa	བརྟན་ཤིག་ལོང་བ
to make fun of	gö long-ya	གོད་ལོང་ཡག
funeral	ku-phoong kyel-wa	སྐུ་གདུང་སྐྱེལ་བ
furnished	nâng-chay zom-pa	ནང་ཆས་འཛོམས་པ
future	ma-wong-pa	མ་འོངས་པ

G

game	tsay-mo	རྩེད་མོ
(games, sport)		
garage	za-re zo-re loog-sa khâng-pa	ཟ་རེ་ཟོ་རེ་ལུག་ས་ཁང་པ
garbage	gay-nyig	གད་སྙིགས
gardens	doom-ra	ལྡུམ་ར
gas cylinder	gas gâm	གྷེས་སྒམ
gate	go	སྒོ
general	chi-tâng	སྤྱིར་བཏང
gift	lâg-tâg	ལག་རྟགས
girl	bu-mo	བུ་མོ
girlfriend	tok-mo	གྲོགས་མོ
to give	trö-pa • te-wa	སྤྲོད་པ • སྟེར་བ

Could you give me ...?
ngah ... tay-da · ངར་ ... སྟེར་དང

glass	ge-la-si	གྷེ་ལ་སི
to go	doh-wa	འགྲོ་བ
to go out with	nyâm-tu chi-lo doh-wa	མཉམ་ཏུ་ཕྱི་ལོག་འགྲོ་བ

Let's go.
ta doh — དགྲོ།

We'd like to go to ...
ngân-tso ...-la don-dhö yö — དཚོ ...ལ་འགྲོ་འདོད་ཡོད།

Go straight ahead.
ka-toog do-shi — ཁ་ཐུག་འགྲོ་ཤིག

goal	mik-yü	དམིགས་ལྱུལ
goalkeeper	go kâg-khen	སྒོ་ལྕགས་ལྡན
goat	ra	ར
God	kön-chok	དཀོན་མཆོག
of gold	say-gi	གསེར་གྱི
good	yâg-po	ཡག་པོ

Good afternoon.
chi-to de-lek — ཕྱི་དྲོ་བདེ་ལེགས།

Good evening.
gong-to de-lek — དགོང་དྲོ་བདེ་ལེགས།

Good morning.
nga-to de-lek — སྔ་དྲོ་བདེ་ལེགས།

Good night.
sim-ja nâng-go — གཟིམ་ཇ་གནང་རྒོ

government	shoong	གཞུང
gram	ga-râm	གྲམ
grandchild	pu-gü pu-gu	ཕུ་གུའི་ཕུ་གུ
grandfather	po-po	པོ་པོ
grandmother	mo-mo	མོ་མོ
grapes	gün-doom	རྒུན་འབྲུམ
grass	tsa	རྩ
grave	du-trö	དུར་ཁྲོད
great	chen-po	ཆེན་པོ

Great!
yâk-po choong-sha — ཡག་པོ་བྱུང་ཤག

green	jâng-gu	ལྗང་ཁུ
greengrocer	ngo-tse tsong-khâng	སྔོ་ཚེ་ཚོང་ཁང
grey	kya-wo	སྐྱ་བོ
to guess	tsö-pâg chay-pa	ཚོད་དཔག་བྱེད་པ

H

guide (person)	lâm-tön-pa	ལམ་སྟོན་པ
guidebook	lâm-tön-teb	ལམ་སྟོན་དེབ
guide dog	long-wa ti-khen-kyi	ལོང་བ་འཁྲིད་
guided trek	kâng-lâm do de-po	རྐང་ལམ་འགྲོ་འདེ་པོ
guitar	da-nyan • pi-wâng	སྒྲ་སྙན • པི་ཝང
gym	lü-tse	ལུས་རྩལ
gymnastics	lü-tse-gi	ལུས་རྩལ་གྱི

H

hair	ta	སྐྲ
hairbrush	ta-shay phâg-se	སྐྲ་བཤད་ཕགས་སེ
half	chay-ka	ཕྱེད་ཀ
half a litre	li-tar chay-ka	ལི་ཊར་ཕྱེད་ཀ
to hallucinate	trü-nâng shâ-wa	འཁྲུལ་སྣང་ཤར་བ
ham	phâg-sha dü-ma	ཕག་ཤ་བསྡུས་མ
hammer	tho-wa	ཐོ་བ
hand	lâg-pa	ལག་པ
handbag	lâg-kay bag-la	ལག་འཁྱེར་འབེགལག
handicrafts	lâg-shay	ལག་ཤེས
handmade	lâg-sö	ལག་བཟོས
handsome	zay-po	མཛེས་པོ
happy	kyi-po	སྐྱིད་པོ

> Happy Birthday!
> kye-kah-nyin ta-shi de-lek   སྐྱེས་སྐར་ཉིན་བཀྲ་ཤིས་བདེ་ལེགས

harbour	dru-ka	གྲུ་ཀ
hard (not soft)	teg-po	མཁྲེགས་པོ
harness	ta-chay	རྟ་ཆས
harassment	nye-chö	བརྙས་བཅོས
to have	yö-pa	ཡོད་པ

> Do you have ...?
> kay-râng-la ... yö-bay   ཁྱེད་རང་ལ ... ཡོད་པ
>
> I have ...
> nga-la ... yö   ང་ལ ... ཡོད

| he | kho | ཁོ |
| head | go | མགོ |

headache	go-na	མགོ་ནད།
health	trö-ten	འཕྲོད་བསྟེན།
to hear	ahm-chog go-wa	ཨམ་ཅོག་གོ་བ
heart	nying	སྙིང་
heat	tsha-wa	ཚ་བ
heater	tsha-log	ཚ་ལོག
heavy	ji-kog	ལྗིད་པོག

Hello.
ta-shi de-lek   བཀྲ་ཤིས་བདེ་ལེགས།

Hello! (answering telephone)
ha-lo   ཧ་ལོ

| helmet | châg sha-mo | ལྕགས་ཞྭ་མོ |
| to help | rog nâng-wa | རོགས་གནང་བ |

Help!
rog nâng-da   རོགས་གནང་དང་།

herbs	men-tsa	སྨན་རྩ
herbalist	men-tsa kay-pa	སྨན་རྩ་མཁས་པ
here	day	འདིར་
heroin	nye-tha hi-ro-yen	ཉེ་ཐ་ཧི་རོ་ཡེན
heroin addict	nye-tha hi-ro-yen-la	ཉེ་ཐ་ཧི་རོ་ཡེན་ལ་སྨྱོ་གཡེང་
	kyâg-lâng shoh tsa-khen	ཁོང་ཚོར་མཁན
high (altitude)	tho-po	མཐོ་པོ
high school	tho-rim lob-ta	མཐོ་རིམ་སློབ་གྲྭ
to hike	kâng-drö gyâk-pa	རྐང་འགྲོས་རྒྱག་པ
hiking boots	kâng-drö gyâk-dü	རྐང་འགྲོས་རྒྱག་དུས
	gyön-ya lhâm-ko	གྱོན་ཡ་ལྷམ་ཀོ
hiking routes	kâng-drö lâm	རྐག་འགྲོས་ལམ
hill	ri	རི
Hindu	hin-du	ཧིན་དུ
to hire	yâr-wa	གཡར་བ
to hitchhike	drü-pa tay-po ten-nay	འགྲུལ་པ་མཐོ་པོ་བསྟེན་ནས
	mo-ta-nâng do-wa	མོ་ཊ་ནང་འགྲོ་བ
holiday (vacation)	goong-seng	གུང་གསེང
homeless	kyim-may	ཁྱིམ་མེད
homosexual	phö pho-la châg-pa chay-pa	ཕོ་ཕོ་ལ་ཆགས་པ་བྱེད་པ
honey	dâng-tsi	སྦྲང་རྩི

horrible	dhuk-cha	སྡུག་ཆགས་
horse	ta	རྟ་
horse riding	ta shön-pa	རྟ་བཞོན་པ་
hospital	men-khâng	སྨན་ཁང་
private hospital	gay-gi men-khâng	རྒྱེ་གི་སྨན་ཁང་
hot	tsha-po	ཚ་པོ་
hot water	chu tsha-po	ཆུ་ཚ་པོ་

It's hot.
tsha-po du ཚ་པོ་འདུག

to be hot	tsha-wa	ཚ་བ་
house	khâng-pa	ཁང་པ་
housework	nâng-lay	ནང་ལས་
how	kân-te-si	གང་འདྲ་སི་

How do I get to ...?
...-la kân-te-si do-gö-ray ...ལ་གང་འདྲ་སི་འགྲོ་དགོས་རེད།

How do you say ...?
... kân-te-si lâb-gö-ray ... གང་འདྲ་སི་ལབ་དགོས་རེད།

hug	tse-way thâm-pa	བརྩེ་བའི་འཐམ་
human rights	do-wa-mee thob-tâng	འགྲོ་བ་མིའི་ཐོབ་ཐང་
hundred	gya • gya tâm-pa	བརྒྱ་/བརྒྱ་ཐམ་པ་
to be hungry	drö-kog tog-pa	གྲོད་ཁོག་ལྟོགས་པ་
in a hurry	tay-way ngâng	སྟེ་བའི་ངང་
husband	kyo-ga	ཁྱོ་ག

I

ice	kyâg-pa	བ་ཁྱགས་པ་
ice axe	kyâg-pa cho-ya ta-re	བ་ཁྱགས་པ་གཅོག་ཡག་ལ་སྟ་རེ་
ice cream	kyâg-pa ngâ-mo	བ་ཁྱགས་པ་མངར་མོ་
identification	ngo-trö	ངོ་སྤྲོད་
identification card	ngo-trö lâg-kay	ངོ་སྤྲོད་ལག་ཁྱེར་
idiot	len-ta-chen	གླེན་ཏ་གས་ཅན་
if	kay-te	གལ་སྲིད་
ill	na-wa	ན་བ་
immigration	chi-gye-la shi châg-pa	ཕྱི་རྒྱལ་ལ་གནས་ཆགས་པ་
important	kay-chen-po	གལ་ཆེན་པོ་

It's important.		
kay-chen-po ray		གལ་ཆེན་པོ་རེད།
It's not important.		
kay-chen-po ma-ray		གལ་ཆེན་པོ་མ་རེད།

included	nâng-tshü	ནང་ཚུད།
incomprehensible	lö pog mi-thoob-pa	བློ་འགོགས་མི་ཐུབ་པ།
indicator	dâ tong-ya	འཛུག་གཏོང་ཡ།
indigestion	kha-la mi-ju-wa	ཁ་ལག་མི་འཇུ་བ།
industry	so-dra	བཟོ་གྲྭ།
inequality	da-nyâm may-pa	འདྲ་མཉམ་མེད་པ།
to inject	men-khâb gyâk-pa	སྨན་ཁབ་རྒྱག་པ།
injection	men-khâb	སྨན་ཁབ།
injury	may-kyön	རྨས་སྐྱོན།
inside	nâng-lâ	ནང་ལ།
instructor	lob-tön-pa	སློབ་སྟོན་པ།
insurance	in-shu-ren gan-gya	ཨིན་ཤུ་རེན་གན་རྒྱ།
intense	shoog-ta chem-po	ཤུགས་དྲག་ཆེན་པོ།
interesting	nâng-wa dro-po	སྣང་བ་སྒྲོ་པོ།
international	gya-chee	རྒྱལ་སྤྱི།
interview	ngo-toog di-len shu-wa	རྔོ་གཏུགས་འདྲི་ལན་ཞུ་བ།
island	tso-ling	མཚོ་གླིང།
itch	sâb-ra lâng-wa	ཟར་ལངས་བ།
itinerary	drü-shü dü-tsö re-mik	འགྲུལ་བཞུད་དུས་ཚོད་རེ་འུ་མིག

J

jail	tsön-khâng	བཙོན་ཁང།
jealous	tâg-tog	ཕྲག་དོག
jeans	jeen	ཇིན།
jeep	mo-ta jeep	མོ་ཊ་འཇིབ།
jewellery	gyen-jâ	རྒྱན་ཆ།
job	lay-ka	ལས་ཀ
joke	gö toh-po	བཞད་གད་པོ།
to joke	gö long-wa	བཞད་གད་ལོང་བ།
journalist	sar-gö-pa	གསར་འགོད་པ།
journey	drü-kyö	འགྲུལ་སྐྱོད།
judge	tim-pön	ཁྲིམས་དཔོན།

juice	shing-toh khu-wa	ཤིང་ཏོག་ཁུ་བ
to jump	chong-wa	མཆོང་བ
jumper (sweater)	ba-len • o-mo-sü tö-toong	སྦ་ལེན • ཨུ་མོ་སུའི་སྟོད་ཐུང
justice	dâng-dhen	དྲང་བདེན

K

key	di-mig	ལྡེ་མིག
kick	dhog-gya	རྡོག་རྒྱག
to kill	sö-pa	གསོད་པ
kilogram	ki-lo-ga-râm	ཀི་ལོ་གྲ་རམ
kilometre	ki-lo-mi-tar	ཀི་ལོ་མི་ཏར
kind	sem sâng-po	སེམས་བཟང་པོ
kindergarten	chi-so-khâng	ཕྱི་སོ་ཁང
king	gyal-po	རྒྱལ་པོ
kiss	kha-kye • woh	ཁ་སྐྱེ • ཝོ
to kiss	kha kye-wa • woh chay-pa	ཁ་སྐྱེ་བ • ཝོ་བྱེད་པ
kitchen	thâb-tsang	ཐབ་ཚང
kitten	shim-toog	ཞིམ་ཐུག
knapsack	phay-kok	ཕད་ཀོག
knee	pü-mo	པུས་མོ
knife	ti	གྲི
to know	ha go-wa	ཧ་གོ་བ

I don't know.
ha go-ki-may   ཧ་གོ་གི་མེད

L

lace	ju-toh	འཇུར་སྟོག
lake	tsho	མཚོ
lamp	shu-mah	བཞུགས་མར
land	sa-cha	ས་ཆ
language	kay-yig	སྐད་ཡིག
large	chen-po	ཆེན་པོ
last	tha-ma	མཐའ་མ
last month	da-wa ngön-ma	ཟླ་བ་སྔོན་མ
last night	ka-sa gong-ta	ཁ་སང་དགོང་དག
last week	dün-ta ngön-ma	བདུན་ཐག་སྔོན་མ
last year	lo ngön-ma	ལོ་སྔོན་མ

late	chi-po	ཕྱི་པོ
laugh	gay-mo shor-wa	གད་མོ་ཤོར་བ
laundry	tu-log trü-khâng	དགུ་ལོག་འཁྲུ་ཁང
law	tim	ཁྲིམས
lawyer	tim-tsö-pa	ཁྲིམས་རྩོད་པ
lazy	nyob-to • lay-lo-chen	ཉོབ་ཏོ • ལེ་ལོ་ཅན
leader	go-ti	འགོ་འཁྲིད
to learn	châng-wa	སྦྱང་བ
leather	ko-wa	ཀོ་བ
leather goods	gyu-cha ko-wa	རྒྱུ་ཆ་ཀོག
to be left (behind/over)	gyâb-la shâg-pa • shâg-pa	རྒྱབ་ལ་བཞག་པ • བཞག་པ
left (not right)	yön	གཡོན
left-wing	yön-chog sho-kak	གཡོན་ཕྱོགས་ཤོག་ཁག
leg	kâng-pa	རྐང་པ
legalisation	tim-tün	ཁྲིམས་མཐུན
legislation	cha-tim	བཅའ་ཁྲིམས
lens	par-shay	པར་ཤེལ
lesbian	mö mo-la châg-pa chay-khen	མོ་མོ་ལ་ཆགས་པ་བྱེད་མཁན
less	nyoong-wa	ཉུང་བ
letter	yi-ge	ཡི་གེ
liar	kyâg-zün shö-khen	སྐྱག་རྫུན་ཤོད་མཁན
library	pan-zö-khâng	དཔེ་མཛོད་ཁང
lice	shig	ཤིག
to lie	kyâg-zün shö-pa	སྐྱག་རྫུན་ཤོད་པ
life	tse • sog	ཚེ • སྲོག
lift (elevator)	log ken-za	གློག་སྐས་འཛེགས
light (bright)	kar-cha	དཀར་ཆ
light (weight)	yang-po	ཡང་པོ
light (sun/lamp)	wö	འོད
light (clear)	tsön-shi tâng-po	ཚོན་གཞི་དྭངས་པོ
light bulb	log shay-tog	གློག་ཤེལ་དོག
lighter	may-par-yak	མེ་སྤར་ཡག
to like	ga-po chay	དགའ་པོ་བྱེད
line	thig	ཐིག
lips	chu-toh	མཆུ་ཏོ
lipstick	chu-toh choog-ya tsö	མཆུ་ཏོ་བྱུག་ཡ་ཚོས

to listen	ahm-chog nyen-pa	ཨམ་ཙོག་ཉན་པ
little (small)	choong-choong	ཆུང་ཆུང
a little (amount)	nyoong-nyoong	ཉུང་ཉུང
to live (somewhere)	dhö-pa	སྡོད་པ

Long live ...!
... ku-tse ten-pa-sho   ... སྐུ་ཚེ་བརྟན་པར་ཤོག

local	sa-nay	ས་གནས
local city bus	dong-kay nâng-kü	གྲོང་ཁྱེར་ནང་ཁུལ་འགྲོ་མཁན་
	do-khen chi-chö lâng-kho	ཉི་སྤྱོད་རླངས་འཁོར་
location	sa-chog	ས་ཕྱོགས
lock	gon-châg	སྒོ་ལྕགས
to lock	gon-châg gyâk-pa	སྒོ་ལྕགས་རྒྱབ་པ
long	ring-po	རིང་པོ
long distance	sa-tâg ring-po	ས་ཐག་རིང་པོ
long-distance bus	sa-tâg ring-po do-khen	ས་ཐག་རིང་པོ་འགྲོ་མཁན་གྱི་
	chi-chö lâng-kho	སྤྱོད་རླངས་འཁོར་
to look	mik ta-wa	མིག་ལྟ་བ
to look after	je-la mik ta-wa	རྗེས་ལ་མིག་ལྟ་བ
to look for	la mik-ta-wa	ལ་མིག་ལྟ་བ
loose change	see-ma	སིལ་མ
to lose	lâg-pa	བརླགས་པ
loser	phâm-khen	ཕམ་མཁན
loss	gyong	གྱོང

Get lost!
phah gyook-shi   ཕར་རྒྱུགས་ཤིག

a lot	mâng-po	མང་པོ
loud	kay-shoog chen-po	སྐད་ཤུགས་ཆེན་པོ
to love	ga-po chay	དགའ་པོ་བྱེད
lover	ga-po chay-khen	དགའ་པོ་བྱེད་མཁན
low	mah-po	དམའ་པོ
loyal	sha-shen-chen	ཞ་ཞེན་ཅན
luck	lâm-do • loong-ta	ལམ་འགྲོ • རླུང་རྟ
lucky	loong-ta tho-po	རླུང་རྟ་མཐོ་པོ
luggage	tog-tay	དོག་གཏད
luggage lockers	tog-tay gon-châg	དོག་གཏད་སྒོ་ལྕགས
left luggage	tog-tay shâg-pa	དོག་གཏད་བཞག་པ

lump	boor-tog	འབུར་ཏོག
lunch	nyin-goong kha-la	ཉིན་གུང་ཁ་ལག
lunchtime	nyin-goong kha-la dü-tsö	ཉིན་གུང་ཁ་ལག་དུས་ཚོད
luxury	ha-châng kyi-po	ཧ་ཅང་སྐྱིད་པོ

M

machine	trü-khor	འཁྲུལ་འཁོར
mad	nyön-pa	སྨྱོན་པ
made (of)	sö-pay	བཟོས་པའི
magazine	dü-teb	དུས་དེབ
magician	jâ-du tön-khen •	ཇ་འདུ་སྟོན་མཁན •
	gyu-ma-khen	སྒྱུ་མ་མཁན
mail	dâg	སྦྲག
mailbox	dâg-gâm	སྦྲག་སྒམ
main road	lâm-chen	ལམ་ཆེན
main square	mi-mâng zom-sa te-wa	མི་མང་འཛོམས་ས་སྟེ་བ
majority	mâng-che-wa	མང་ཆེ་བ
to make	so-wa	བཟོ་བ
make-up	gün-sâb	གྱུན་གསབ
man	pho	ཕོ
manager	u-zihn	དབུ་འཛིན
manual worker	nge-tsö lay-ka chay-khen	དངལ་རྩོལ་ལས་ཀ་བྱེད་མཁན
many	mâng-po	མང་པོ
map	sâp-ta	ས་བཀྲ

Can you show me on the map?
(sâp-ta di-nâng) tön nâng-da (ས་བཀྲ་འདི་ནང་) སྟོན་གནང་དང

marijuana	nye-ta may-ra wa-na	ཉེ་ཏ་མེ་ར་ཝ་ན
marital status	châng-sa gyâb yö-may	ཆང་ས་བརྒྱབ་ཡོད་མེད
	nay-bâb	གནས་བབ
market	trom	ཁྲོམ
marriage	châng-sa	ཆང་ས
to marry	châng-sa gyâk-pa	ཆང་ས་བརྒྱབ་པ
marvellous	hang-sâng yâk-po	ཧང་སང་ཡག་པོ
massage	lü phur-nye tong-wa	ལུས་ཕུར་ཉེ་གཏོང་བ
mat	sa-den	ས་གདན
to match	chig-pa	གཅིག་པ

matches	tsâg-ta • mu-si	ཙགྶྐ • སུ་སེ

It doesn't matter.
kay chay-ki ma-ray ཀྱེ་བྱེད་ཀྱི་མ་རེད།

What's the matter?
kâ-ray chay song ག་རེ་བྱུས་སོང་།

mattress	bö-den	འབོལ་གདན
maybe	chig chay-na	གཅིག་བྱེད་ན
mayor	dong-kay mi-pön	གྲོང་ཁྱེར་མི་དཔོན
mechanic	trü-lay-pa	འཕྲུལ་ལས་པ
medal	tâg-ma	རྟགས་མ
medicine	men	སྨན
meditation	gom	སྒོམ
to meet	thoog-tay chay-pa	ཐུག་འཕྲད་བྱེད་པ
member	tsog-mi	ཚོགས་མི
menstruation	dha-tsen	ཟླ་མཚན
menu	kha-la-tho	ཁ་ལག་ཐོ
message	kha-len	ཁ་ལན
metal	châg	ལྕགས
meteor	nâm-dho	གནམ་མདའ
metre	mi-tar	མི་ཏར
midnight	tsen-goong	མཚན་གུང
migraine	go-se na-tsa	མགོ་གཤེད་ན་ཚ
military service	dâ-mâg shâb-shu	དམག་མིའི་ཞབས་ཞུ
milk	oh-ma	འོ་མ
millimetre	mi-li-mi-tar	མི་ལི་མི་ཏར
million	sa-ya-chig	ས་ཡ་གཅིག
mind	sem	སེམས
mineral water	te-chu	གཏེར་ཆུ
minute (time)	ka-ma-chig	སྐར་མ་གཅིག
in (five) minutes	ka-ma (ngay) nâng	སྐར་མ་(ལྔའི་)ནང

Just a minute.
teh-si gu-ah ཏོག་ཙམ་སྒུག་ཨ།

mirror	shay-go	ཤེལ་སྒོ
miscarriage	pu-gu nge-nay shor-wa	ཕྲུག་གུ་ངེས་ནས་ཤོར་བ
to miss (feel absence)	den-pa	དྲན་པ

mistake	non-trül	ནོར་འཁྲུལ།
to mix	se-wa • toog-pa	སྲེབ་ • དཀྲུགས།
mobile phone	lâg-pa kye-ya kha-pa	ལག་པར་འཁྱེར་ཡག་ཁ་པར།
modem	mo-dem	མོ་ཌེམ།
moisturising cream	shâb-sö	ཞབ་གསོས།
monastery	gom-pa	དགོན་པ།
money	ngü	དངུལ།
monk	ta-pa	གྲྭ་པ།
month	da-wa	ཟླ་བ།
this month	da-wa-di	ཟླ་བ་འདི།
monument	den-ten	རྟེན་རྟེན།
moon	da-wa	ཟླ་བ།
more	mâng-wa	མང་བ།
morning	nga-toh	སྔ་དྲོ།
mosque	kha-che lha-khâng	ཁ་ཆེ་ལྷ་ཁང་།
mosquito	duk-drâng	དུག་སྦྲང་།
mosquito coil	doog-dâng-pö	དུག་སྦྲང་སྤོས།
mosquito net	nye-gur	ཉལ་གུར།
mother	ah-ma	ཨ་མ།
motorboat	trü-khor-dru	འཕྲུལ་འཁོར་གྲུ།
motorcycle	bâhg-bâhg	སྤག་སྤག
mountain	ri	རི།
mountain bike	ri shön-ya kâng-ga-ri	རི་ར་བཞོན་ཡག་ཀང་ག་རི།
mountain path	ri-lâm	རི་ལམ།
mountain range	ri-gyü	རི་རྒྱུད།
mountaineering	ri gâng zâg-ya	རི་རྒྱང་འཛེགས་ལས་ཡག
mouse	tsi-tsi	ཙི་ཙི།
mouth	kha	ཁ།
movie	log-nyen	གློག་བརྙན།
mud	dâm-pâg	འདམ་པག
mum	ah-ma	ཨ་མ།
muscle	sha-gyü	ཤ་རྒྱུད།
museum	dem-tön-khâng	འགྲེམས་སྟོན་ཁང་།
music	rö-ja	རོལ་ཆ།
musician	rö-ja tong-khen	རོལ་ཆ་གཏོང་མཁན།
Muslim	kha-che	ཁ་ཆེ།
mute	koog-pa	ལྐུགས་པ།

English	Tibetan (romanized)	Tibetan script
name	ming	མིང
nappy (diaper)	chu-den	ཆུ་གདན
nappy rash	chu-den thor-sib	ཆུ་གདན་ཐོར་སྱིབ
national park	mi-mâng ling-ga	མི་དམངས་གླིང་ག
nationality	gye-khâb	རྒྱལ་ཁབ
nature	râng-joong	རང་བྱུང
nausea	kyoog-me lâng-wa	སྐྱུག་མེར་ལངབ
near	tih-la	འཐྱིལ་ལ
necessary	gö ngay-chen	དགོས་ངེས་ཅན
necklace	ke-gyen	སྐེ་རྒྱན
to need	gö-pa	དགོས་པ
needle (sewing)	khâb	ཁབ
needle (syringe)	men-khâb	སྨན་ཁབ
neither	nyi-ka min-pa	གཉིས་ཀ་མིན་པ
never	tsa-wa-nay	རྩ་བ་ནས
new	sar-ba	གསར་པ
New Year's Day	lo-sar	ལོ་གསར
news	sân-gyur	གསར་འགྱུར
newsagency	tsâg-sho nyo-sa	ཚགས་ཤོག་ཉོ་ས
newspaper	tsâg-ba	ཚགས་པར
next	je-ma	རྗེས་མ
next month	da-wa je-ma	ཟླ་བ་རྗེས་མ
next week	dün-ta je-ma	བདུན་ཕྲག་རྗེས་མ
next year	lo je-ma	ལོ་རྗེས་མ
next to	je-la	རྗེས་ལ
nice	yâk-po	ཡག་པོ
nickname	ming-dok	མིང་འདོགས
night	gong-da • tsen	དགོང་དག • ཚན
no	min • may •	མིན • མེད •
	ma-ray • min-du	མ་རེད • མིན་འདུག
noise/noisy	kay-choh • kay-choh tsha-po	སྐད་ཆོ • སྐད་ཆོ་ཚ་པོ
none	chig-kyâng-may •	གཅིག་ཀྱང་མེད •
	chig-kyâng-min	གཅིག་ཀྱང་མིན
noon	nyin-goong	ཉིན་གུང
north	châng	བྱང
nose	na-khoog	སྣ་ཁུག

notebook	di-teb	འབྲི་དེབ
nothing	gâng-yâng-may •	གང་ཡང་མེད •
	gâng-yâng-min	གང་ཡང་མིན
not yet	tân-da-yâng may	ད་དུང་ཡང་མེད
now	tân-da	ད་ལྟ
nuclear energy	dü-tren nü-pa	རྡུལ་ཕྲན་ནུས་པ
nuclear testing	dü-tren tsön-cha	རྡུལ་ཕྲན་མཚོན་ཆ་ཚོད
	tsö-ta chay-pa	བཟོ་བྱེད་པ
nun	ah-ni	ཨ་ནི
nurse	nay-yog	ནད་གཡོག

O

obvious	ngön-say tö-po	མངོན་གསལ་དོད་པོ
ocean	gyâm-tsho	རྒྱ་མཚོ
offence	phog-toog	ཕོག་ཐུག
office	lay-koong	ལས་ཁུངས
office work	lay-koong lay-ka	ལས་ཁུངས་ལས་ཀ
office worker	lay-koong lay-chay-pa	ལས་ཁུངས་ལས་བྱེད་པ
often	yâng yâng • yâng-se	ཡང་ཡང • ཡང་སེ
oil (cooking)	kha-noom	ཁ་སྣུམ
OK	di-gi-ray	འགྲིག་གི་རེད
old	nying-pa	རྙིང་པ
Olympic Games	oh-lim-pik tse-mo	ཨོ་ལིམ་པིཀ་རྩེད་མོ
on	gâng-la	སྒང་ལ
once; one time	teng-ray • teng-chig	ཐེང་རེ • ཐེང་གཅིག
one-way (ticket)	ya-lâm chig-po	ཡར་ལམ་གཅིག་པོ་འགྲོ
	do-ya ti-ka-si	ཡའགྲོ་ཊི་ཀ་སི
only	chig-po • ma-tog	གཅིག་པོ • མ་གཏོགས
open	kha-chay	ཁ་ཕྱེ
to open	kha chay-wa	ཁ་ཕྱེ་བ
opening	gon-zoog	འགོ་འཛུགས
opera	rö-gar tâb-tön	རོལ་གར་འཐབ་སྟོན
opera house	rö-gar-khâng	རོལ་གར་ཁང
operation	lay-gü	ལས་འགུལ
operator	trü-cha tong-khen	འཕྲུལ་ཆ་གཏོང་མཁན
opinion	sâm-tshül	བསམ་ཚུལ
opposite	gan-dha • dog-chog	བགལ་བཟློ • ལྡོག་ཕྱོགས

P

or	yâng-na	ཡང་ན
oral	ngâg-tog	ངག་ཐོག
orange (colour)	li-ti	ལི་ཏི
order (stage)	bâng-rim	བང་རིམ
to order	kâ tong-wa	བཀའ་གཏོང་བ
ordinary	kyü-ma	དཀྱུས་མ
to organise	go-dig chay-pa	གོ་སྒྲིག་བྱེད་པ
original	ngo-ma	ངོ་མ
other	shen-da	གཞན་དག
outgoing	chee do-khen	ཕྱིར་འགྲོ་མཁན
outside	chi-log	ཕྱི་ལོགས
over	tog-la	ཐོག་ལ
overdose	men thün-tsay-lay ge-wa	སྨན་ཐུན་ཚད་ལས་བརྒལ་བ
overseas	chi-gye	ཕྱི་རྒྱལ
to owe	trö-jay chay-pa	བློ་འཁུར་བྱེད་པ
owner	dâg-po	བདག་པོ
oxygen	sog-zin-loong	སོག་འཛིན་རླུང

P

pacifier (dummy)	jib-ru	འཇིབ་རུ
package	châg-pa • di-thoom	ཁུག་པ • སྒྲིལ་ཐུམ
packet	châg-pa chig • gâm-chig	ཁུག་པ་གཅིག • སྒམ་གཅིག
packet of cigarettes	tha-ma châg-pa	ཐ་མག་ཁུག་པ
padlock	gon-châg	སྒོ་ལྕགས
page	shog-dâng	ཤོག་གྲངས
pain	nay-soog	ན་ཟུག
painful	nâ-soog chem-po	ན་ཟུག་ཆེན་པོ
painkillers	nay-soog cho-ya	ན་ཟུག་བཅོས་ཡག
to paint	tsön-tsi tong-wa	ཚོན་རྩི་གཏོང་བ
painter	tsön tong-khen	ཚོན་གཏོང་མཁན
painting (art)	ri-mo di-wa	རི་མོ་འབྲི་བ
pair (a couple)	cha-chig	ཆ་གཅིག
palace	gye-khâng	རྒྱལ་ཁང
pan	tse-lâng	ཚེ་ལང
pap smear	chay-shay-tog tâg-chay	སྐྱེ་ཤེད་ཐོག་བརྟག་དཔྱད
	chay-ya zay	སྐྱེད་ཡག་ཟས
paper	shu-gu	ཤོག་གུ

paraplegic	may-dib	སྨད་གྱིབ
parcel	cha-lâg • to-po	ཅ་ལག • དོ་པོ
parents	pha-ma	ཕ་མ
park	ling-ga	གླིང་ག
to park	mo-ta jog-pa	མོ་ཊ་འཇོག་པ
parliament	gya-yong trö-tshog	རྒྱལ་ཡོངས་གྲོས་ཚོགས
part	cha-shay	ཆ་ཤས
party (fiesta)	thoog-toh	ཐུགས་སྤྲོ
party (politics)	si-dön tshog-pa	སྲིད་དོན་ཚོགས་པ
pass	pa-say • lâg-kye	པ་སེ • ལག་ཁྱེར
passenger	drü-pa	འགྲུལ་པ
passport	pa-se-pot • chi-kyö lâg-teb	པ་སེ་པོ • ཕྱི་སྐྱོད་ལག་དེབ
passport number	pa-se-pot ahng-dâng	པ་སེ་པོ་ཨང་གྲངས
past	day-pa • ngön-ma	འདས་པ • སྔོན་མ
path	lâm-ga	ལམ་ག
patient (adj)	sö-sen-chen	བཟོད་སྲན་ཅན
to pay	rin trö-pa	རིན་སྤྲོད་པ
payment	rim-pa • la-phog	རིན་པ • གླ་ཕོགས
peace	shi-wa	ཞི་བ
peak	tse-mo	རྩེ་མོ
pedestrian	kâng-tâng dro-khen	རྐང་ཐང་འགྲོ་མཁན
pen (ballpoint)	nyu-gu	སྙུག་གུ
pencil	sha-nyoog	ཞ་སྙུག
penis	lig-pa • je	ལིག་པ • མཇེ
penknife	teb-di	དེབ་གྲི
pensioner	gen-yö	རྒན་ཡོལ
people	mi-mâng	མི་མང
pepper	ey-ma	གཡེར་མ
period pain	dha-tsen bâ-kâb nay-soog	ཟླ་མཚན་བབས་ཀབས་ནད་ཟུག
permanent	ten-châg	གཏན་འཆགས
permission	chog-chen	ཆོག་མཆན
permit	chog-chen trö-pa	ཆོག་མཆན་སྤྲོད་པ
person	mi	མི
personality	shi-ka	གཞིས་ཀ
to perspire	ngü-nâg thön-pa	རྔུལ་ནག་ཐོན་པ
petition	nyen-shu	སྙན་ཞུ
pharmacy	men tsong-khâng	སྨན་ཚོང་ཁང

P

phone	kha-pah	ཁ་པར
phone book	kha-pah-teb	ཁ་པར་དེབ
phone box	kha-pah tong-say khâng-choong	ཁ་པར་གཏོང་ས་ཁང་ཆུང
phonecard	kha-pah tong-ya lâg-kye	ཁ་པར་གཏོང་ཡ་ལག་ཁྱེར
photo	par	པར

Can I take a photo (of you)?
(kay-râng) par-chig gyâb-na
di-giy ray-bay

(ཁྱེད་རང་)པར་ཅིག་རྒྱབ་ན
འགྲིག་གི་རེད་པས

photographer	par-pa • par	པར་པ • པར
photography	par-lay • pâh gya-khen	པར་ལས • པར་རྒྱག་མཁན
pick/pickaxe	doog-pa • tog-tsay ko-wa	རྡུགས་པ • ཏོག་ཙེ་ཀོ་བ
to pick up	len-pa	ལེན་པ
piece	toom-bu • cha-shay	དུམ་བུ • ཆ་ཤས
pig	phâg-pa	ཕག་པ
pill	ri-bu	རིལ་བུ
the Pill	kye-gok-men	སྐྱེ་འགོག་སྨན
pillow	nyen-go	སྔས་མགོ
pillowcase	nyen-shoob	སྔས་ཤུབས
pine	tâng-shing	ཐང་ཤིང
pink	sing-kya	སིང་སྐྱ
pipe	boob-dong	སྦུབས་གདོང
place	sa-cha	ས་ཆ
place of birth	kye-yül	སྐྱེ་ཡུལ
plane	nâm-du	གནམ་གྲུ
planet	gyu-kar	རྒྱུ་སྐར
plant	tsi-shing	རྩི་ཤིང
to plant	zoog-pa • deb-pa	འཛུགས་པ • འདེབས་པ
plastic	pö-kar	སྦོལ་དཀར
plate	tha-pa	ཐ་བ
plateau	sa-thö tang-shong	ས་མཐོའི་ཐང་གཤོང
platform	ding-cha	སྟིང་ཆ
play (theatre)	tâb-tön	འཁྲབ་སྟོན
to play (a game)	(gyen) tse-wa	(རྒྱན་)རྩེ་བ
to play (music)	(rö-ja) tong-wa	(རོལ་ཆ)གཏོང་བ
player (sports)	tse-mo-wa (tse-mo)	རྩེད་མོ་བ(རྩེད་མོ)

D
I
C
T
I
O
N
A
R
Y

222

playing cards	tah-se	ཏ་སེ།
plug (bath)	trü-shong kha tig-ya	ཁྲུས་གོང་ཁ་དྲིག་ཡག
pocket	bâ-khoog	སྦ་ཁུག
poetry	nyen-ngâg	སྙན་ངག
to point	kha-chog tön-pa	ཁ་ཕྱོགས་སྟོན་པ།
police	kor-soong-wa	སྐོར་སྲུང་བ།
politics	si-dön • châb-si	སྲིད་དོན་ • ཆབ་སྲིད།
politicians	si-dön-pa	སྲིད་དོན་པ།
pollen	sen-drü-dü	ཟེ་འབྲུའི་རྡུལ།
polls	wön-du	འོས་བསྡུ།
pollution	du-lâng-ki dib-pa	དུད་ལངས་ཀྱི་སྒྲིབ་པ།
pool (swimming)	kye-zing	རྐྱལ་རྫིང་།
poor	kyo-po	སྐྱོ་པོ།
popular	yong-ta	ཡོངས་གྲགས།
possible	sih-pa	སྲིད་པ།

It's possible.
si-ki ray ཞེས་ཀྱི་རེད།

It's not possible.
thoob-ki ma-ray ཐུབ་ཀྱི་མ་རེད།

post office	dâg-khâng	སྒྲག་ཁང་།
postage	dâg-la	སྒྲག་གླ།
postcard	dâg-shog	སྒྲག་ཤོག
postcode	dâg-chang ahng-dâng	སྒྲག་ཕྲང་ཨང་གྲངས།
poster	di-tâg jar-yig	རི་མོ་སྒྲགས་སྦྱར་ཡིག
pot (ceramic)	(zay) khog-ma	(ཟའི་)ཁོག་མ།
pottery	za-chay	ཟ་ཆས།
poverty	wü-phong	དབུལ་ཕོངས།
power	nü-shoog	ནུས་ཤུགས།
prayer	mön-lâm • kha-dhön	སྨོན་ལམ་ • ཁ་འདོན།
prayer book	kha-dhön-teb	ཁ་འདོན་དེབ།
to prefer	dâm-ga chay-pa	འདམ་ག་བྱེད་པ།
pregnant	pu-gu kye-ya yö-pa	ཕྲུ་གུ་སྐྱེ་ཡག་ཡོད་པ།
premenstrual tension	dha-tsen mâ-bâb-gong ngâng-tsâb	ཟླ་མཚན་མ་བབས་གོང་གདངས་ཚབ།
to prepare	da-dig chay-pa	གྲ་སྒྲིག་བྱེད་པ།
present (gift)	ngen-pa • lâg-ta	ཟྣས་པ་ • ལག་རྟགས།

present (time)	tân-da	ད་ལྟ་
presentation	ngo-trö	ངོ་སྤྲོད་
presenter (TV etc)	ngo-trö chay-khen	ངོ་སྤྲོད་བྱེད་མཁན་
president	si-zin	སྲིད་འཛིན་
pretty	nying-jay-po	སྙིང་རྗེ་པོ་
to prevent	ngön-gok chay-pa	སྔོན་འགོག་བྱེད་པ་
price	gong • rim-pa	གོང་ • རིན་པ་
pride	nga-gye	ང་རྒྱལ་
priest	la-ma	བླ་མ་
prime minister	si-lön	སྲིད་བློན་
print (artwork)	par-shü	པར་ཤུས་
prison	tsön-khâng	བཙོན་ཁང་
prisoner	tsön-pa	བཙོན་པ་
private	gay	གྱེར་
privatisation	gay-la gyu-wa	གྱེར་ལ་འགྱུར་བ་
to produce	thön-kye chay-pa	ཐོན་སྐྱེད་བྱེད་པ་
profession	tso-tâb lay-rig	མཚོ་ཐབས་ལས་རིགས་
profit	keb-sâng	ཁེབ་བཟང་
profitability	keb-sâng yö-pa	ཁེབ་བཟང་ཡོད་པ་
program	lay-rig	ལས་རིམ་
promise	kay-len	ཁས་ལེན་
proposal	drö-shi	གྲོས་གཞི་
to protect	kyob-pa-chay • soong-wa-chay	སྐྱོབ་པ་བྱེད་ • སྲུང་བ་བྱེད་
protest	ngo-gö	ངོ་རྒོལ་
to protest	ngo-gö chay-pa	ངོ་རྒོལ་བྱེད་པ་
public toilet	mi-mâng sâng-chö	མི་དམངས་གསང་སྤྱོད་
to pull	ten-par-chay	འཐེན་པར་བྱེད་
pump	phun-dâ	ཕུན་དཱ་
puncture	yi-koong • khor-lo dö-wa	ཡི་ཀུང་ • འཁོར་ལོ་རྡོལ་བ་
to punish	nye-pa tong-wa	ཉེས་པ་གཏོང་བ་
puppy	kyib-toog	ཁྱི་ཕྲུག་
pure	lhay-may • dâng-ma	ལྷད་མེད་ • དྭངས་མ་
purple	mu-man	སྨུག་མན་
to push	bü-gya tong-wa	འབུད་རྒྱག་གཏོང་བ་
to put	jog-pa	འཇོག་པ་

Q

qualifications (person's)	shay-tse	ཤེས་ཚད
quality	pü-ka	སྤུས་ཀ
quarantine	nay-yâm ngon-gok-che	ནད་ཡམས་སྔོན་འགོག་ཆེད
	su-kâg chay-pa	སྲུང་བཀག་བྱེད་པ
quarrel	toog-pa gyák-pa	འཐུག་པ་རྒྱག་པ
quarter	shi-cha-chig	བཞི་ཆ་གཅིག
queen	gyal-mo	རྒྱལ་མོ
question (topic)	leng-shi	གླེང་གཞི
question (enquiry)	di-wa	དྲི་བ
to question	di-da di-wa	དྲི་བ་འདྲི་བ
queue	len dig-pa •	ལན་སྒྲིག་པ •
	ray-mö chay-pa	རེས་མོས་བྱེད་པ
quick	gyok-po	མགྱོགས་པོ
quiet (adj)	kha-khu sim-bu	ཁ་ཁུ་སིམ་པོ
to quit	pong-wa	སྤོང་བ

R

rabbit	ri-bong	རི་བོང
race (people)	rig-gyü	རིགས་རྒྱུད
race (sport)	gyook-tse den-du	རྒྱུགས་རྩལ་འགྲན་འདུར
racing bike	gyook-den kâng-ga-ri	རྒྱུགས་འགྲན་རྐང་གཱ་རི
racism	mi-rig ten-kay	མི་རིགས་བརྟན་བཀའ
radio	hru-yin-ji • loong-tin	རྡུང་འཕྲིན • རླུང་འཕྲིན
railway station	ri-lee bâb-tsoog	རི་ལི་འབབ་ཚུགས
rain	chah-pa	ཆར་པ

> It's raining.
> **chah-pa bâb-ki du**   ཆར་པ་འབབ་ཀྱི་འདུག

to rape	tsen-yem chay-pa	བཙན་གཡེམ་བྱེད་པ
rare	kön-po	དཀོན་པོ
rash	thor-sib	ཐོར་སིབ
rat	tsi-tsi	ཙི་ཙི
rate of pay	gong-tsay	གོང་ཚད
raw	jen-pa	རྗེན་པ

R

razor	ta-di	སྟ་དི།
razor blades	ta-di-kha	སྟ་དི་ཁ།
to read	log-pa	ཀློག་པ།
ready	da-dig	གྲ་སྒྲིག
to realise	go-tön tog-pa	གོ་རྟོགས་ཐོགས་པ།
reason	gyoom-tshen	རྒྱུ་མཚན།
receipt	choong-zin	བྱུང་འཛིན།
to receive	choong-wa • jor-wa	བྱུང་བ་ • འབྱོར་བ།
recent/recently	nye-char	ཉེ་ཆར།
to recognise	ngö zin-pa	ངོས་འཛིན་པ།
to recommend	ngo-trö gyâb-nye	ངོ་སྤྲོད་རྒྱབ་ཉེ།
recyclable	kyâr-tu bay-chö chay chog-pa	བསྐྱར་དུ་བེད་སྤྱོད་བྱེད་ཆོགཔ།
recycling	kyâr-tu bay-chö chay-pa	བསྐྱར་དུ་བེད་སྤྱོད་བྱེད་པ།
red	mah-po	དམར་པོ།
referee	tse-den dig-tim soong-khen	རྩེད་འགྲན་སྒྲིག་ཁྲིམས་སྲུང་མཁན།
reference	ngo-jor	ངོ་སྦྱོར།
reflection (mirror)	sog-nyen	གཟུགས་བརྙན།
reflection (thinking)	sâm-lo ting-sâb tong-wa	བསམ་བློ་གཏིང་ཟབ་གཏོང་བ།
refrigerator	kyâk-gâm	འཁྱག་སྒམ།
refugee	kyâb-chö-wa	སྐྱབས་བཅོལ་བ།
refund	chi-log	ཕྱིར་ལོག
to refund	chi-log chay-pa	ཕྱིར་ལོག་བྱེད་པ།
to refuse	kay-len mi-chay-pa	ཁས་ལེན་མི་བྱེད་པ།
regional	sa-khü-gi	ས་ཁུལ་གྱི།
registered mail	teb-kyel-dâg	དེབ་སྐྱེལ་སྒྲག
to regret	gyö-pa kye-wa	འགྱོད་པ་སྐྱེ་བ།
relationship	de-wa	འབྲེལ་བ།
to relax	lhö-lhö chay-pa	ལྷོད་ལྷོད་བྱེད་པ།
religion	chö-loog	ཆོས་ལུགས།
religious	chö-loog-ki	ཆོས་ལུགས་ཀྱི།
to remember	den-pa	དྲན་པ།
remote	loong-koog • ta-kob	ལུང་ཁུག • མཐའ་འཁོབ།
rent	khâng-la • yâr-la	ཁང་ལ་ • གླ་ཡར་གླ།
to rent	yâr-wa	གླ་ཡར་བ།
to repair	so-chö gyâk-pa	བཟོ་བཅོས་རྒྱགཔ།
to repeat	kyar-dhö chay-pa	བསྐྱར་ཟློས་བྱེད་པ།

republic	chi-thün gya-kâb	སྤྱི་མཐུན་རྒྱལ་ཁབ
reservation	ngön-ngâg	སྔོན་མངགས
to reserve	ngön-ngâg chay-pa	སྔོན་མངགས་བྱེད་པ
resignation	tsa-gong shu-wa	རྩ་དགོངས་ཞུ་བ
respect	gü-shâb	གུས་ཞབས
rest (relaxation)	nge-so	ངལ་གསོ
rest (what's left)	lhâg-ma	ལྷག་མ
to rest	ngay so-wa	ངལ་གསོ་བ
restaurant	sa-khâng	ཟ་ཁང
resume (CV)	shay-tsay	ཞེས་ཚད
retired	gen-yö	རྒན་ཡོལ
to return	chih log-pa	ཕྱིར་ལོག་པ
return (ticket)	ya-lâm ma-lâm	ཡར་ལམ་མར་ལམ་འགྲོ
	do-ya ti-ka-si	ཡྭ་ཏི་ཀ་སི
review	kyâr-shib	བསྐྱར་ཞིབ
rhythm	da-dâng chay-tsâm	སྒྲ་མདངས་བཅད་མཚམས
rice	dray	འབྲས
rich (wealthy)	choog-po	ཕྱུག་པོ
rich (food)	kha-la shag-tsi-chen	ཁ་ལག་ཞག་ཚིལ་ཅན
to ride	shön-pa	བཞོན་པ
right (correct)	tâg-tâg • den-pa	དྲང་དྲང • འདེན་པ

> **You're right.**
> **kay-râng tâg-tâg ray** ཁྱེད་རང་དྲང་དྲང་རེད

right (not left)	yeh	གཡས
right-wing	yeh-chog sho-kak	གཡས་ཕྱོགས་ཚོགས་ཁག
ring (on finger)	tsih-kok	ཚིགས་ཁྱོས
ring (of phone)	kha-pah-kay	ཁ་པར་སྐད

> **I'll give you a ring.**
> **ngay kha-pah tang-gi-yin** ངས་ཁ་པར་གཏང་གི་ཡིན

rip-off	go-kor tong-wa	མགོ་སྐོར་གཏོང་བ
risk	nyen-ga	ཉེན་ག
river	tsâng-po	གཙང་པོ
road (main)	lâm-chen	ལམ་ཆེན
road map	lâm-kay sâb-ta	ལམ་གྱི་ས་བཀྲ
to rob	tog-chom chay-pa	འཇོག་འཆོམ་བྱེད་པ

rock	dâg	ཐྭག
rock climbing	dâg-la zek-pa	བྲག་ལ་འཛེག་པ
rolling	dil-wa	དྲིལ་བ
romance	pho-mo tse-doong	ཕོ་མོ་རྩེ་གདུང
room	khâng-mi	ཁང་མི
room number	khâng-mi ahng-dâng	ཁང་མི་ཨང་གྲངས
rope	tâg-pa	ཐག་པ
round	go-gor	སྒོར་སྒོར
rowing	dru tong-wa	གྲུ་གཏོང་བ
rubbish	kay-nyig	གད་སྙིགས
rug	room-den	རུམ་གདན
ruins	shig-rü	ཞིག་རལ
rules	dig-lâm	སྒྲིག་ལམ
to run	gyuk-sha lö-pa	རྒྱུག་ཤ་རྒྱོད་པ

sad	sem kyo-wa	སེམས་སྐྱོ་བ
safe (n)	rin-tâng chen-pö cha-la jog-sa	རིན་ཐང་ཆེན་པོའི་ཅ་ལག་འཇོག་ས
safe (adj)	nyen-ga may-pa	ཉེན་ཁ་མེད་པ
safe sex	nyen-soong tig-jor	ཉེན་སྲུང་འཇིག་སྦྱོར
saint	kye-bu dâm-pa	སྐྱེས་བུ་དམ་པ
salary	la-phog	གླ་ཕོགས
(on) sale	tshong(-chay)	ཚོང་(ཆེད)
salt	tsha	ཚ
same	chig-pa	གཅིག་པ
sand	chay-ma	བྱེ་མ
sanitary napkins	tsâng-day shu-gu	གཙང་སྦྲའི་ཤོག་གུ
to save (money)	ngü sog-pa	དངུལ་གསོག་པ
to say	lâb-pa • shö-pa	ལབ་པ • ཞོད་པ
to scale (climb)	tsay jay-wa • zek-pa	ཚད་བཟབ་བ • འཛེག་པ
scarves	kha-ti	ཁ་ཏིག
school	lob-ta	སློབ་གྲ
science	tsen-rig	མཚན་རིག
scientist	tsen-rig-pa	མཚན་རིག་པ
scissors	jâm-tse	བྱམ་ཙེ
to score	ahng-dâng thob-pa	ཨང་གྲངས་འཐོབ་པ

scoreboard	ahng-dâng tsi-sa shog-pâng	འང་གྲངས་རྩིས་ས་ཤོག་པང་
script	tsu-yig	རྩོམ་ཡིག
sculpture	bu-kö	འབུར་རྐོས་
sea	tsho	མཚོ་
seasick	tsho-nâng do-nay shen-log gyâk-pa	མཚོ་ནང་འགྲོ་ནས་ཞེན་ ལོག་རྒྱག་པ་
seat	koob-kya	སྐུབ་རྐྱ་
seat belt	koob-kya tâg-pa	སྐུབ་རྐྱ་ཐག་པ་
second (n)	nyi-pa	གཉིས་པ་
secretary	doong-yig	དྲུང་ཡིག
to see	mik tâ-wa	མིག་ལྟ་བ་

self-employed	tso-wa rang-kyong	འཚོ་བ་རང་སྐྱོང་
selfish	râng-shay tsâ-po	རང་ཞེན་ཚ་པོ་
self-service	râng-gö rang-dem	རང་དགོས་རང་འདེམས་
to sell	tsong-pa	བཙོང་པ་
to send	tong-wa	གཏོང་བ་
sensible	go-dön-chen	གོ་དོན་ཅན་
sentence (words)	tsig-doob	ཚིག་གྲུབ་
sentence (prison)	tim-tâg chö-pa	ཁྲིམས་ཐག་བཅད་པ་
to separate	ka-ka so-wa	ཁ་ཁ་བཟོ་བ་
series	mu-tü gyü-del	མུ་མཐུད་རྒྱུད་འབྲེལ་
serious	tshâb-che	ཚབས་ཆེ་
service (assistance)	rog chay-ya	རོགས་བྱེད་ཡག་
service (religious)	cho-ga tong-wa	ཆོ་ག་གཏོང་བ་
several	ka-shay • ka-chen	ཁ་ཤས་ • བཀའ་ཅན་
to sew	tsem-po-gyâk-pa	འཚེམ་པོ་རྒྱག་པ་

S

sex	pho-mo tâg	ཕོ་མོ་རྟགས
sexy	châg-nyâm dö-po	ཆགས་ཉམས་འདོད་པོ
shade/shadow	dib-nâg	གྲིབ་ནག
shampoo	ta-trü-ya shâm-bu	སྐྲ་འཁྲུད་ཤ་མ་པུ
shape	sob-ta	བཟོ་དབྱིབས
to share (with)	go-sha gyâk-pa	འགོ་ལ་བར་རྒྱག་པ
to share a dorm	chi-khâng-nâng nyâm-tu dhö-pa	སྤྱི་ཁང་ནང་ཉམས་དུ་སྡོད་པ
to shave	shar-wa-chay	གཤར་བ་བྱེད
she	mo	མོ
sheep	loog	ལུག
sheet (bed)	cha-tah	ཅ་ལ་དར
sheet (paper)	shog-leb	ཤོག་ལྗེབ
shelves	bâng-ti	བང་ཏི
ship	dru-zing	གྲུ་གཟིངས
to ship	tong-wa	གཏོང་བ
shirt	tö-toong	སྟོད་ཐུང
shoe shop	lhâm-ko tsong-khâng	ལྷམ་ཀོ་ཚོང་ཁང
shoes	lhâm-ko	ལྷམ་ཀོ
to shoot	phen-pa	འཕེན་པ
shop	tsong-khâng	ཚོང་ཁང
to go shopping	nyob-cha gya-ga-do	ཉོ་ཆ་རྒྱག་ག་འགྲོ
short (height)	mâ-po	དམའ་པོ
short (length)	toong-toong	ཐུང་ཐུང
short films	log-nyen toong-toong	གློག་བརྙན་ཐུང་ཐུང
short stories	doong toong-toong	སྒྲུང་ཐུང་ཐུང
shortage	ma-dâng-pa • nyoong-ta-pa	མི་འདང་པ • ཉུང་དྲགས་པ
shorts	ha-pan • gö-toong wog-dho	ཧ་པན • གོས་ཐུང་འོག་དོ
shoulders	poong-pa	དཔུང་པ
to shout	kay-cho gyâk-pa	སྐད་ཆོ་རྒྱག་པ
show	tay-mo	ལྟད་མོ
to show	tön-pa	སྟོན་པ

Can you show me on the map?
(sâp-ta di-nâng) tön nâng-da   (ས་བཀྲ་འདི་ནང་) སྟོན་གནང་དང

shower	soog-po tru-ya tor-cho	གཟུགས་པོ་འཁྲུ་ཡ་ཏོར་ཆུ
shrine	lha-khâng	ལྷ་ཁང
to shut	kha gyâk-pa	ཁ་རྒྱག་པ

230

S

shy	ngo tsha-wa	ངོ་ཚ་བ
sick	nah-wa	ནད་བ
sickness	na-tsa	ནད་ཚ
side	chog	ཕྱོགས
sign	tâg	རྟགས
to sign	sa-yig gyâk-pa	ས་ཡིག་རྒྱག་པ
signature	sa-yig	ས་ཡིག
silk	dru-zi	གྲུབ་རྩི
of silver	ngü-gi	དངུལ་གྱི
similar	chig-pa	གཅིག་པ
simple	lay la-po	ལས་སླ་པོ
sin	dig-pa	སྡིག་པ
since (May)	(chin-da nga-pa) nay	(ཕྱི་ཟླ་ལྔ་པ)ནས
to sing	shay tong-wa	གླུ་ལེན་གཏོང་བ
singer	shay tong-khen	གླུ་ལེན་གཏོང་མཁན
single (person)	mi-hreng	མི་ཧྲེང
single (unique)	chig-kyâng	གཅིག་ཀྱང
single room	khâng-mi-chig	ཁང་མི་གཅིག
sister	pün-kya bu-mo	སྤུན་སྐྱ་བུ་མོ
to sit	dhö-pa	སྡོད་པ
size	tsay	ཚད
to ski	gang-shü-tong	གངས་ཤུད་གཏོང
skiing	gang-shü tong-wa	གངས་ཤུད་གཏོང་བ
skin	pâg-pa	པགས་པ
sky	nâm	གནམ
to sleep	nyi nyay-wa	གཉིད་ཉལ་བ
sleeping bag	nye-koog	ཉལ་ཁུག
sleeping pills	nyi-men	གཉིད་སྨན
sleepy	nyi doh-po	གཉིད་རོ་པོ
slow/slowly	ka-lee ka-lee	ག་ལེ་ག་ལེ
small	choong-choong	ཆུང་ཆུང
smell	ti-ma	དྲི་མ
to smell	ti-ma noom-pa	དྲི་མ་སྣོམ་པ
to smile	gay-mo tse-tse chay-pa	དགད་མོ་ཚ་ཚ་བྱེད་པ
to smoke	tha-ma ten-pa	ཐ་མག་འཐེན་པ
smoking	tha-ma ten-pa	ཐ་མག་འཐེན་པ
soap	yi-tsi	ཡི་རྩི

D I C T I O N A R Y

soccer	kâng-pol	ཀང་པོལ
social sciences	chi-tsog rig-nay	སྤྱི་ཚོགས་རིག་གནས
social security	chi-tsog de-soong	སྤྱི་ཚོགས་བདེ་སྲུང
social welfare	chi-tsog de-dön	སྤྱི་ཚོགས་བདེ་དོན
socialist	chi-tsog ring-loog-pa	སྤྱི་ཚོགས་རིང་ལུགས་པ
solid	trâg-po	བྲག་པོ
some	ka-shay	ཁ་ཤས
someone	mi-chig	མི་གཅིག
something	gang chig	གང་ཅིག
sometimes	tshâm-tshâm	མཚམས་མཚམས
son	bu	བུ
song	lu	གླུ
soon	gyok-po	མགྱོགས་པོ

| I'm sorry. | | |
| gong-da | | དགོངས་དག |

sound	da	སྒྲ
south	lho	ལྷོ
souvenir	dren-ten cha-lâg	དྲན་རྟེན་ཅ་ལག
souvenir shop	dren-ten cha-lâg tsong-khâng	དྲན་རྟེན་ཅ་ལག་ཚོང་ཁང
space	bar-nâng	བར་སྣང
to speak	kay-cha shö-pa	སྐད་ཆ་ཤོད་པ
special	mik-say	དམིགས་བསལ
specialist	mik-say kay-pa	དམིགས་བསལ་མཁས་པ
speed	gyok-po	མགྱོགས་པོ
speed limit	gyok-tsay	མགྱོགས་ཚད
spicy (hot)	men-na	སྨན་ན
sport	lü-tsay	ལུས་རྩལ
sportsperson	lü-tsay kay-pa	ལུས་རྩལ་མཁས་པ
sprain	tsig chü-pa	ཚིགས་འཆུས་པ
spring (season)	chi-ka	དཔྱིད་ཀ
square (shape)	toob-shi	གྲུ་བཞི
square (in town)	(dong-kay)	(གྲོང་ཁྱེར)
	zom-sa te-wa	མི་མང་འཛོམས་ས་སྟེ་བ
stadium	lü-tsay tang	ལུས་རྩལ་ཐང
stage	ding-cha	སྟེང་ཆ
stairway	kay-zek-lâm	སྐས་འཛེགས་ལམ

stamp	dâg-tâg • ti-ka-si	སྒྲ་དགས་ • ཊི་གསི
standard (usual)	tsay-den	ཚད་ལྡན
standard of living	tso-way nay-tâng	འཚོ་བའི་གནས་སྟངས
stars	kar-ma	སྐར་མ
to start	go zoog-pa	འགོ་འཛུགས་པ
station	bâb-tsoog • ti-sing	འབབ་ཚུགས • ཊི་སིང
stationery shop	yig-chay tsong-khâng	ཡིག་ཆས་ཚོང་ཁང
statue	ku-da	སྐུ་འདྲ
to stay (remain)	dhö-pa	སྡོད་པ
to steal	ku-wa	རྐུ་བ
steam	lâng-pa	རླངས་པ
steep	sah-po	གཟར་པོ
step	gom-pa	གོམ་པ
stomach	drö-kog	གྲོད་ཁོག
stomachache	drö-kog na-soog	གྲོད་ཁོག་ན་ཟུག
stone	dho	རྡོ
stop	tsâm jog-pa	མཚམས་འཇོག་པ
to stop	kâg-pa	བཀག་པ

stork	toong-toong kâ-mo	གྲུང་གྲུང་དཀར་མོ
storm	char-loong dâg-po	ཆར་རླུང་དྲག་པོ
story	doong	གྲུང
stove	tâb	ཐབ
straight	ka-toog	ཁ་ཐུག
strange	ken tsâ-po	ཁྱད་མཚར་པོ
stranger	gyü may-pay-mee	རྒྱུ་མེད་པའི་མི
stream	gyoog-chu	རྒྱུག་ཆུ
street	lâm-ga	ལམ་ག
strength	tob	སྟོབས
strike	lay-tsâm ngo-gö	ལས་མཚམས་ངོ་རྒོལ
on strike	lay-tsâm ngo-gö chay-pa	ལས་མཚམས་ངོ་རྒོལ་བྱེད་པ
string	kü-pa	སྐུད་པ
stroll	châm-châm	འཆམས་འཆམས
strong	shoog chen-po	ཤུགས་ཆེན་པོ
stubborn	go teg-po •	མགོ་ཁྲིགས་པོ •
	wu-tsoog tsa-po	ཡུ་ཚུགས་ཚ་པོ

student	lob-toog	སློབ་ཕྲུག
studio	par-khâng •	པར་ཁང་ •
	ri-mo di-khâng	རི་མོ་སྒྲིག་ཁང་
stupid	koog-ta-chen	གུགས་རྟགས་ཅན
style	sob-ta	བཟོ་བཀོད
suburb	dong-kay sa-kü	གྲོང་ཁྱེར་ས་ཁུལ
suburbs of ...	... gi dong-kay sa-kü	... གྱི་གྲོང་ཁྱེར་ས་ཁུལ
success	doob-day thön-pa	གྲུབ་འབྲས་ཐོན་པ
to suffer	doog-nge nyong-wa	སྡུག་བསྔལ་མྱོང་བ
sugar	chay-ma-ka-ra • chi-ni	ཅེ་མ་ཀ་ར • ཅི་ནི
suitcase	gâm	སྒམ
summer	yar-ga	དབྱར་ཁ
sun	nyi-ma	ཉི་མ
sunblock	nyib-ta gok	ཉི་འབྱུགས་འགོག
sunburn	nyib-ta teb-pa	ཉི་འབྱུགས་འཐེབས་པ
sunglasses	mik-shay nâg-po •	མིག་ཤེལ་ནག་པོ •
	nyi-dib mig-shay	ཉི་སྒྲིབ་མིག་ཤེལ
sunny	nyin-ma tsa-po	ཉིན་མ་ཚ་པོ
sunrise	nyi-shar	ཉི་ཤར
sunset	nyi-noob	ཉི་ནུབ

Sure.		
ngön-nay • yin-dâng-yin		དངོས་གནས། • ཡིན་དང་ཡིན།

surface mail	sa-tog tong-ya-dâg	ས་ཐོག་གཏོང་ཡ་དག
surname	kyim-ming	ཁྱིམ་མིང
surprise	ha lay-pa • hâng sâng-wa	ཧ་ལས་པ • ཧང་སངས་བ
to survive	sön-pa	གསོན་པ
sweet	ngah-mo	མངར་མོ
to swim	chu-kye gyâk-pa	ཆུ་རྐྱལ་རྒྱག་པ
swimming pool	kye-zing	རྐྱལ་རྫིང
swimsuit	kye-chay	རྐྱལ་ཆས
sword	di	གྲི
sympathetic	sha-tsay	ཤ་ཚེ
synagogue	ju-yi lha-khâng	ཇུ་ཡི་ལྷ་ཁང
syringe	men-khâb	སྨན་ཁབ

T

table	chog-tse • gya-chog	ཅོག་ཙེ • རྒྱ་ཅོག
table tennis	ping-pong	པིང་པོང
tail	nga-ma • shu-gu	རྔ་མ • གཤུག་གུ
to take (away)	kyer-wa • len-pa	འཁྱེར་བ • ལེན་པ
to take photographs	par gyāk-pa	པར་རྒྱབ་པ
to talk	kay-cha shö-pa	སྐད་ཆ་བཤད་པ
tall	ring-po	རིང་པོ
tampons	ma-kha gok-chay sin-bay	མ་ཁ་འགོག་བྱེད་སྲིན་པས
tasty	to-wa chen-po	ཟོ་བ་ཆེན་པོ
tax	tay	ཁྲལ
taxi	tek-si	ཊེགསི
taxi rank	tek-si dhö-sa	ཊེགསི་སྡོད་ས
teacher	gay-gan	དགེ་རྒན
teaching	lob-ti	སློབ་ཁྲིད
team	ru-kâg	རུ་ཁག
tear (crying)	mik-chu	མིག་ཆུ
technique	tâb-tsü	ཐབས་རྩལ
teeth	so	སོ
telegram	tar	ཏར
telephone	kha-pah	ཁ་པར
telephone centre	kha-pah lay-khoong	ཁ་པར་ལས་ཁུངས
to telephone	kha-pah tong-wa	ཁ་པར་གཏོང་བ
telescope	gyāng-shay	རྒྱང་ཤེལ
television	dian-shi •	ཊེ་ལི •
	soog-tong nyen-tin	གཟུགས་མཐོང་ཉན་བརྙན་འཕྲིན
to tell	lâb-pa	ལབ་པ
temperature (fever)	tsha-wa	ཚ་བ
temperature (weather)	nâm-shi	གནམ་གཤིས
temple	lha-khâng	ལྷ་ཁང
tennis	te-ne-si	ཊེ་ནེ་སི
tennis court	te-ne-si tse-tâng	ཊེ་ནེ་སི་རྩེད་ཐང
tent	gur	གུར
tent pegs	phoor-pa	ཕུར་པ
tenth	chu-pa	བཅུ་པ
terrible	pay dhuk-cha	དཔེ་སྡུག་ཆགས
test	tsö-ta	ཚོད་ལྟ

| to thank | tu-jay-chay shu-wa | ཐུགས་རྗེ་ཆེ་ཞུ་བ |

Thank you.
tu-jay-chay ཐུགས་རྗེ་ཆེ།

theatre	tâb-tön-khâng	བལྟ་སྟོན་ཁང་
thermos flask	cha-dâm	ཅ་དམ་
they	khong-tso	ཁོང་ཚོ་
thick	thoog-po	མཐུག་པོ་
thief	ku-ma	རྐུན་མ་
thin	tâb-po	སྲབ་པོ་
to think	sâm-lo tong-wa	བསམ་བློ་གཏོང་བ་
third	soom-pa	གསུམ་པ་
thirsty	kha kom-po	ཁ་སྐོམ་པོ་
this (one)	di (chig)	འདི་(གཅིག)
thought	sâm-lo	བསམ་བློ་
throat	mik-pa	མིད་པ་
ticket	ti-ka-si • pa-say	ཊི་ཀ་སི • པ་སེ
ticket collector	ti-ka-si shib-shay chay-khen	ཊི་ཀ་སི་ཞིབ་ཞེ་བྱེད་མཁན
ticket office	ti-ka-si lay-khoong	ཊི་ཀ་སི་ལས་ཁུངས་
tide	dü-lâb	དུས་རླབས་
tight	dâm-po	དམ་པོ་
time	dü-tsö	དུས་ཚོད་
on time	dü-tog	དུས་ཐོག
timetable	dü-tsö re-mig	དུས་ཚོད་རེའུ་མིག
tin (can)	châg-tin	ལྕགས་ཏིན་
tin opener	châg-tin kha chay-ya	ལྕགས་ཏིན་ཁ་བྱེད་ཡག་ལ
tip (gratuity)	ngen-pa • sö-ray	བཞེན་པ • གསོལ་རས
tired	tâng chay-pa	ཐང་ཆད་པ་
tissues	tsâng-ta shu-gu	གཙང་བྱ་ཤོག་གུ
toast	may-ta bâk-lay	མེ་ལྟག་བག་ལེབ
tobacco	doh-thâg	དོ་བ
today	te-ring	དེ་རིང་
together	nyâm-du	མཉམ་དུ་
toilet	sâng-chö	གསང་སྤྱོད་
toilet paper	sâng-chö shu-gu	གསང་སྤྱོད་ཤོག་གུ

tomorrow	sa-nyin	᠌
tomorrow afternoon	sa-nyin chi-toh	
tomorrow evening	sa-nyin gong-da	
tomorrow morning	sâng-nyi nga-to	
tonight	toh-gong	
too (as well)	yâng	
too expensive	gong chay-tâg-pa	
too much/many	mâng dâg-pa	
tooth (front)	(dün) so	
tooth (back)	(gyâb) so	
toothache	so na	
toothbrush	so-trü	
toothpaste	so-men	
torch (flashlight)	log-shu	
to touch	reg-pa • châng-wa	
tour	ta-kor	
tourist	yu-kor to-châm-pa	
tourist information office	yu-kor to-châm-pay lay-khoong	
towards	chay-tu	
towel	ah-choh	
track (car-racing)	(den-tse mo-ta) gyuk-sa	
track (footprints)	(kâng-je) shü-lâm	
track (sports)	(den-tse) gyuk-lâm	
track (path)	kâng-lâm	
trade union	so-lay kyi-doog tsog-pa	
traffic	dim-drü	
traffic lights	dim-drü log-da	
trail (route)	lâm-shü • lâm-chog	
train	ri-li	
train station	ri-li bâb-tsoog	
transit lounge	drü-pa nye-so gyâk-sa dön-khâng	
to translate	phâb-gyur chay-pa	
to travel	drü-shü chay-pa	
travel agency	dim-drü lay-koong	

travel sickness	drü-shü-la ten-nay	འགྲིམ་འགྲུལ་ལ་བརྟེན་
	go-yom dâng	ནས་མགོ་ཡོམ
	kyoog-may lâng-wa	དང་སྐྱུག་མེད་ལངབ
travellers cheques	drü-shü ngü-zin	འགྲུལ་འགྲུལ་དངུལ་འཛིན
tree	shing-dong	ཤིང་སྡོང
trek	ri-loong-doh-wa	རི་ལུང་འགྲོབ
trendy (person)	mi ta-so dö-po	མི་ལྟ་སོ་འདོད་པོ
trip	drü-shü	འགྲུལ་འགྲུལ
trousers	gö-toong • dho-ma	གོས་ཐུང • དོར་མ
truck	do-kye lâng-khor •	རྡོ་སྐྱེལ་རྡུངས་འཁོར •
	lo-ri	ལོ་རི

It's true.
ngön-nay ray • den-pa ray   དངོས་གནས་རེད • བདེན་པ་རེད

trust	yi-chay	ཡིད་ཆེས
to trust	yi-chay chay-pa •	ཡིད་ཆེས་བྱེད་པ •
	lo gay-wa	བློ་བགེས་པབ
truth	den-pa	བདེན་པ
to try (to taste)	tsö-ta chay-pa	ཚོར་ལྟ་བྱེད་པ
to try (to attempt)	bay-tsö chay-pa	འབད་ཙོལ་བྱེད་པ
T-shirt	gong-may tö-toong	གོང་མེད་སྟོད་ཐུང་ཕུ་ཆེད
	phu-che	
tune	da-dâng	སྒྲ་གདངས

Turn left.
kha yön-la kyog   ཁ་གཡོན་ལ་བསྐོར

Turn right.
kha ye-la kyog   ཁ་གཡས་ལ་བསྐོར

TV	dian-shi •	ཌེན་ཞི •
	soog-tong loong-tin	གཟུགས་མཐོང་ལུང་འཕྲིན
twice	teng-nyi	ཐེངས་གཉིས
twin beds	nye-ti cha-chig	ཉ་ཁྲི་ཆ་གཅིག
twins	tsib-toog	མཚེ་ཐུག
to type	châg-par gyâk-pa	ལྕགས་པར་རྒྱབ་པ
typical	trü-may	འཕྲུལ་མེད
tyre	gyik-gi khor-lo	འགྱིག་གི་འཁོར་ལོ

U

umbrella	nyi-du	ཉི་གདུགས
to understand	ha go-wa chay-pa	ཧ་གོ་བར་བྱེད་པ
unemployed	lay-ka may-pa	ལས་ཀ་མེད་པ
unemployment benefits	lay-may-phog	ལས་མེད་ཕོགས
unfurnished	nâng-chay may-pa	ནང་ཆས་མེད་པ
universe	jig-ten-khäm	འཇིག་རྟེན་ཁམས
university	tsoog-la lob-ta	གཙུག་ལག་སློབ་གྲྭ
unsafe	nyen-ga yö-pa	ཉེན་ཁ་ཡོད་པ
until (June)	(chin-da doog-pa) bah-tu	(ཟླ་བ་དྲུག་པ)བར་དུ
unusual	cha-chen min-pa	ཕལ་ཆེར་མིན་པ
up	yah • gâng-la	ཡར • སྒང་ལ
uphill	ri gâng-la	རི་སྒང་ལ
urgent	kay chen-po	གལ་ཆེན་པོ
useful	bay-chö-chen	ཁེ་ཕན་ཅན

V

vacant	tong-pa	སྟོང་པ
vacation (holiday)	goong-seng	གུང་གསེང
vaccination	nay ngön-gok men-khâb	ནད་སྔོན་འགོག་སྨན་ཁབ
valley	loong-shong	ལུང་གཤོངས
valuable	rin-tâng chen-po	རིན་ཐང་ཆེན་པོ
value (price)	gong-tsay • rin-tâng	གོང་ཚད • རིན་ཐང
vegetable	ngo-tsay	སྔོ་ཚལ
vegetarian	sha mi-sa-khen	ཤ་མི་ཟ་མཁན

I'm vegetarian.	
nga sha mi-sa-khen yin	ང་ཤ་མི་ཟ་མཁན་ཡིན

vegetation	tsi-shing	རྩི་ཤིང
vein	tâg-tsa	ཁྲག་རྩ
venereal disease	tig-jor-lay choong-way gö-nay	འབྲིག་སྦྱོར་ལས་འབྱུང་བའི་འགོས་ནད
venue	zom-sa • tsog-sa	འཛོམས་ས • འཚོགས་ས
very	shay-ta	ཞེ་དྲག
view	tong-tsül	མཐོང་ཚུལ
village	dong-seb	གྲོང་གསེབ

vine	gün-doom	ཀུན་འབྲུམ
vineyard	gün-doom shing-ra	ཀུན་འབྲུམ་ཞིང་ར
virus	nay-bu ta-mo-shig	ནད་འབུ་ཚོ་ཞིག
visa	vi-za • tong-chen	ཝི་ཟ • མཐོང་མཆན
to visit	do-wa • thoog-tay	འགྲོ་བ • ཕྲད་འཕྲད
vitamins	tob-kye-men	སྟོབས་སྐྱེད་སྨན
voice	kay	སྐད
volume	da-shoog	སྒྲ་ཤུགས
to vote	wö-shog loog-pa	འོས་ཤོག་བླུགས་པ

W

Wait!
gu-dâng-da སྒུག་དང་ད

waiter	se-dim shâb-shu-wa	ཟས་འབྲི་ཞབས་ཞུ་བ
waiting room	drü-pa gook-dhö-khâng	འགྲུལ་པ་སྒུག་དོད་ཁང
walk	châm-châm	འཆམས་འཆམས
to walk	gom-pa gyâk-pa	གོམ་པ་རྒྱག་པ
wall (inside)	gyâng	རྒྱང
wall (outside)	châg-ri	ལྕགས་རི
to want	gö-pa • dhö-pa	དགོས་པ • འདོད་པ
war	mâg	དམག
wardrobe	du-log jog-sa al-mi-ra	དུག་ལོག་འཇོག་ས་ཨལ་མི་ར
warm	drö-po	དྲོད་པོ
to warn	nyen-da tong-wa	ཉེན་བརྡ་གཏོང་བ
to wash (something)	trü gyâk-pa	ཁྲུས་རྒྱག་པ
to wash (oneself)	soog-po tru-wa	གཟུགས་པོ་འཁྲུད་བ
watch	chu-tsö	ཆུ་ཚོད
to watch	mik ta-wa	མིག་བལྟ་བ
water	chu	ཆུ
mineral water	tay-chu	གཏེར་ཆུ
water bottle	chu shay-tâm	ཆུ་ཤེལ་དམ
wave	ba-lâb	རྦ་རླབས
way	lâm-ga	ལམ་ག

Please tell me the way to ...
...-la do-ya-gi lâm-ga tön ...ལ་འགྲོ་ཡ་གི་ལམ་ག་སྟོན
nâng-da གནང་དང

Which way?		
lâm-ga ka-gi		འལམ་ག་ག་གི

Way Out		
chi-lo dön-sa		ཕྱི་ལོག་འདོན་ས

we	ngân-tso	ངེད་ཚོ
weak	soog-po kyo-po	གཟུགས་པོ་སྐྱོ་པོ
wealthy	choog-po • gyu chen-po	ཕྱུག་པོ་ • རྒྱུ་ཆེན་པོ
to wear	gyön-pa	གྱོན་པ
weather	nâm-shi	གནམ་གཤིས
wedding	châng-sa	ཆང་ས
week	dün-tâ	བདུན་ཕྲག
this week	dün-tâ di	བདུན་ཕྲག་འདི
weekend	sa pen-pa dâng nyin-ma	གཟའ་སྤེན་པ་དང་ཉིན་མ
to weigh	ji-tse dheg-pa	ལྗིད་ཚད་འདེགས་པ
weight	ji-tse	ལྗིད་ཚད
welcome	ta-shi de-lek •	བཀྲ་ཤིས་བདེ་ལེགས •
	ka-su-shu	དགའ་བསུ་ཞུ
welfare	de-dhuk	བདེ་སྡུག
well	de-po	བདེ་པོ
west	noob	ནུབ
wet	lön-pa	རློན་པ
what	kâ-ray	ག་རེ

What is he saying?		
khö kâ-ray lâb-ki-du		ཁོས་ག་རེ་ལབ་ཀྱི་འདུག

What time is it?		
chu-tsö kâ-tsay ray		ཆུ་ཚོད་ག་ཚོད་རེད

wheel	kho-lo	འཁོར་ལོ
wheelchair	kho-lö koob-gya	འཁོར་ལོ་ཀྲུབ་རྒྱ
when	ka-dü	ག་དུས

When does it leave?		
ka-dü tön-gi ray		ག་དུས་འཐོན་གྱི་རེད

where	ka-bah	གབར

Where is the bank?		
ngü-khâng ka-bah		དངུལ་ཁང་ག་བར

W

| white | kar-po | དཀར་པོ |
| who | su | སུ |

Who is it?
su yim-pa སུ་ཡིན་པ།

Who are they?
khong-tso su ray ཁོང་ཚོ་སུ་རེད།

| whole | tshâng-ma | ཚང་མ |
| why | kâ-ray chay-nay | ག་རེ་བྱས་ནས |

Why is the museum closed?
kâ-ray chay-nay dem-tön-khâng
goh gyâb yö-ray
ག་རེ་བྱས་ནས་འགྲེམ་སྟོན་
ཁང་གི་སྒོ་བརྒྱབ་ཡོད་རེད།

wide	gya-chem-po	རྒྱ་ཆེན་པོ
wife	kye-man	སྐྱེ་དམན
wild animal	ri-dâg	རི་དྭགས
to win	gya-ka tob-pa	རྒྱལ་ཁ་འཐོབ་པ
wind	loong	རླུང
window	gay-koong	སྐྱེ་ཁུང
to go	trom-la ta-ga-si	འཁྲོམ་ལ་འདུག་གི་སེ་འགྲོ་
window-shopping	kyâm-kyâm do-wa	འཆམ་འཆམ་འགྲོ་བ
wine	gün-doom châng-râk	རྒུན་འབྲུམ་ཆང་རག
winery	châng-râk so-sa	ཆང་རག་བཟོ་ས
wings	shog-pa	གཤོག་པ
winner	gya-ka tob-khen	རྒྱལ་ཁ་འཐོབ་མཁན
winter	gün-ga	དགུན་ཀ
wire	châg-kü	ལྕགས་སྐུད
wise	lo-drö-chen • kay-pa	བློ་གྲོས་ཅན • མཁས་པ
to wish	re-wa chay-pa	རེ་བ་བྱེད་པ
with	nyâm-tu	མཉམ་དུ
within	nâng-ngö-su	ནང་ངོས་སུ
within an hour	chu-tsö-chig nâng	ཆུ་ཚོད་གཅིག་ནང
without	may-pa • min-pa	མེད་པ • མིན་པ
woman	kye-man	སྐྱེ་དམན
wonderful	ha lay-pay yâk-po	ཧ་ལས་པའི་ཡག་པོ
wood	shing	ཤིང
wool	bay	བལ
word	ming-tsig	མིང་ཚིག

DICTIONARY

work	lay-ka	ལས་ཀ
to work	lay-ka chay-pa	ལས་ཀ་བྱེད་པ
work permit	lay-ka chay-ya chog-chen	ལས་ཀ་བྱེད་ཡག་ཆོག་མཆན
workshop	so-lay-khâng	བཟོ་ལས་ཁང
world	zâm-ling	འཛམ་གླིང
worms	bu-sin	འབུ་སྲིན
worried	sem-tel chay-pa	སེམས་ཁྲལ་བྱས་པ
worship	châg-chö mön-lâm	ཕྱག་མཆོད་སྨོན་ལམ
worth	pen-tog • rin-tâng	ཕན་ཐོགས • རིན་ཐང
wound	ma-may	རྨ་ཁ
to write	ti-wa	འབྲི་བ
writer	tsom-pa-po	རྩོམ་པ་པོ
wrong (fault)	non-trül	ནོར་འཁྲུལ

> I'm wrong. (my fault)
> **ngay non-trü ray**   ངའི་ནོར་འཁྲུལ་རེད
>
> I'm wrong. (not right)
> **ngay nor sha**   ངས་ནོར་ཤག

Y

year	lo	ལོ
this year	lo-di	ལོ་འདི
yellow	say-po	སེར་པོ
yesterday	kay-sa	ཁ་སང
yesterday afternnoon	kay-sa chi-toh	ཁ་སང་ཕྱི་དྲོ
yesterday evening	kay-sa gong-da	ཁ་སང་དགོང་དག
yesterday morning	kay-sa shoh-gay	ཁ་སང་ཞོགས་ཀར
yet	ta-toong • tân-da yâng	ད་དུང • ད་ལྟའང
you (pol)	kay-râng-tso	ཁྱེད་རང་ཚོ
young	shön-shön	གཞོན་གཞོན
youth (collective)	shön-kye	གཞོན་སྐྱེ
youth hostel	shön-nü don-khâng	གཞོན་ནུའི་མགྲོན་ཁང

Z

| zodiac | kar-kyim chu-nyi | སྐར་ཁྱིམ་བཅུ་གཉིས |
| zoo | chen-sig-khâng | སྐྱུ་གཟིགས་ཁང |

INDEX

I
N
D
E
X

245

I
N
D
E
X

Phrasebooks

L onely Planet phrasebooks are packed with essential words and phrases to help travellers communicate with the locals. With colour tabs for quick reference, an extensive vocabulary and use of script, these handy pocket-sized language guides cover day-to-day travel situations.

- handy pocket-sized books
- easy to understand Pronunciation chapter
- clear & comprehensive Grammar chapter
- romanisation alongside script to allow ease of pronunciation
- script throughout so users can point to phrases for every situation
- full of cultural information and tips for the traveller

'...vital for a real DIY spirit and attitude in language learning'
– *Backpacker*

'the phrasebooks have good cultural backgrounders and offer solid advice for challenging situations in remote locations'
– *San Francisco Examiner*

Arabic (Egyptian) • Arabic (Moroccan) • Australian *(Australian English, Aboriginal and Torres Strait languages)* • Baltic States *(Estonian, Latvian, Lithuanian)* • Bengali • Brazilian • Burmese • British *(English, dialects, Scottish Gaelic, Welsh)* • Cantonese • Central Asia *(Kazakh, Kyrgyz, Pashto, Tajik, Tashkorghani, Turkmen, Uyghur, Uzbek & others)* • Central Europe *(Czech, German, Hungarian, Polish, Slovak, Slovene)* • Costa Rica Spanish • Czech • Eastern Europe *(Albanian, Bulgarian, Croatian, Czech, Hungarian, Macedonian, Polish, Romanian, Serbian, Slovak, Slovene)* • East Timor *(Tetun, Portuguese)* • Egyptian Arabic • Ethiopian *(Amharic)* • Europe *(Basque, Catalan, Dutch, French, German, Greek, Irish, Italian, Maltese, Portuguese, Scottish Gaelic, Spanish, Turkish, Welsh)* • Farsi *(Persian)* • Fijian • French • German • Greek • Hebrew • Hill Tribes *(Lahu, Akha, Lisu, Mong, Mien & others)* • Hindi/Urdu • Indonesian • Italian • Japanese • Korean • Lao • Latin American Spanish • Malay • Mandarin • Mongolian • Moroccan Arabic • Nepali • Papua New Guinea • Pidgin • Pilipino (Tagalog) • Polish • Portuguese • Quechua • Russian • Scandinavian *(Danish, Faroese, Finnish, Icelandic, Norwegian, Swedish)* • South-East Asia *(Burmese, Indonesian, Khmer, Lao, Malay, Tagalog Pilipino, Thai, Vietnamese)* • South Pacific *(Fijian, Hawaiian, Kanak languages, Maori, Niuean, Rapanui, Rarotongan Maori, Samoan, Tahitian, Tongan & others)* • Spanish *(Castilian, also includes Catalan, Galician & Basque)* • Sri Lanka • Swahili • Thai • Tibetan • Turkish • Ukrainian • USA *(US English, vernacular, Native American, Hawaiian)* • Vietnamese

COMPLETE LIST OF LONELY PLANET BOOKS

AFRICA Africa on a shoestring • Cairo • Cape Town • East Africa • Egypt • Ethiopia, Eritrea & Djibouti • The Gambia & Senegal • Healthy Travel Africa • Kenya • Malawi • Morocco • Mozambique • Read This First: Africa • South Africa, Lesotho & Swaziland • Southern Africa • Southern Africa Road Atlas • Tanzania, Zanzibar & Pemba • Trekking in East Africa • Tunisia • Watching Wildlife East Africa • Watching Wildlife Southern Africa • West Africa • World Food Morocco • Zimbabwe, Botswana & Namibia

AUSTRALIA & THE PACIFIC Aboriginal Australia & the Torres Strait Islands • Auckland • Australia • Australia Road Atlas • Bushwalking in Australia • Cycling Australia • Cycling New Zealand • Fiji • Healthy Travel Australia, NZ and the Pacific • Islands of Australia's Great Barrier Reef • Melbourne • Micronesia • New Caledonia • New South Wales & the ACT • New Zealand • Northern Territory • Outback Australia • Out to Eat – Melbourne • Out to Eat – Sydney • Papua New Guinea • Queensland • Rarotonga & the Cook Islands • Samoa • Solomon Islands • South Australia • South Pacific • Sydney • Sydney Condensed • Tahiti & French Polynesia • Tasmania • Tonga • Tramping in New Zealand • Vanuatu • Victoria • Walking in Australia • Watching Wildlife Australia • Western Australia

CENTRAL AMERICA & THE CARIBBEAN Bahamas, Turks & Caicos • Baja California • Bermuda • Central America on a shoestring • Costa Rica • Cuba • Dominican Republic & Haiti • Eastern Caribbean • Guatemala • Guatemala, Belize & Yucatán: La Ruta Maya • Havana • Healthy Travel Central & South America • Jamaica • Mexico • Mexico City • Panama • Puerto Rico • Read This First: Central & South America • World Food Mexico • Yucatán

EUROPE Amsterdam • Amsterdam Condensed • Andalucía • Austria • Barcelona • Belgium & Luxembourg • Berlin • Britain • Brussels, Bruges & Antwerp • Budapest • Canary Islands • Central Europe •Copenhagen • Corfu & the Ionians • Corsica • Crete • Crete Condensed • Croatia • Cycling Britain • Cycling France • Cyprus • Czech & Slovak Republics • Denmark • Dublin • Eastern Europe • Edinburgh • England • Estonia, Latvia & Lithuania • Europe on a shoestring • Finland • Florence • France • Frankfurt Condensed • Georgia, Armenia & Azerbaijan • Germany • Greece • Greek Islands • Hungary • Iceland, Greenland & the Faroe Islands • Ireland • Istanbul • Italy • Krakow • Lisbon • The Loire • London • London Condensed • Madrid • Malta • Mediterranean Europe • Milan, Turin & Genoa • Moscow • Mozambique • Munich • The Netherlands • Normandy • Norway • Out to Eat – London • Paris • Paris Condensed • Poland • Portugal • Prague • Provence & the Côte d'Azur • Read This First: Europe • Rhodes & the Dodecanese • Romania & Moldova • Rome • Rome Condensed • Russia, Ukraine & Belarus • Scandinavian & Baltic Europe • Scotland • Sicily • Slovenia • South-West France • Spain • St Petersburg • Sweden • Switzerland • Trekking in Spain • Tuscany • Venice • Vienna • Walking in Britain • Walking in France • Walking in Ireland • Walking in Italy • Walking in Spain • Walking in Switzerland • Western Europe • World Food France • World Food Ireland • World Food Italy • World Food Spain